Bikes, Bombs and Bunny Girls

Tales of a Long, Hot Summer

By

Graham Bone and Viv Moore

Disclaimer

We have tried to recreate events, locales and conversations from our memories of them. In order to maintain their anonymity in some instances we have changed the names of individuals. ***WARNING*** *- A number of activities contained in this book are dangerous, please do not try them yourselves – the authors exclude all liability associated with this book to the extent permitted by law.*

Contents

FOREWORD

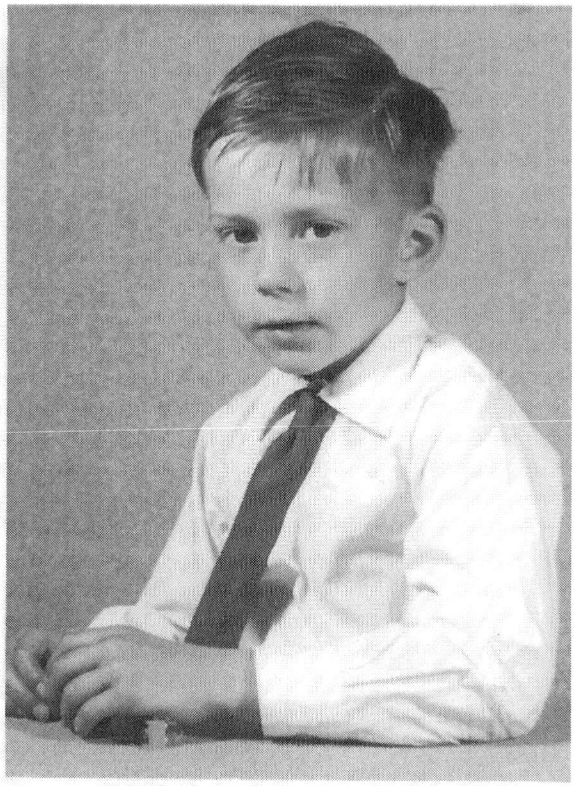

Graham's first school photo

I will start at the beginning, 1961. (I don't actually remember this bit, having just been born. I'm relying on my sister who's older than me and, in the way of all sisters, has an uncanny knack of remembering a lot about my life that I had thought safely forgotten.)

Anyway, picture the scene, The Preston Hawe Council Estate, in Tadworth, Surrey. The Church Hall, dusty wooden floorboards, high windows, strong smell of disinfectant.

"Hello, Edith! We haven't seen you for a couple of weeks," my mum Iris called out as Mrs Johnson came into the hall pushing a large navy bassinet pram. "Baby finally arrived then? What did you have?"

"Another boy!" said Mrs Johnson, proudly showing off her new son.

"So we've all had boys," put in their friend Mrs Haste. "If we carry on like this we'll have a football team!"

Three boys - Graham (that's me), Danny and now Gary, and as our mums gossiped our three prams stood side by side in the draughty Church Hall. The visit became a weekly event and somehow a bond of friendship grew between us as we waited to be weighed. Perhaps it was the effect of the National Dried Milk, or the bottles of free orange juice and cod liver oil. We all grew strong on Farley's Rusks and spoonfuls of malt as our mum's swapped stories of sleepless nights, boiling endless dirty nappies and the general ineptitude of our respective fathers.

Together we took our first tentative steps exploring our small world. Toddling soon turned to running, then pushing and fighting, but always making up. As we grew in confidence we learnt each others strengths and weaknesses. Three very different boys: me of course stunningly handsome and highly intelligent (listen to my mum and ignore my two elder sisters), with brown hair and eyes, inquisitive, a non-stop chatterbox, with an urgent need to take anything mechanical to pieces; Danny, lithe, dark and skinny, incessantly on the go, never walking when he could run, with a sunny disposition, making friends wherever he went; and last but certainly not least, Gary, tall for his age and with the frame of a future wrestler, auburn (never ginger!) hair and freckles, a dare devil with absolutely no idea where his passion for mischief would lead him and certainly never understanding that it might have 'consequences'!

Preston Hawe was a typical council estate, built in the 1950's to take the post-war overflow from London. Terraces of yellow brick houses, each with neat gardens front and back, interspersed with three storey blocks of flats, surrounded by large greens to play on and with a small parade of shops to supply everyday needs. On one side the rolling South Downs, on the other acres of wild heathland. Life was idyllic for us three lads, as we rode our second-hand tricycles and pedal cars along wide pavements, learnt to kick a ball and spent our pocket-money pennies on black jacks and fruit salad chews.

Then that fateful September arrived when, aged five, we all started school - Merland Rise Infants School that is. There were no Nursery classes then to get kids used to going to school, so this was a big event and had been talked about for weeks. School uniform had been gathered via catalogues, jumble sales and hand-me downs. Our three mums had been busy with their knitting needles making the regulation grey v-necked pullovers. We all ran excitedly into the red brick building together. The first hour passed pleasurably enough, finding our classroom, meeting our teacher called 'Miss', recognising other kids from the estate. Drinking little bottles of milk was a novelty, although we all thought it unfair that a *'girl'* had been chosen to hand out the straws. We had all put our hands up, there had only been a little bit of pushing and shoving, none of us had any idea how those chairs had fallen over. Besides anyone who cried because a stupid little chair had fallen on them was a cissy. There had been no need for Miss to split us up so we were all sitting at different tables.

Break time was fun, charging around the playground being Spitfire pilots. Rat-a-tat-a-tat. Firing at the girls and making them screech, using the coke heap as an enemy stronghold to attack. How were we to know it was out of bounds? Fancy making such a fuss about a little dirt. Fancy making us wash our hands. With soap!

Worse was to come. Sit still. No talking. Share those crayons nicely. No you can't just use black, or just the brown. What are you colouring then? Nice boys do not use the word 'shit'. No 'poo' is not a better word. BE QUIET!

Eventually the bell rang for lunch and it was time to go home, thank goodness.

"Go back? But I went to school this morning! No...ooo!!" My screams rent the air as the total horror of the situation dawned on me. It was a conspiracy. I had been tricked. Having finished my lunchtime sandwich and packet of crisps I was all prepared to get down to the real business of the day – playing.

"Your sisters are ready to go back to school, and you have to go too," explained my mother patiently.

"But they're girls!" I shrieked. "I'm a BOY and I don't like school. I went this morning and I DON'T WANT TO GO AGAIN!"

I'm sorry to admit I wept, well I was only five. Then I screamed, I kicked, I cajoled, I hung grimly onto every lamppost. Smack. SCREAM. Smack. SCREAM. My education expanded with a few choice words my mum hadn't even realised she knew. I learnt the terrible news that big boys of five had to go *every* weekday to school, and even worse every single year until they were at least sixteen, which was years, and years away. I learnt that my mum had a strong right arm, and that those new short trousers, the ones I had been so proud of wearing that very morning, left a large amount of flesh exposed for painful chastisement. I learnt that life was UNFAIR.

When I finally reached my new, and now hated, classroom a whispered conversation with my two best buddies revealed the terrible truth – they had also been duped. The bond grew stronger. The war against the establishment had begun!

Chapter 1

The Tank

Fast forward ten years of falling out of trees, off bikes and into ponds. Danny, Gary and I had been to the District Hospital so often we were on first name terms with the nurses. The long, hot summer of 1975 has passed and 1976 was set fair. Barry Sheen was well on his way to becoming World Motor Cycle Champion and James Hunt's intrepid motor racing style was inspiring us to ever more daring bicycle stunts. Easter was over and the summer term just begun and we three lads, now all fourteen, were out for trouble, or as we preferred to call it, fun! Naturally, none of us had overcome our aversion to school, teachers, rules or anything else that kept us from enjoying that fun.

We had left the delights of infant and junior school. Entrance exams had taken the place of the eleven plus. Naturally, given our engrained habits of non-attention, larking about and general apathy none of us passed said entrance exams to the Grammar school, so the local Secondary it had to be. De Burgh Secondary Modern School - built for the baby-boomers of the 1950's in a modern, progressive design of red brick under a flat roof, surrounded by playgrounds, tennis courts, football/cricket/hockey pitches and a running track, blah, blah, blah, – or so said the spiel in the school brochure. Unfortunately the baby-boomers had done more booming than originally envisioned and the school was ringed with wooden huts, while the new sixth form block took up most of the front lawn. News of our many talents had gone before us and the Headmaster, Mr. Mather, (well known psychopath and lover of the cane[1]) had taken the totally ridiculous decision to once again split us up. Not just separate tables, but separate forms. Of course we still met up occasionally, in the playground, on the sports field, and in detention.

We had soon figured out that Physical Education was something to be survived rather than enjoyed. There had already been two serious accidents – no, you are completely wrong – neither of them involved us, although I admit that was probably more by luck than any good judgement on our part. The first was the eye incident, and I'm sure any boy reading this would completely understand why a lad would remove the bungee hooks from around the side of a trampoline, stretch them, and fire at an attractive girl who was studiously ignoring him. However, instead of hitting the object of his lust the hook twanged back yanking out his eyeball, sending it flying across the sports hall. Blood splattered everywhere. I don't know whose screams were the loudest, the boy who'd just lost his eye, or the poor girl standing innocently at the side of the Hall who suddenly found this blood dripping eyeball heading straight for her. It certainly got her attention! I suppose the good thing about it was it did get the boy time off school, although even I have to admit it was a bit drastic. He had to have a glass eye fitted which sometimes moved around in its socket of its own accord, to end up pointing in the wrong direction - fascinating.

Then there was the javelin incident, again totally understandable, I mean what was a boy to do when he was caught short half way around the running track? Naturally he dashed around the back of one of the huts for a quick pee. How was he to know that the girls would have started javelin practice when he came running out again? He had the shock of his life when twenty javelins rained down on him. Of course he put

---

[1] Mr Mather had written a book on the value of corporal punishment. A copy was kept in the school library for our edification.

his hand out to protect himself, it was just unfortunate he got skewered, the javelin pinning him to the ground. All the girls screamed, and one of them pretended to faint and had to be carted off to the nurse, which is typical of girls making every little incident into a drama (for safety reasons I omit my sisters from that observation!). You wouldn't believe the amount of fuss they made, while the poor lad waited stoically for the ambulance. We considered the lad lucky as none of the other javelins penetrated his body and he survived with only a hole in his right hand. Even so we decided that 'Games' as it was called was a very dangerous activity and to be avoided at all costs.

All that changed the day the Army came to school on a recruitment drive. Not that any of us had any intention of joining the army you understand – discipline was not our strong point. However, they bought with them a Chieftain[2] tank.

We watched from the edge of the school field as the officer in charge chatted with a couple of teachers, while his men jumped down from a large camouflaged truck and began unloading an interesting assortment of equipment.

"What do you think they're doing?" asked Danny.

"No idea," I answered, "but I wouldn't mind a go in that tank."

Danny nodded agreement as we both looking longingly at the Chieftain.

"They're never going to let you two loose in a tank," jeered Gary. "Not with your puny arms. You need muscles to drive one of those." He flexed his biceps, so we both jumped on him. Unfortunately the bell for afternoon lessons went before we could have more than a quick skirmish.

---

[2] The Chieftain FV4201 was the main battle tank of the UK during the 1960s/70s/80s.

As we queued up waiting to go back into the school, Physics Jones, our Head of Year, came out and stood at the top of the steps. "Quiet please," he yelled. "I've got an important announcement. Would all boys from year four come to the Sports Hall immediately after registration, and bring your games kit with you."

"What's it about, Sir?" I asked. "Is it anything to do with that tank?"

Jones looked down his nose as though I'd just farted. "If you come to the Sports Hall Bone, as I've just requested, you'll find out."

Typical teacher, I thought, every one a comic.

It seemed to take Mr. Parker ages to call the register, I was sure he was taking his time on purpose, but eventually we all filed into the Sports Hall. 'Bloodsucker' Leech, Head of Games, was showing off his hairy knees and equally hairy arms, bouncing up and down on the spot like a demented yoyo. He stuck his whistle in his mouth and blew an ear piercing blast that got the attention of all of us. "Sit down," he yelled, and then beckoned forward the Army Officer. "This is Sergeant Walker," he introduced the man with a smarmy grin. "He and his men are giving up their valuable time to talk to you about life in the Army. Give them a warm welcome, please."

The clapping was enthusiastic, well we were missing lessons and there was a tank involved, which beat French and Maths any time.

The Sergeant was alright, he kept his talk brief, unlike most of the windbags that came to school to talk about careers. Danny, Gary and I huddled at the back of the hall, none of us were interested in joining the Army, you could get shot at, which might be OK as kids playing cowboys and Indians, but in real life it meant you could end up dead. Suddenly our ears pricked up. "We have set up an assault course, if any of you would like to try it would you please divide yourselves into teams of three. The winners with the fastest time will be allowed to drive the tank."

That caused a cheer to go up, lethargy overcome in a flash.

"We should enter this," I said, immediately imagining us as winners and the damage we could do to the school in that tank!

It was obvious the others were thinking the same.

"Yeah, with our skills we'll walk it," agreed Danny, nodding enthusiastically.

Easy," added Gary with a grin, as we hurried off to the changing rooms to get into our kit.

Outside the sports field had been transformed with various obstacles consisting of tunnels, tyres, rope swings and nets. We stood shivering in our aertex shirts and cotton shorts as we watched some of the other teams having a go, and our confidence began to ebb a little.

"That wall looks tricky," muttered Gary, sounding worried. "Look at Harper struggling."

Harper, known more for his ability to blow smoke rings than for his sporting prowess, tried once more to climb the final wall, before giving up and jogging tiredly around it.

"Nah, you just need a decent run at it," I said, firmly fixated on the glory of winning. "We'll do it easy."

"Just don't fall over when you run through those tyres," added Danny. "Look at Bates he's tiptoeing through like a ballet dancer."

We began to giggle and mess about, pirouetting around with our arms above our heads.

The Sergeant spotted us immediately and called us over. "You seem to have a lot of energy," he said. "You can go next."

"We can do this," I muttered as we stood waiting on the line. "Let's show 'em how it's done."

"Ready. Steady. Go!"

We were off. Dan went like a rocket, me a close second and Gary right behind us. The tyres slowed us down, left, right, left, right, left, right, then balancing along a log, then diving down under a tarpaulin, on our stomachs, elbows and knees going like mechanical frogs. We were neck and neck, all our practicing tearing around the woods and up trees paying off. The swings were a doddle, we swarmed easily over the nets, then through another tunnel. Finally it was just the wall. Dan and I made it easily, but as we reached the top and looked back we could see Gary struggling. He was carrying more weight and it was beginning to slow him. Quickly I jumped back down and made a cup with my hands. "Here, Gary." I yelled. Up he went, with Danny grabbing him by the shirt for a final heave. I took another run up and was over. We dashed for the finishing line together.

"Well done, lads," said the Sapper with the stop-watch. "That was a good time."

Eventually all of the teams had finished and we went back into the Sports Hall for the verdict.

"We have a tie for first place," announced the Sergeant. "However, because of the excellent teamwork involved we have decided to present the prize to the green team." He glanced down to look at a piece of paper in his hand. "That's Graham Bone, Danny Haste and Gary Johnson." He stepped forward and presented each of us with a winning medal.

It was great! We couldn't believe it. At long last we had been given something other than a detention. 'Bloodsucker' Leech looked gobsmacked and then more than a little worried. You could see his little brain going into overdrive at the though of us three in a tank!

Puffed up with pride we followed the Sergeant outside. The tank was painted in camouflage with nets on the side. A soldier was sitting snugly inside and at a nod from the Sergeant he fired it up. At once a large cloud of smoke emitted from the back, choking us all and setting our eyes watering.

"Let's be 'aving you then," yelled another soldier over the noise of the engine. Reaching down he grabbed us by our polo shirts and hauled us up onto the top of it.

"Hang on," yelled the Sergeant, and off we went across the school field, the tank vibrating and shaking so badly it was all we could do not to fall off.

I looked down into the turret and could see the driver working the levers with both hands to steer. "Can we have a go?" I shouted.

"OK," replied the Sergeant. He lifted Danny down onto the lap of the driver, where he was allowed to put his hands on the levers and turn the tank from side to side. "That's enough," said the Sergeant. Then it was Gary's go. With a huge smile on his face he was lowered down and took over. He turned out to be a natural and was so good he was allowed to turn the tank around at the top of the field. Next it was me, trundling the vast tank down the field towards the school. "Turn left," instructed the Sergeant. Unfortunately, I was a little slow, not on purpose of course! The tank blundered over the edge of the footpath, making a huge track shaped dent in it, leaving my mark on the school for eternity. We went back to look at it after, gathering around and putting our foot into the gaping hole.

"I suppose you are pleased with yourselves for damaging school property?" said the Sergeant, who had wandered over to join us.

"Yes," we all agreed laughing. "Who wouldn't be?"

The Sergeant smiled knowingly. "We had a great day," he said. "You three did well for a first attempt. You should come and join the army."

However, none of us did, and I think the Army probably had a lucky escape!

Chapter 2

Detention

As I've explained, the school did its best to keep Danny, Gary and I separate during school hours, putting each of us in different forms. Of course we didn't abide by this mind-numbingly stupid decision, once registration was over we quite often tagged along to each others classrooms, particularly if the teacher in charge was young and innocent (how we loved that type of teacher!). Detention was one of the few times teachers were actually forced to allow the three of us to be together, which was how we all came to be in the History room one particular lunchtime.

"Ouch!" I yelled, grabbing my neck. I hadn't noticed the piece of chalk whipping across the class room until it landed with well aimed accuracy.

"Bone, get your eyes off those girls and onto your work. If you'd behaved yourself in class you could have spent your lunchtime chatting up Debbie Smith instead of us all wasting our time up here." As I've mentioned, Mr. Watson, Head of the History Department, was one of the few teachers it was wise not to mess about, especially when he was missing his midday fag.

Still clutching my neck I picked up my pen and feigned diligence. Old Watson's right about something I thought, lunchtime detention is dead boring. Almost as boring as the hundred year war he'd been gabbling on about that morning, no wonder my mind had begun to wander. Looking across at Gary, who was staring into space with a blank look on his face, I began to ponder the merits of detention. What future life was a detention meant to be preparing us for - a long stay in prison perhaps, or a boring office job? Could it be that exercising our right to 'free speech' would set us off into a life of crime, or worse a career in accountancy stuck in an office for the rest of our lives! It was confusing, our teachers were always telling us it was our 'right' to speak out about how we felt, according to them democracy meant freedom of speech for all, however, when we did speak out it always ended in detention for questioning school policy or 'answering back'. Life was unfair!

The windows were open, and the scent of new mown grass drifted in, reminding us that Easter was over and the summer term was already heading towards May. The school bordered Burgh Heath and the opportunities offered by ponds and trees beckoned enticingly. Outside the babble of over a thousand kids, all intent on making the most of their last ten minutes of playtime, mocked us three prisoners trapped at our desks.

Salvation came in the form of a scruffy first former.

"Yes, Bennett." Watson eyed him with disfavour.

"I've got a note for you from Mr. Mather, sir."

"Well don't stand there dithering, give it here."

Watson took the proffered piece of paper, scanned it quickly, and then looked up. "You'll be relieved to hear that I'm wanted elsewhere. However, that does not mean that your detention is over. You will complete your essays on why you should keep your seething hormones under control and concentrate on your work, instead of drooling over the fourth form girls playing netball. I shall expect those essays on my desk when I return, or you will be back here again tomorrow. Do I make myself understood?"

"Yes, sir." We all nodded earnestly.

We gave him two minutes.

"I'll just make sure he's gone," I whispered, heading for the door. I stuck my head over the banisters just in time to see Watson disappearing around the corner towards the Head's office. As I turned back I noticed something hanging on the wall. It was then I had my light bulb moment.

“Hey, you lot,” I called over my shoulder. “Come and see what’s out here.”

“What’s that then?” asked Danny, as he and Gary followed me onto the landing.

Hanging on the wall was a fire hose enclosed in a glass case. No explanation was needed! We swiftly had the lock undone and it was the work of a moment to unwind the hose and take it through the classroom to the open window.

“We’ll wait until the girls are lined up and then we’ll get ‘em,” said Danny, taking hold of the nozzle.

“Duck down or they’ll see us,” urged Gary. “You turn on the water Gra’. We’ll tell you when.”

Moments later the bell sounded.

I gripped the red wheel that fed the water into the hose and waited.

“Now” yelled Gary.

I yanked the wheel. Nothing. The blasted thing wouldn’t budge.

“Come on Gra’, we’ll miss ‘em.”

Taking the wheel in both hands I yanked with all my might. The wheel suddenly began to move, slowly at first, then faster. I could feel the water filling up the hose, so I turned the wheel some more, and then some more.

Suddenly I heard screams coming from the playground, so I left the wheel and rushed into the classroom.

The pressure from the hose was so strong it was taking both Danny and Gary to hold it. Water was streaming out of the window, arcing high into the blue sky and pouring in a deluge on the line of girls below. They were getting absolutely soaked.

“Look at Suzie’s top, you can see her tits!” cried Danny joyfully, as the water plastered the girls blouses.

The screams were getting louder as the girls, drenched from head to foot, squealed and shouted. Some ran, others sank to the floor in a wet heap, Pam

Forrest, the wimp, burst into tears. It was brilliant. We stood at the window rocking with laughter.

Then Danny noticed someone dashing across the playground. "It's the Head," he yelled. "Quick, turn it off."

I sped out onto the landing, grabbed the wheel and spun it. The next second I was staring in horror – the wheel had come off in my hand!

"The wheel, it's bloody broken," I yelled as I pounded back into the classroom. "I can't turn it off."

Dan and Gary turned round immediately, yanking the hose back into the room. Danny, thinking quickly, put his hand over the spout, attempting to stop the water spraying everywhere. At that moment Gary fell backwards, crashing hard against Dan and the hose came out of their hands. It seemed to take on a life of its own, squirming around like a demented snake, spraying water over walls and ceiling, and anything else in its path. Papers shot off Watkins desk, tumbling in a sodden pile to the floor. Desks and chairs began to slither drunkenly as the force of the water pushed them backwards towards the classroom wall.

"Run!" I yelled.

Gary stumbled again, becoming even more entangled in the hose, which I swear had come to life and seemed determinedly out to get him.

We turned back to help him, reaching for the hose and attempting desperately to untangle it.

"Get out," shouted Gary. "Save yourselves. Go on!"

Within seconds Danny and I were out of the classroom and skidding down the stairs that were fast turning into Niagara Falls. We leapt wetly into the boy's cloakroom, hearts going twenty to the dozen. As we banged the door shut behind us we could hear footsteps pounding from all directions as teachers and prefects raced along corridors and up the stairs.

Quickly we dried ourselves on the roller-towels, and headed for our own classrooms. By the time our form teachers returned we were sitting angelically waiting for afternoon registration.

Gary, great mate that he is, assured the Head he had acted alone, although I'm sure Watkins wasn't so easily taken in. We told him we had left our completed essays on his desk, it wasn't our fault if the water had ruined them, but he gave us all an extra detention anyway.

Gary brushed aside our thanks for taking the inevitable caning (we shall always be grateful to him for that). To cheer him up Danny and I offered to walk home with him after school. It was a slow walk!

Chapter 3

Late Night Shopping

Thursday night on our estate was a good time to get up to mischief. It was the night most parents did their supermarket shop as the stores opened late and stock was sold cheaply before the Friday re-stock for the weekend. A convoy of cars could be seen disappearing towards the towns of Epsom or Sutton, and we kids felt safe in the knowledge that our parents would be out of the way for several hours as they searched the shelves for bargains.

"Hey, what's that noise?" asked Danny, as he and Gary watched me cleaning out the rabbit hutch (mum's vain attempt to keep me out of trouble).

We all listened. The noise seemed to be coming from Joe Brown's house in the next street.

"I wonder what he's up to?" asked Gary. "Shall we go and find out?"

I didn't need much encouragement to leave off the mucking out. Quickly I shoved the rabbit back into its run and we went to investigate. Minutes later we were clambering through Jo's garden gate and found him with his dad's Puch Maxi[3] moped. He had it up on its stand and was pedalling furiously, trying to start it.

"You won't get it going like that," said Danny helpfully, having immediately seen what the problem was. "Not until you've turned the fuel tap on!"

This was swiftly remedied and soon the engine barked into life.

---

[3] Puch Maxi moped – manufactured by the Austrian company Puch throughout the 1970s and 80s, with a 50cc air cooled engine. Very economical to run and could be ridden like a bicycle when the engine was disengaged.

"Are you going out on it?" asked Gary, always quick to spot an opportunity.

"Just over the field," Joe replied. "I thought I'd have a quick ride before mum and dad get back."

"Can we come too?"

"Sure."

We knew he'd let us have a go. Joe was the most easy-going boy you could ever meet, always up for a laugh no matter what the consequences.

Soon we were over the field taking turns riding up and down on the moped. Of course word got around and more kids turned up, all keen to take their first ride on a motorised bicycle which needed hardly any pedalling. Bumping over the soft turf, one lap of the field was all you got before being dragged off so someone else could have a go.

Eventually Joe decided it was getting late. "Sorry, everyone," he said. "That will have to be the last go. I'd better get the bike back before my dad gets home, he'll be wanting it for work in the morning."

"Can we do it again next week?" asked young Jonathan from the flats.

"Yeah," said Joe breezily. "I'll bring it over next Thursday."

As Joe rode the bike home everyone said what a good bloke he was for letting us all have a go, and how much fun it had been, and how fast it felt tearing around on the grass. Suddenly Joe became the most popular boy on the estate, and the following Thursday was eagerly awaited by everyone keen to have a ride on the moped.

Finally the long for day arrived. As soon as Joe's parents drove off he got the bike out and, looking like the Pied Piper of Hamelin with a string of kids in tow, he led the way to the field. More boys and girls were waiting on the green, all eager for a chance to emulate everyone's hero Barry Sheen. The nights riding went well, without a single accident and we got the bike back just before his dad pulled up. We left Joe helping to unload the shopping.

The following week the weather turned foggy and a low mist covered the field. We were worried that Joe would not be willing to risk damaging his dad's bike in those conditions. We needn't have been concerned as soon the high pitched whine of an engine was heard, and Joe came racing up the path with the bike's headlight on and a big smile on his face.

Only a small group had gathered this time, so we all got two or three laps of the field each. With the fog thickening it was hard to see where we were going, which added to the excitement.

Gary, always keen to take things a stage further, realised that if you turned the headlight off and rode straight at the group, then turned the light back on and jabbed the horn at the last minute, you could scare everyone into running out of the way. This literally sorted the boys from the girls, as the girls immediately screamed and ran, while the boys, keen to prove how brave (or stupid) they were, waited until the last second to jump.

As the evening wore on it began to get dark as well as foggy, which added an extra element of danger. The girls quickly realised how hazardous the game was becoming.

"We're going home," said Penny.

"What for?" asked Danny.

"Someone's going to get hurt the way you boys are carrying on."

"Nah, we know what we're doing," boasted Gary.

"You're mad, all of you, just mad," said Sue. "Come on let's leave these idiots to kill themselves."

We watched the girls as they strolled towards the flats, soon becoming swallowed up in the fog. Pride and pig-headedness dictated that not one of us boys was going to follow them. There was no way any of us were going to be laughed at or be called ‘chicken’. To go would be to loose face - we were in it until the end.

My turn was next. I went flying down the field, totally miscalculating where the group was. I felt Gary’s arm brush mine as, completely by luck rather than judgement, I turned the light back on at the last minute to see everyone scatter. With the dark and thickening fog it had been impossible to see a thing, and I was glad my turn was over and I (and everyone else) had survived.

“My go next,” said Danny, picking up the bike.

We could hear him turn the bike at the end of the field and then head towards us. We all poised ourselves ready to run, but then Dan got carried away with the horn which totally spoilt the surprise and we easily jumped out of his way. Annoyed at his failure he chased after Gary and tried to kick him, probably not the best move as it was Gary’s turn next.

As soon as Gary got on the bike we knew there would be trouble. He had that look in his eyes, you know, the one that meant normal rules did not apply. This would be one ride which would end either in Gary being declared utterly fearless, or someone getting seriously hurt.

A long way off, at the top of the field, we could hear him winding the bike up for a flat out run straight at us.

“He’d better not smash that bike,” said Joe, sounding worried. “My dad’ll kill me.”

We could see the bike’s headlight very dimly pointing towards us. Then it went out. The engine began to scream, getting closer and closer. Holding onto each other we were all shaking, but determined not to be the first to run. We waited in the pitch dark as the bike hurtled towards us. The air filled with the deafening scream of the engine. For a moment it seemed as if Gary would miss us, but suddenly the lamp came on and he was right there on top of us, the light almost blinding us as he rode straight at us.

Immediately we scattered, running in all directions. I saw Gary turn at the last second; desperately trying to avoid crashing into us, but Danny was already heading in 'that' direction. The bike went over his foot with a 'thud'. Danny fell to the ground; the bike went one way and Gary went face first the other.

Joe went running for the bike. "You bloody idiot," he yelled at Gary. "You've smashed the back light."

Gary sat up, coughing and spluttering. Danny hobbled to his feet, looked at Gary and started laughing. Soon he was holding his side, in hysterics.

"What is it?" I asked, helping Gary to his feet. Then I saw it and began to laugh too.

"What is it?" asked Gary. "What is it?"

By now the entire group was giggling and pointing.

"What the feck is it?"

"You seem to have something on the side of your face," I spluttered, trying hard not to laugh, but failing.

Hanging from the side of Gary's mouth was the biggest dog turd we had ever seen.

"What! WHAT!"

Suddenly he must have got the smell or the taste or something and tried to flick the turd off, but it got stuck to his hand, which just made us laugh more. We were rolling on the grass it was so funny, although Gary didn't seem to share our amusement.

"Yuck, shit, get it off me!" Gary began leaping around, flapping his hand, trying to get rid of the turd while we just doubled up.

Eventually, Danny, proving there were no hard feelings, produced a handkerchief so that Gary could clear himself up.

"No, I don't want it back!"

Well, that cheered Joe up and he started to push the moped towards home. Unfortunately, his parents chose just that moment to return from their shopping trip. His dad was not pleased. We could hear him shouting all the way back to their house, until their front door slammed shut with a BANG that set every dog in the street barking.

Walking back to my house to get cleaned up, (Danny limping as his foot had swollen to almost twice its normal size) we all decided riding mopeds was great. As soon as we were sixteen we would all get one and ride around together, and then the whole world would be ours to explore.

We told mum our plans as she examined the bruising to Danny's foot.

"It's a good idea, isn't it mum? With one of those mopeds we could go anywhere. It's only just over a year 'til we're sixteen."

"Mm," muttered mum, as she held a bag of frozen peas to Danny's ankle. "If you live that long!"

"Just think of all the girls we could meet if we had mopeds," I said, ignoring her.

Gary grinned. "I'm getting a Mulaguti[4] as soon as I can," he announced.

"Fizzies[5] are faster and more reliable," asserted Danny, with all the confidence of an expert who had never ridden one in his life.

"Malaguti's look better," I argued. "And if you want to impress the girls, then looks are important."

The others nodded, it was most important to impress the girls!

---

[4] Malaguti – Italian scooter.

[5] Fizzy – Yamaha FS1 moped

Chapter 4

Girls

We didn't have much luck with girls at school; they never seemed to like us, apart from one – Debbie Smith. She was the prettiest girl in the school, with short blond hair cut in a bob, a fantastic body, really fit and guaranteed to turn any lad's head. Unfortunately, Debbie had a temper and was definitely not one to cross. I went to judo club with her and knew she was strong enough to toss a man twice her size. She was not someone to get on the wrong side of - beautiful, but deadly.

I've no idea why she decided to be friends with us, probably because we were always in trouble like her. Her dad was the local builder and had turned their end-of- terrace home into a country mansion with a swimming pool in the back garden. He didn't mind her having friends over so, having nothing to do on a Thursday night now that Joe's dad had forbidden him to even look at the Puch Maxi, we went around to Debbie's house to watch Top of the Pops[6].

"Why do you think girls don't like us?" I asked, ogling Pan's People[7] as they gyrated energetically.

Debbie gave me a very critical look, her eyes flicking disparagingly over my collar length brown hair, none-too-clean t-shirt and flared jeans.

"It's your hair," she decided. "You should have it cut to look more like a pop star."

---

[6] Top of the Pops – A popular weekly TV programme on the BBC, with some of the week's best selling music artists and bands, and a run-down of the music charts.

[7] Pan's People – All girl dance group, which performed weekly on Top of the Pops.

Seems reasonable to me, I thought, watching as the TV screen switched to Paul Simon belting out 'Fifty ways to leave your lover'. He was surrounded by girls crowding around the stage, flicking back their hair and flashing their eyes at him.

"OK," I said, "cut it then."

I knew that Debbie's mum owned a hairdressing salon and that Debbie worked there at the weekend, sweeping up and making cups of tea for the clients.

"Really?" asked Debs, her eyes lighting up at a chance to practice her skill with the scissors.

I nodded.

"You couldn't make it worse," put in Danny, with all the helpfulness mates are known for. But as his mum still insisted he went to the local barber's at Burgh Heath for a short back and sides, everyone ignored him.

"Just let me get some scissors then."

She gave me the full works, first dragging me into the bathroom where I had to put my head over the sink while she gave my hair a wash. Well, I don't know what her mum had been teaching her at that salon, but I thought my head was going to come off the way she attacked my scalp.

"Hey, I haven't got nits," I spluttered through a mouth full of soap.

"Just making sure," said Debbie.

My, that girl had some muscles on her.

Then she towelled me so briskly I'm surprised there was any hair left to cut.

Next she hustled me into the kitchen. "Sit there," she demanded, pointing to a chair.

Well, you didn't argue with Debbie when she told you to do something. I sat!

A towel was draped around my shoulders, and then she picked up a lethal looking pair of scissors and went in for the kill. Hair flew everywhere as I sat immobile in that chair, terrified to move a muscle in case I lost an ear.

Danny and Gary sat at the kitchen table smirking as Debbie finished me off with a blast from a burning hot hair dryer, curling my hair around a brush that I swear was invented by the Devil to strip the skin from my scalp. Then she proudly produced a mirror.

I looked like Elvis Presley!

The lads could hardly suppress their laughter, but a look from Debbie soon stopped that.

"You look great," spluttered Danny, swiftly.

"It really suits you," added Gary, sounding as if his underpants were strangling him.

I was not so sure.

Debbie was surveying me critically again. "It needs something else," she decided, thinking hard. "I know – an earring."

"OK," I said quickly, hoping to impress her. "Have you got one?"

"Loads! Come on up into the bathroom," she replied. "Gary, get some ice out of the fridge."

"Ice?" I questioned.

"To numb the skin and stop the bleeding."

"Oh!" I looked at her dubiously, beginning to think this might not be such a good idea. "Have you done this before?"

"No," she said nonchalantly. "But I've seen my sister do it."

"That's all right then," said Danny.

He and Gary stood there grinning, both giving me a gleeful pat on the back.

"We'll make sure you don't bleed to death," Gary assured me cheerfully, egging me on as only a true mate would.

I was not feeling confident, but there was no way I could back out of it now, the lads would never let me forget it, and worse, neither would Debbie! She'd be on the phone to her friends as soon as I walked out of the door.

"Hold this ice cube on your ear until it goes numb," ordered Debbie. "Then I'll stick this needle through into a cork behind it and then we can put a stud in and you will have an earring. Easy."

Easy, she said. Easy for her no doubt, but I manfully submitted to the torture. Actually the pain was not so bad, although there was a lot of blood as she pushed the stud through. However, it soon stopped when she grabbed a tissue and pinched my ear, pinched it so tightly I was sure the blood would never flow through it again and my ear would fall off.

"How do I look now?" I asked, gingerly feeling the gold stud and wondering when the throbbing feeling would stop.

"Don't ask me," she retorted. "You all look ugly to me! But I'll ask my sister."

She stuck her head out of the door and yelled.

Her sister Angie worked in a casino in London as a bunny girl[8]. She came into the bathroom wearing her outfit, complete with ears and fluffy tail, breasts proudly and unselfconsciously on display. Gary nearly passed out! With no sisters he'd led a very sheltered life.

Angie grabbed hold of my chin and turned my face from side to side before giving her opinion. "Yeah, he's not bad."

This was too much for Danny. "We should go," he spluttered. "It's getting late."

At the front door I thanked Debbie for the haircut, and the earring. She bent over and quickly kissed me on the cheek.

I floated home with her sister's laughter ringing in my ears, my two best mates ribbing me all the way.

The next day I went to school full of delightful expectation, convinced that now I looked like a film star I would have the girls falling at my feet. However, life is cruel, all I got was a lot of mickey taking from the boys and the girls all ignored me - as usual.

---

[8] Bunny Girl – Originally a waitress at The Playboy Club, London. The girls wore a very skimpy outfit called a 'bunny suit'.

Chapter 5

Cross Country Running

Although we hated PE, Games and Athletics generally, we were always first to volunteer for cross country running. This really puzzled our teachers because the three of us did not appear the athletic type; Gary built like a rugby scrum half, Danny wiry but small and me who hated being *made* to do anything and refused to do Games just to be awkward. However, as soon as cross country running was mentioned up our hands would go. The course involved running out of the school gates, across the fields, down to Tattenham Corner, across Epsom Downs, around the clock tower and then back again. What the teachers failed to realise was that my house overlooked the fields, which meant a short run before ducking through my back gate and into the kitchen. There we spent the afternoon cooking beefburgers and sausages, drinking mum's homemade wine, watching TV and lying on the sofa with our feet up. There is a lot to be said for having a mum who goes out to work. We could see the others run back past and would simply join in with the rest of the pack somewhere towards the back, jumping in some puddles to get dirty on the return to school.

Never coming first was a tradition at De Burgh, because if you won anything it was the responsibility of the other lads to drag you naked out of the showers, push and kick you out of the changing room and then jam the door so the girls, (whose changing room was next-door) would see you standing there with no clothes on. This of course occasioned great hilarity. It also occasioned numerous spiteful and derogatory comments (never let anyone tell you that girls are sweet), as you tried desperately to cover your embarrassment. However, on this particular day of cross country running Gary had something to prove – someone had been teasing him about his extra weight and his lack of physical ability. So, after a lovely afternoon relaxing, we joined the pack as usual for the short trot back to school, only this time Gary decided that, just for a change, he was going to win. Well, we couldn't let him win on his own, so we ran as fast as we could after him and some other joined in too, so it looked like we were really racing for the line.

You could see the astonishment in the Games master's face as we arrived in first, second and third!

"Well done, lads," he said, "That was a really good time. It's the Inter School Sports on Friday - you must run for the school. It's against Nork Park and Epsom College."

We were horrified, not only would we have to run, but against the two schools we hated the most. This was definitely news we did not want to hear. We had only once run the entire course and it had nearly killed us, and on principal we hated everyone who went to 'Dork' Park, and the posh kids at Epsom 'Private' College.

Gary, as tradition dictated, was pushed naked out of the changing room just as the girls were lining up after netball. He ran around chasing them until the teacher heard all the screaming and pushed him back in. Strangely enough he enjoyed this experience, and his return to the changing room with a big grin on his face was accompanied by much patting on the back.

Friday came around far too quickly and we got onto the maroon and cream coach supplied by Epsom Coaches and headed across the Downs towards Epsom town. We were all in a right stew and sat on the back seat looking glumly out of the windows.

"Those posh kids are weird," said Gary dejectedly. "You know they actually seem to like going to school?"

To us this seemed disgraceful; the only thing we liked about De Burgh was the final bell.

"And they are *so* polite," he continued, putting on a hoity-toity voice, "with oh such perfect manners. La-di-da-di-dah."

"I saw one of their boys in town last week when I went to the dentist," put in Danny. "He was talking to a teacher. By choice!"

We stared at him in amazement. That was truly horrific.

"Dork Park are worse though," I said "Look at them." I pointed to the coach that was pulling through the gates to Epsom College ahead of us. A row of lads were giving us the finger through the back window.

"My sister said when she was at school Nork Park was called Piquet's Way School," Danny informed us, "but it had such a bad reputation they had to change the name."

"Didn't do any good, did it?" said Gary disparagingly.

We shook our heads, watching as the Nork Park contingent continued to stick out their tongues and make obscene gestures, copied of course by us.

"I'm not going to let any of that lot beat me," I decreed.

"So how are we going to beat them?" asked Gary.

"Well, Danny's the fastest of us three," I said. "If he can get in front of them and slow them down a bit, I'll trip them up and you can jump on them."

"What about that posh black kid?" asked Danny, immediately spotting a flaw in my immaculate plan, "I bet he goes like a rocket; I won't be able to catch him."

"Just keep up with him and wear him down," suggested Gary, making it sound easy.

"OK, then, that's the plan, let's try to stick with it this time," I said, knowing we rarely, if ever, kept to a set plan.

The first setback to this amazing plan was at the start – we found out that three teachers would be joining us on the run to make sure there was fair play. Trust a teacher to think of something ridiculous like that.

"Just stick to the plan," I muttered. "Those two fat morons we saw smoking will never keep up."

"That tall ginger teacher might give us some trouble," murmured Danny.

"I'll keep my eye on him," I whispered. "You worry about the black kid."

Off we ran, taking it easy at first, as though we were pacing ourselves, which of course we were. We passed one or two stragglers, and then put on a burst of speed, shooting on ahead. Soon a pack of five of us got into the lead. The black kid was in front, followed by the ginger teacher, then the three of us.

"Catch him, Danny," I said with a quick nudge. "Tell him someone's fallen."

I'll say one thing for Dan he's quick on the uptake. Immediately he ran forward and tugged the teacher's shirt. "Please, Sir, one of your team has tripped."

"Yes, Sir," joined in Gary, panting a little already. "It's the red haired boy back there; we heard a terrible crack as he landed. I think he might have broken something."

"Thanks, lads," he said. "You carry on and I'll go back."

"OK, Sir," we called, trying to keep a straight face.

"Good luck then," he shouted, as he sprinted back.

"Cheers, Sir."

Now it was just the black kid who was in the distance and we were struggling to catch him. Just as we came over the top of the hill we saw him turn left and run off the track and into the trees.

"Where's he going?" asked Gary.

"He's taking a short cut," I answered. "Come on, let's follow him."

Quick as a flash we were off the track too and heading into the wood.

"Oi! Where are you going?" I shouted, as we scrambled through the trees towards him.

He stopped and leant against an old oak tree, trying to catch his breath.

"I'm running away," he explained, sounding really choked up. "I hate it at that boarding school, they all pick on me. I want to get back to Tadworth. I've got a sister there and I can stay with her for the summer."

"Alright," I said, thinking furiously. "You let us win and we'll smuggle you onto our coach. My uncle drives it and he can drop you off on the way back."

"Really?" he asked.

"Of course," I replied. "Here, shake on it. What's your name?" I added as I held out my hand.

"James." He sounded really posh.

"Well, I'm Graham," I explained, "and this is Gary and Danny.

We all shook his hand that looked so different from ours.

"Are you always so black?" I asked in my usual blunt way, I'd never met a black person before.

"Yes," he replied, looking surprised.

"Cool," we said, stretching out our arms to match his.

"I thought I had a good tan until I met you," I said and he laughed.

"I come from Africa," he explained. "Everyone I know back home is black."

That seemed reasonable to us, everyone we knew in England was white, except Mr Patel and his family who ran the shop, and they were so much a part of the Estate that we didn't notice what colour they were, to us they were just the Patels. We had never really questioned it, but thinking about it now we decided it was natural that there might be other countries where everyone was black.

"We'd better get on if we want to win," said Danny. "Is there a way through here?"

"Yes," said James. "It's a short-cut. It'll bring us out near the finish. I always cut through here."

I was beginning to like James, he thought like one of us, and he hated the posh school, so we would have to help him escape.

We rejoined the race at a bend in the track and went straight up the hill to the school gates a mile away. The short-cut was not so short and a pack of other runners were catching us up now, so we all picked up speed and sprinted towards the gates. The last part was very steep and I could feel my heart beating so fast I though my lungs would explode. This racing lark was for idiots.

James was lagging behind us as we entered the school. A large crowd had gathered around the finish line. They all went quiet when they saw we were in front and as we crossed the line together there was a lot of mumbling about possible cheating, particularly from the supporters of Nork Park. Then James shook our hands. "You've beaten me fair and square," he said loudly, with a big grin.

The ginger teacher came over and thanked us for alerting him to the problems behind as there had been a fight between Nork Park and a posh kid when they had tried to do exactly what we had planned. They were sent home in disgrace, much to our delight.

Gary was declared the winner, with Danny second and me third. Old Mather, our Head, was there of course, and for once seemed as delighted as we were. He always turned up in his Rolls Royce when someone from the school won something. It gave him a chance to get in the news. Sure enough he had brought along the photographer from the local paper who took a picture of us with our medals.

"You must all stay for dinner," said the Epsom College Head.

"Come on," said James. "I'll show you where the showers are and then you can have a look around."

The school was enormous, very old and dark, with lots of wood panelling. We really liked it and were surprised to find that everyone was friendly and made us feel welcome. The food was unbelievable, four courses, soup, then salmon, followed by roast beef with all the trimmings and ice-cream to finish.

"Do you eat like this all the time?" I asked James.

"Yes, of course." He looked at us curiously. "What do you eat?"

"Beans on toast mainly," said Gary, and we all laughed, but James didn't get the joke. Gary's mum thought all boys needed feeding up, and every time we went to his house she would make us beans on toast. I don't suppose James had ever eaten that council estate staple.

My cunning plan to help James escape drove out of the gates when the coach we were going to smuggle him onto left with the rest of our school team. Mr. Mather had decided that we were to be driven back to the school in his chauffeur driven car.

"We'll see you tomorrow," I whispered to James as we left. "Don't worry we'll soon get you free.

In the car on the way home we all agreed James must be mad for wanting to leave Epsom College, it was an amazing school and we would all love to have gone there. It was completely different to how we had imagined and De Burgh seemed shabby in comparison, although we were sensible enough to keep our observations from Mr. Mather!

Chapter 6

The Great Escape

I've no idea how we managed to get up at five-thirty the following morning for our paper-rounds. I don't know about Dan and Gary, but I was feeling completely bushed. My legs felt like lead as I pushed my bike out of our shed and rode stiffly over to the Newsagents in Kingswood to collect the papers. Luckily the others looked just as knackered as me as we all arrived at the front of the shop.

A couple of hours later we caught the bus to Epsom to rescue James. Unfortunately, after knocking at the door of Epsom College we were told to come back later as James was in lessons!

"OK, we'll come back at twelve," I said.

"Can you believe that?" asked Danny as we walked back down the long drive. "Fancy having lessons on a Saturday and we thought De Burgh was strict."

"You wouldn't catch me doing lessons on a Saturday," declared Gary. "Weekends are for fun!"

Danny and I agreed. Doing school work for five days a week was more than enough for anyone, especially with the amount of homework we got, not that we did much of it.

We decided to go to the park and spent the morning walking around the boating lake and watching the model boats being sailed. The cool wind of the day before had given way to sunshine and the yachts had to be pushed across the water with the help of long sticks. We were far more interested in a remote controlled launch, as we had not seen one before.

Eventually we returned to the College and knocked once again for James. He was given some money to spend and told to be back by six.

"Have you hidden your clothes?" I asked furtively; as we strolled nonchalantly back down the drive, enjoying the warm sun on our backs.

James looked embarrassed. "I've decided not to run away," he admitted.

"Why not?" asked Gary, with a look of surprise. "We'll help you escape if you want to."

"Yeah, we can soon get you to Tadworth," added Danny.

"No, it's alright now," said James. "As soon as I lost that race everyone seemed to warm to me."

He looked down and shuffled his feet. "I was trying very hard to win at everything," he explained, "because I thought they would like me more if I was good at things. But instead everyone got fed up with me."

"They probably thought you were showing off," said Danny frankly. "No-one likes a smart ass."

We all nodded.

"Anyway, no-one wants to win at our school, not at sports anyway," I said.

"Why's that?" asked James, looking totally confused. "I thought everyone wanted to win."

"You get thrown out of the changing rooms naked if you win," explained Danny, "and all the girls laugh at you."

"Have you got girls at your school?" asked James, looking surprised.

"Loads of 'em," I said. "And they can be a complete pain in the neck. Aren't there any at your school then?"

James shook his head.

We looked at him in amazement, a school without girls, how cool was that? Merland Rise (our primary school), De Burgh and even Dork Park were all co-ed, it hadn't occurred to us that there might be schools where girls were excluded.

"That's why it's so quiet," stated Danny, thinking of his sisters at home. "Without girls screeching all the time it must be *so* peaceful."

I nodded in agreement, my house was certainly quieter since my two sisters had got married, and no doubt school would be the same without hoards of girls twittering on. Although the view from the history room might not be quite as interesting!

"What are we going to do then?" asked Gary.

"I'd still like to see my sister," said James.

"Whereabouts in Tadworth does she live?" I asked.

"At the end of Vernon's Walk."

I looked at Gary. That was his paper route.

"Yeah, I know it," he said with a laugh, "The house with the gates - Fir Tree Cottage. I've been delivering newspapers there for the last two years."

"OK, let's get the bus then," I said.

"What's a bus?" asked James, looking puzzled.

All three of us stared at him.

"You're winding us up," I said.

James shook his head.

"You must know what a bus is," put in Danny.

James shook his head again. "I've really no idea what you're talking about. What is a bus?"

"Blimey," said Gary. "What country are you from?"

"Africa," answered James, he went red again and looked embarrassed, then looked around cautiously. "Can I trust you?" he whispered.

We all nodded vigorously.

He looked around nervously again. Then in a low voice so that only we could hear, he said, "I suppose I'd better explain, but please promise to keep quiet about it," he paused and his dark eyes seemed to bore into us. "It could be dangerous."

Dangerous! That sounded interesting. We stared at him goggled eyed and solemnly promised. With all the things we had to keep quiet about one more wouldn't be a problem!

"My father is a Prince," explained James. "We are in exile here because of the trouble at home."

"Really?" we asked, still thinking he might be pulling our leg.

"Really," he said, looking deadly serious. "There was a coup, a really bloody coup, and many people were killed."

"Blimey!" said Gary again.

I wasn't at all sure what a coup was, but it didn't sound good.

"Never mind, mate," I said, giving him a friendly shove. "You're safe enough here."

"Nothing interesting ever happens here," added Gary gloomily.

"What's it like in Africa then?" asked Danny, changing the subject.

"Well, it is hot all the time," explained James, "and there is no winter. There is never any snow."

"That's a shame," I said. "We love the snow."

We were soon telling him how we had ridden down Box Hill on the bonnet of an old car last winter, and had snow ball fights against Dork Park, and savage coups were forgotten.

The bus arrived and we bundled up stairs. James seemed fascinated by the experience, and insisted on paying our fares. It wasn't far to the village and we soon found Fir Tree Cottage and were let in by the butler who made us all fruit drinks. James's sister was tall, slim, with a long neck and very elegant looking. She had a baby daughter who was soon being passed around the four of us. My eldest sister had a baby boy about the same age so I was quite used to babies and this one was lovely, happy to go to any of us, although she especially loved James and kept smiling at him. We sat outside in the warm May sunshine and talked about Africa. James and his sister told us about the different wild animals, and how they had lived as part of a royal family, their life was so very different from ours, but at least we didn't have to worry about being shot. Eventually the baby fell asleep, so we thanked James's sister for having us (my mum would have been pleased that her lessons in manners had not been completely wasted!) and promised to return again soon with our new friend James.

"What shall we do now?" Danny chipped in, as we walked through the village centre.

"What do you normally do on a Saturday afternoon?" asked James.

"Football!" we chorused.

"Have you ever played football, James?" Danny asked, as we strolled towards the playing fields opposite my house.

"Not at school," he replied. "They only let us play rugby. But at home in Africa I was the star player for my team."

"Well, I bet you've never played a game of football like this before," I laughed. "And if you've as good as you say you'd better be on our side."

We led him to the field opposite my house. It was bordered by hedges of hawthorn, weighed down with May blossom and their perfume scented the warm afternoon air. Unfortunately Dutch Elm Disease was beginning to decimate many of the tall elm trees, but the oak trees were just beginning to unfurl their leaves, and the edges of the field were lacy with cow parsley, stitchwort and red campion (or to us lads, pink and white flowers!).

We usually played at the end of the field where a fence separated it from the new estates garages, the advantage being that when a goal was scored the ball would hit the fence and bounce back. The goal at the other end was more moveable depending on how many people were playing, with little kids on tricycles or with toddlers in tow being persuaded to collect any balls that got past the goalie.

When we arrived a game was already in progress, as it was every Saturday afternoon. Jackets had been set out to mark the goal posts, and teams were recognised by removing tops on one side (Skins) and keeping tops on (Shirts) for the other.

"Hi, Gra', you going to play for us?" yelled one of the Skins.

"Yeah," I yelled back, beginning to strip off my t-shirt. "This is James; he'll play for us too."

There was a bit of disagreement when James stripped off and the others realised how fit he looked, but a quick reshuffle of players, with Shirts being allowed a couple of extra kids, soon sorted things out.

Harold was keeping goal at the estate end, aged about twenty-five and built like a tank, no-one argued with him, so he doubled up as referee, ably assisted by my next-door-neighbour Clive who was goalie at the other end. They also broke up any fights, and insisted dogs and motorbikes were kept off the field. A bucket of water and a cup that was used for refreshment by everyone was on hand by the fence, and play only stopped for a while after a goal was scored to regroup or have a wee in the trees.

"There's a woman with no top on," whispered James, giving me a nudge.

"Oh, that's Joan," I explained as she dashed past, dribbling the ball like an expert, her breasts looking like they might bounce out of her bra. "She's on our side, Skins. Don't worry, she's really good."

James looked rather bemused but jogged willingly onto the pitch.

"Here, Joan, here," I yelled, dodging around a couple of little kids. One immediately grabbed hold of my leg and clung on.

Gary ran around me, scooping the other kid out of the way, swinging him in the air for me to catch, while Danny raced past heading up the field. Joan tapped the ball towards him, and he swiftly passed it on to James. Weaving around a couple of young mums and a drunken pensioner James took aim and gave a mighty kick. Harold made a noble effort, but the ball just grazed his fingers and banged loudly against the fence. GOAL!

I tucked the kid under my arm and went over to pat James on the back. "Great work." I said, dumping the kid on the ground. "Keep that up and you'll have to play for us every Saturday."

The kid immediately saw a new idol and attached himself to James. "Up, up," he demanded, lifting up his sticky hands.

"Good idea," said Harold, "I think your new friend needs to play with a handicap, or you'll be romping away. Got to keep things fair"

James grinned good-naturedly and lifted the kid up onto his shoulders. He spent the next twenty minutes running backwards and forwards along the pitch with young Ben gripping on for grim death, yelling "Goal! Goal!", until his mum came to take him home for his tea. We could hear the little lad's screams until his front door shut.

We played for the rest of the afternoon, the two teams expanding and contracting as people joined in or went home. Mums went to put the dinner on, while dads tried to recapture the glories of their youth, pretending they had to look after their kids when they got out of breath. Word got around that James was playing, and some of the girls gave off titivating themselves for the Church social and strolled over to the field, clapping and fluttering their eye lashes every time he ran towards the goal. In, out and around everyone ran kids of all shapes and sizes - boys and girls, toddlers and teens, Jon who had learning difficulties but loved football and Andy an expert in blocking with his wheelchair, if they could kick a ball or even if they couldn't they could play in a team. There was some really good football played, some totally rubbish passes, and some excellent goals, although we stopped counting when it got to double figures.

"That was great," said James as we walked him back to the bus.

"We're here every Saturday," I said, "just come over and join in."

We waited until the bus arrived to see James off, and then walked back to my house across the fields. The football game had fizzled out as more people went home to get their tea, leaving just a few stragglers sprawled out on the grass.

"That new friend of yours was good," yelled one. "You want to bring him again."

"We're trying to get him along next week," I assured him.

"Good job we had James on *our* side," put in Danny. "He scored a couple of cracking goals.

"Pity he goes to Epsom College," added Gary. "If he lived with his sister he could go to our school, then we could see him during the week."

"We'd soon show him a few tricks," said Danny with a grin.

"I bet he has to knuckle down at that College," I said. "Did you hear him saying he gets reams of homework and they have something called 'Prep' after school, where one of the teachers makes sure they do their homework – ALL of it!"

The others looked horrified.

"That wouldn't suit me," asserted Danny.

"Nor me," agreed Gary.

We walked in silence for a moment as we imagined having to stay at school each night until our homework was finished. It was enough to give us nightmares!

"We can find better things to do with our evenings than homework," stated Danny emphatically. And Gary and I, equally emphatically, agreed.

Chapter 7

The Footballing Granny

It was the May Bank Holiday and the weekend stretched ahead of me. I was sitting in the kitchen clutching a mug of tea. Our dog, Joe, sat waiting expectantly, nose on my knee, trying to mesmerise me into sharing my breakfast toast and marmalade.

"We're going into Banstead later on," said mum, filling the kettle again (our house ran on tea). "Do you want to come?"

"Are you going shopping?" I asked suspiciously, thinking it might be a cunning plan to get me to help with the weekend shop. Mothers are tricky creatures.

"No, it's the Lion's Club; they're having a summer fete."

"I won't have to stay with you, or help out?" I asked, still suspicious. It is just as well to be completely clear about these things. Mum was likely to have me helping on the cake stall, or even worse, selling raffle tickets.

"No. Dad will give you some money and you can go off on your own."

That was all right then. I got on the phone to Danny and Gary immediately. Of course their parents were going too. The Preston Hawe Estate wasn't exactly humming with social opportunities at the weekend, or at any other time come to that.

We met up by the refreshments tent and, after conning mum into buying us all a cake and a can of coke, getting my dad to grudgingly hand over some money.

"Don't come back to me asking for more," said dad, watching mum nervously as she headed for the plant stall.

"No," I assured him. "And we'll find our own way home."

He hurried after mum, eager to stop her spending spree, while we strolled around looking at what was on offer.

Summer fetes usually followed a similar formula, with lots of stalls all trying to part you with your money:- cake stalls, plant sales, second hand books, the white elephant stall (i.e. loads of old junk). Guess the weight of the cake – I always suspected someone had hidden a brick inside it. Guess how many jelly beans in a jar was a favourite with the kids. There was bash the ferret, pick a duck, and a bran tub (a prize every time for the toddlers). The local brass band was usually wheeled out. The primary school put on a country dancing display (that was usually worth watching as they bumped into each other and fell over, and some kid ended up with a nose bleed). However, this year they had laid on something special – Beat the Granny!

The Granny was obviously a man dressed in fancy dress with a wig and make-up. The idea was to pay your money, take five shots from the penalty spot into a full sized goal, and if you managed to get three goals past the Granny you would win a prize. This was the funniest thing we had seen, and we were soon creased up as one after another man and boy walked up to the penalty spot and took aim, only to be defeated by the Granny. We had some very good players locally, some even professional, but in their casual shoes not one could score the required three goals. This Granny was obviously something special.

Eventually Granny took a break and headed for the toilets.

"Come on," said Danny. "Let's follow him."

Dan was obviously up to something, so into the 'Gents' we all trooped, to find Granny battling with her long skirts and petticoats to relieve 'herself' in the urinal.

"Hello, Peter," said Danny with a grin,

Granny gave us a startled look - then realisation dawned.

"Sussed!" he said and smiled.

"Come with me," he beckoned, as soon as he had adjusted himself.

We followed him into a tent, which he carefully zipped shut behind us.

"Have these, lads," he said and handed us each footballs, gloves, scarves, boots and key-rings. They were all signed Peter Bonetti. 'Granny' was only the Chelsea and England goalkeeper, probably the best goalkeeper in the entire world at the time!

"Now keep quiet all of you, or I'll get into trouble with the manager for this. It's just a favour for a friend to raise some money for charity, but if the FA find out I'll be up shit creek, so you keep your mouths shut and I might let you score some goals."

We were delighted and nodded our heads eagerly.

"Thanks very much," said Danny, as we gathered around to shake Peter's hand.

"And we promise not to tell a soul," I added.

"Good lads," he said and turned to Danny. "Don't be late with the papers!"

We realised then that this was one of the celebrities from Danny's paper round. What a bit of luck!

The Union Jack bags he had given us to put the gifts in stood out and some friends from school asked what was in them, but of course we couldn't tell, so we walked up to the shops and sat on a bench to see what we'd been given. We'd done really well and, after we had swapped them around so they fitted, we each had a super pair of football boots, much better than we could have afforded to buy ourselves.

"Let's go back to the Beat a Granny and have a go with our new boots," I suggested.

"Good idea," agreed Gary.

We made our way back to the field. It was still very busy, with families and couples walking around enjoying the sunshine and the side shows, and kids running everywhere. The refreshment tent was packed, and people spilled out onto the grass.

We dumped our bags on the ground beside the goal mouth and put on our new boots.

"Are you going to have a go?" called Granny.

"Yes," replied Danny, walking up to the spot and placing the ball.

A small crowd had gathered to watch the fun. There was utter amazement when Danny managed to put in three consecutive goals.

"It must be the boots," said Danny.

Next went Gary. Three more goals went into the back of the net.

"Saturday football's obviously paying off," I shouted to him.

Then it was my turn. Surely I couldn't do a hat trick. But I did. Three more goals!

I'd like to think I had the skill as I was a better than average player, but there was absolutely no way I should have been able to put even one of those balls past an England goalkeeper of Peter Bonetti's calibre - even if he was dressed as a granny! We were each given a long, thin envelope as a prize for scoring our hat-tricks.

We caught the bus home and rushed up to the top deck as usual.

"Let's have a look in these envelopes," said Danny.

Swiftly we ripped them open.

"Tickets," announced Gary, holding his up.

"Two tickets," said Danny.

"And not just any tickets," I said, reading the wording on them.

We had each received two VIP tickets to see the Harlem Globetrotters, an all black professional basketball team, who were playing at the Wembley

Sports Arena. It was a special 50th anniversary show, and there was to be a juggler as well. A coach had been laid on, leaving from Burgh Heath the following Friday at 4.00pm.

"Basketball?" said Gary, looking faintly disappointed. "Is that like Netball? Like the girls play at school."

"No," replied Danny. "It's American; it's a man's sport."

"That's OK then," I said with relief. We all loved anything from America, Coca Cola, Mohammad Ali, and of course Evel Knievel.

"If it comes from America it must be good, just look at their cars," I added, knowing that we all loved the Ford Mustang one of my sister's boyfriends had driven around in.

"We'll have a great time," agreed Danny. "And we can take a friend as we've got two tickets each."

"Who will you take?" I asked Gary.

"My brother," he said immediately. "What about you?"

"It might be worth asking Debbie," I said casually. Debbie Smith, as you must now realise, was easily the best looking girl at our school and every boy wanted to take her out, including me. I'd hoped that my new haircut and earring might have attracted more than her usual scathing mockery, but no such luck. Perhaps free tickets might do the trick.

"Debbie! You've not got a hope in hell," retorted Danny scornfully, with the brutal honesty of a good mate. "She'd probably punch you for suggesting it.

"Or kick you in the nuts," added Gary cheerfully.

"It's worth a try," I said, with all the foolish optimism of youth. "She's been good to us lately."

"Well, if you're taking a girl I shall ask my sister," decided Danny. "She has a hard time living with Tim. I'm sure she'd like a night out for a change."

We all knew Pam's husband Tim was a hippy and floated through life as though he was on another planet, which of course most of the time he was!

As soon as we reached home we got our bikes out, cycled around to Debbie's house and knocked on the door.

"Afternoon Mrs. Smith," I said politely, it being always wise to keep on the good side of a girl's parents. "Is Debbie at home please?"

The 'please' obviously worked. "Debbie!" Mrs Smith yelled up the stairs.

Debbie did not look impressed to see us, but that was nothing new. However, she *was* impressed by the tickets - particularly with the V.I.P. bit, and with them being free.

"OK," she said nonchalantly, "I'll come with you. BUT," she looked me firmly in the eye, so that I was under no illusions that the Harlem Globetrotters were the attraction and definitely not me. "I'll take my ticket. I'm not getting dressed up just to find that you've lost it!"

I was so pleased that she'd actually said 'yes' that I was happy to ignore any slurs on my character. With two elder sisters I was quite used to female put downs.

The following Friday, spruced up and dressed in our best we all waited at the bus stop at Burgh Heath. It was a lovely evening, with the sun shining and swallows dipping and diving over the pond. A skylark sang high overhead and the chestnut trees that edged the main road were covered in large candles of cream blossom. Of course Debbie was late, and I had almost been convinced by my trusty mates that I'd been dumped, when I spotted her crossing the road. I gave Danny and Gary a superior grin as she hurried towards us, looking stunning in a long red dress she had borrowed from her sister.

Wembley was brilliant; there was no other word for it. We clambered off the coach and were shown into a spacious reception room, where an enormous buffet was laid out. Dainty finger food, huge platters of cold meats, different salads, sausage rolls, trifles, gateaux and cakes, the long table was overflowing with goodies.

"This is better than school dinners," I said, as we all tucked in with enthusiasm.

"Look he's got champagne!" squeaked Debbie, for once shaken out of her superior attitude.

The Wembley official who'd been looking after us called a waiter over and offered us a glass of champagne each, although he insisted it was almost drowned with orange juice. Still it was real champagne and the first time any one of us had tasted it.

Eventually we were shown into our ringside seats in the Arena and the show began.

We were glued to our seats. It was amazing, so much faster than netball, although Debbie was sure it was not beyond her. Up and down the pitch, turning and weaving around other players, with Curly bouncing the ball using his right hand then his left, and Bobby Joe dribbling the ball so fast it was almost impossible to see. My favourite was 'Meadowlark' Lemon who kept hiding the ball from the referee, he had us in stitches.

At the intermission the Harlem Globetrotters were behind on points. While they caught their breath we were mesmerised by a Juggler who could balance four balls at once and spin them around as well. Then it was back to the game. What we saw that night was the impossible, at times the ball just seemed to fly, and 'Meadowlark' Lemon scoring a basket from the other side of the court by just throwing a ball over his head, without even looking, was just unbelievable. Of course the Globetrotters won in the end and we had the best time ever.

But perhaps the best of all was on the way home in the coach, when Debbie fell asleep resting her head on my shoulder. I felt like a king! As I watched out of the coach window at the cars overtaking I didn't even move as a red Ferrari went past, only my favourite sports car. Smugly I smiled at Danny and Gary who had seen it too and expected me to react. However, I was more than content with Debbie resting on my arm, much to the disgust of my two friends.

Chapter 8

Our Very Own Champion

Cars were important to us in 1976 and you could tell a lot about someone by the type of car they owned. Danny's dad drove a Ford Capri 1600 which was a bit flash and not really a family man's car. Gary's dad had a Morris Oxford which he kept spotless, every Sunday morning he was out cleaning and polishing it until it shone. We decided it was a good reliable car for a family man. My dad owned a Morris Marina, which was a reasonable car at the time and a big improvement over the Hillman Minx he had owned before.

Danny, Gary and I all had Observer pocket books which we filled in religiously. Mine was a 1968 edition with an MGB on the front, Danny's had a MG1300 on the cover and Gary had the Motorbike book. As well as pictures the books had all the important specifications such as fuel consumption, top speed, engine size, and BHP so we could compare and work out which we thought the best.

We kept the books with us all the time and would sign off each vehicle as we saw it, with the time, date and where we had seen the car on the bottom of the page. Some were easy to spot, being popular, but others were nearly impossible to see in our area, so we always took our books if we travelled in the hope of signing an elusive one off. We would swap stories of where we had seen a hard to find vehicle and get really excited if we saw a new one locally.

"Did you see Bob the baker?" asked Gary as we walked through the school gates. "He's got a new van."

"About time," I retorted. "That old Morris of his was out of the Ark."

“He said he’s going to keep that,” put in Danny. “Recons it'll be worth something one day.”

“What, that old rust bucket? He must be bonkers,” I said dismissively. “Anyway, what’s his new one?”

“A Ford Transit,” answered Gary enthusiastically. “One of the new Mark 1’s. It looks alright.”

“My dad likes the Fords,” said Danny. “They’re easy to get spares for.”

We all nodded knowledgeably as we strolled past the teachers’ car park, giving the cars there a once over. The class of car had improved recently, since the teachers had received whopping pay rises the last couple of years, (my dad was always complaining about it – ‘part-time hours and all those holidays, money for sitting on their backsides’). My form teacher now had a John Player Special Capri which he considered to be the business, but we knew it had the rubbish V4 engine that let it down badly. The best car at school was the red, white and gold Lotus Élan that a Chemistry teacher owned, a real sports car that he drove fast everywhere and we looked up to him for that.

“How are Rob’s Jensons?” I asked as we paused by the Lotus. Robert, a lad in Gary’s class owned two Jenson Interceptors[9] but they were always breaking down so we hardly ever saw them on the road.

“One of them’s got an oil leak,” replied Gary. “He was working on it when I went past on Saturday.”

“Lucky him,” I said, and the others nodded. We all wished we had a car we could work on, or a motorbike. On Saturdays, if we went into Epsom, we’d visit Arthur Wheeler’s Motorbike shop just to see if a new bike had come in for Gary to tick off in his book. The shop had a Moto Guzzi[10] that Arthur had won a

---

[9] Jenson Interceptor – GT (Grand Tourer) class car, handbuilt between 1966-1976 by Jenson Motors.

[10] Moto Guzzi – Italian motorbike built by Mandello Del Lario since 1921.

race on at the Isle of Man TT[11] and we touched it for good luck every time we went in.

Later that day I had my usual Maths lesson. Chris Medler was the teacher in charge, a plain looking man with ginger hair and beard. As he wrote the equations on the blackboard I sneaked out my Observer pocket book and began to read. Seconds later it was snatched out of my hands.

"What's this?" he asked, looking at the book. "Get up to the front of the class and explain."

This was a God given opportunity! I had never mentioned my strange addiction to sports cars and, with the fervour of a born enthusiast, I seized my chance to explain in detail the cars in the book. In *lots* of detail! Where I had seen different cars; who in the area had them; which were my favourites and why; and also the cars that you never saw. Most of my classmates were amazed to see this side of me. I expected Mr. Medler to be annoyed, but he seemed interested and kept asking questions. He even showed us the equation to work out BHP (brake horsepower), which was Torque x Revs, and explained what this was. It was the best maths lesson I had ever had. I was surprised that he was so interested. He had never struck me before as a car man as he drove a Citroen D1 with self-levelling suspension, which was just plain weird.

The bell bought the lesson to a close.

"Stay behind Bone," said Medler as he began to rummage in his desk.

Oh, oh, I thought, here comes the detention.

"Here," he said, handing me a newspaper cutting.

I couldn't believe it as I stared at the photograph. There was my maths teacher sitting on the bonnet of a stock car with a chequered flag in his

---

[11] Isle of Man TT (Tourist Trophy) Race, motorcycle event held yearly since 1907.

hand. It turned out that in his spare time he was a racing driver!

"I'm in the final at Wimbledon Stadium on Saturday," he said. "I'm hoping to retain the Championship this year."

He handed me some free tickets. "Come and cheer me on if you like."

Would I like? What sort of question was that? I was delighted.

Word soon got around the school and even the girls in his class promised to meet there, along with most of my friends. Danny's dad offered to drive us three to the Stadium. On the way we passed the garage owned by Mr. Medler's brother, which had a large banner hanging outside saying 'Chris Medler Stock Car Champion', so we gave a big cheer.

Chris's team consisted of himself, his brother and their mate, and they all had cars painted green. Chris's car was a Volvo 122S, with number 211 painted on the side, and his brother and friend had Hillman Hunters. Their main opposition was a team with black Ford Zephyrs and Zodiacs that had spikes on the front and clearly wanted to do Chris some damage.

We found a good spot to watch the action, on a bend and close to the fence. As the cars took off around the oval track we clung to the wire and cheered every time Chris came past. People had bought air horns that blasted out and the girls all screamed and jumped up and down at the sight of him. It was a hare and tortoise type race, with Chris driving flat out and the black team blocking and trying to ram him but unable to catch him as he skidded sideways around the corners. He won the first heat by miles, hardly getting hit, to everyone's delight.

In the interval Danny and I went to the pits to see him, but he was far too busy to talk to us. He brother had not been so lucky in the race; the black team had ganged up on him, pinning him on each side then ramming his car from behind, making large holes.

Chris was working frantically, a large cut on his hand soaking blood through the greasy rag tied around it. He hammered the car back into shape, sweating and swearing at it. He obviously took the race very seriously. We had never seen him like this and were most impressed.

We made our way back to our seats and joined Gary watching the motorbike stunt team. They rode through glass and a tunnel of fire, to much applause from us. This was followed by the midget racers, small racing cars that crashed a lot and had to keep stopping. Fireworks were let off to announce the start of the final.

We had quickly picked up the colour coding of stock cars. Chris being a 'red roof' had to start at the back and for the first few laps he kept out of the way. Every other driver got stuck in, crashing all over the track, leaving only a narrow path. Chris stayed behind his brother who cleared a path for him by spinning out cars on the bends. Soon there were only two green and two black cars running on opposite sides of the track. Chris was keeping his distance, but a black car cut across the centre and tried to ram him in the side. Swiftly Chris yanked on his steering wheel to dodge him. The black car rammed into his brother instead, right in the driver's door, pinning him in the car. On the next lap Chris saw what had happened to his brother and started driving like a mad man, soon catching the last car that was swerving to get in his way. Everyone cheered as they got side by side, going faster and faster. Then Chris braked, letting the black car turn in towards him, and then swiftly accelerated hitting its back wheel. The black car span, then turned over and the driver was thrown out, luckily unhurt. The chequered flag came down. Chris had won!

We all ran onto the track and lifted Chris out of his car. After he was given the cup we all jumped onto his car and his brother, who was amazingly unhurt, drove us round the track with everyone cheering. It was a brilliant night.

Back at school on Monday Chris acted like nothing had happened and was teaching maths as usual, but we thought he should have been instantly put in charge of the school at the very least.

On Thursday we all got copies of the Banstead Herald. On the front page was a picture of us sitting on Chris's stock car under a heading 'Local Teacher Wins Championship in front of his Class'. We were so proud at last to have a teacher we could all look up to, but Chris had reverted to being Mr. Medler and seemed embarrassed by the fuss and attention his success had bought.

School was back to normal.

"Old Watson's given me extra homework," said Danny indignantly, as we caught up with each other at the school gate.

"Not that hundred years war again?" I asked.

Danny nodded gloomily.

"Caught you looking out of the window," surmised Gary knowingly.

"Fifth form netball," agreed Dan.

He need say nothing more, we understood the problem completely.

"It wouldn't be so bad if the lessons were interesting," Danny carried on, still angry. "But what use to anyone is the stupid hundred year war? If they taught us something useful like, I don't know, how to strip down a car engine, *then* we might actually enjoy the lesson and take notice."

Gary and I nodded in agreement. It was definitely being bored that got us into trouble, that and the netball pitches being placed right next to our classroom windows!

Chapter 9

Arson!

Yes, boredom, that was our problem – and, as you probably all know, when fourteen year old kids suffer from boredom it leads to trouble, BIG trouble.

Danny started it – setting fire to things with a lighter. You never knew when the urge would take him, although if you were lucky the giggling might give you a clue. Suddenly you would feel a pain or smell burning and realise he'd done it again – set you on fire! He would do it when you least expected it and at the most inopportune moments, like that time in morning assembly.

I was standing in the Hall, pretending to sing the hymn while looking out of the window. Suddenly I felt a nudge in the back, so naturally I ignored it.

People are always trying to get me into trouble, I thought, it'll take more that to catch me out.

Another nudge.

"Piss off," I whispered, half turning.

"Graham, Graham," whispered Pam urgently behind me.

I turned slowly. "What?" I mouthed silently. I could already feel the eyes of several teachers up on the stage as their heads swivelled in my direction.

Pam grimaced and pointed towards the floor.

My bag! Smoke was coming from my bag. Small flames began to lick around the corner of my maths exercise book. He'd f'ing set fire to my bag! Swiftly I stamped on it, terrified that the curtains next to me would catch fire. Then I got down on my knees and pounded it. All around me people were moving back. Luckily I'd got there quickly and the fire was soon out.

Was I thanked? Was I hell. Even though I reckoned I'd saved over a thousand kids from almost certain death, not to mention the mangy teachers, and old Mather. As I knelt, panting and surrounded by smoke, a hand appeared and grabbed my ear, giving it a vicious twist and I was heaved to my feet.

Physics Jones, former rugby scrum half, dragged me protesting from the hall.

Another detention!

I thought I'd be safe from Danny after that, but no, he thought it so funny he only waited to the afternoon before putting paper in my pocket and setting fire to it while I lined up for woodwork.

Double detention!

It wasn't only me who suffered; he picked his victims randomly so you never knew who would be next. He though it hilarious and fell about laughing if you got burnt or had to dash off to the toilets to get some water to put it out. Odd that he even had a lighter because he didn't smoke, none of us did, we all thought smoking a mugs game and had much better things to spend our hard earned cash on. Danny just loved setting fire to stuff.

Of course he caught Gary too, sticking a lighted loo roll under the toilet door while he was sitting on the bog.

Gary was not prepared to let Danny get away with this, and soon got his own back, but this just made things worse because now Gary realised how much fun it was and began setting little fires of his own. First it was the rubbish bins in the playground, and then the loo rolls in the girls' toilets. Suddenly no-one was safe from the phantom fire setters.

"What's going on?" I asked one morning, seeing the main school gates closed and a huddle of kids waiting to go in.

A group of teachers and prefects were on the other side of the gates, each holding a plastic bucket.

"Line up," yelled Geography Jones (we had three teachers called Jones). "Get in an orderly queue and come through one at a time."

We hung back and watched. As kids went in they were ordered towards a junior teacher or prefect. Bags were searched, pockets were turned out and occasionally something was chucked into a bucket.

"They're looking for something," said Danny suspiciously.

"Well, we can't just stand out here," I said. "We're pretty obvious hovering by the pond. We'd better join the queue and see what they're looking for."

We joined the line of other kids waiting and eventually shuffled through the gate.

"Over here Bone," said Jevans, the senior prefect. "Open up your bag."

"What are you looking for?" I asked innocently.

"Lighters," he said. "There have been too many fires lately. The Head's clamping down."

Now it made sense. Luckily I wasn't carrying anything incriminating, but of course Danny and Gary were, and their lighters were immediately confiscated.

"Well, that's the end of that," said Gary, as we walked into the school.

After registration we all trooped into the Hall for assembly. Old Mather marched onto the stage, black gown flapping, and gave us all a long lecture on the evils and dangers of fire, etc., etc. Boring, boring.

"From now on ALL lighters are BANNED from school premises. If any of you are found in possession of a lighter or caught causing a fire you will be immediately bought before me." Mather gave us all the evil eye. We knew exactly what he meant – the cane. He kept a collection in his office, and favoured a particularly flexible little number about the width of his thumb and had honed his caning technique on many a boy's backside. It hurt. I knew! We all knew!

I was quite relieved that Danny's and Gary's arson reign was over for a while, not that I hadn't egged them on of course, but mum was beginning to be seriously annoyed at the burn marks on my school clothes and bag, and had refused to give me any more money for replacement exercise books. Mum was usually fairly easygoing, but she could make life dead uncomfortable if pushed. She had been muttering about the garden shed needing painting and the hedge needing trimming; just to let me know there were plenty of little jobs if I stepped out of line.

I didn't think anything more about it, and I don't suppose Danny or Gary did either – until mid-morning break.

"Here, Danny, we want a word with you!"

We had all visited the tuck shop under the loggia and, armed with wagon wheels and packets of crisps, walked down to our usual playground spot, a bench in the far corner by the tennis courts, (as far from the teacher's common room as possible). Suddenly we were surrounded by a very angry looking mob.

"What's the matter," asked Danny, wide eyed and innocent – his usual look when confronted with trouble.

"You're the matter!" A finger was jabbed in his chest.

Danny stumbled back a couple of steps, but kept his cool. "What?"

More kids joined the mob.

"Because of you, our lighters have all been nicked."

"'Ow are we gonna 'ave a fag? Eh?"

"Yeah!" "Yeah!" "We're missin' out on our fags cos' of you."

All became clear! The smokers were in revolt. This could turn really nasty.

"Ah!" said Danny. Calmly he reached down and fished around in his sock. "This any good?" he asked, holding up a brand new lighter.

It was snatched out of his hand and moments later the mob had dispersed to the back of the bike sheds. Emergency over.

"I thought we were in for a fight then," I said, watching a straggler disappear around the corner.

"Yeah," agreed Gary. "Pity."

All went well for a couple of days. My sister came over and cut the hedge, she likes gardening - odd. Mum and I negotiated a price for the shed, to be painted at the weekend. School wound its usual way towards the weekend, with me dodging the lessons I hated (many!), and handing in as little homework as possible. Eventually it was Friday afternoon – Biology.

I didn't really mind biology, sometimes it was interesting if you could get the teacher talking about sex and blushing. On one memorable occasion, in the middle of the female reproductive system, Stuart had to go up and tell Mr Clarke his flies were undone! That was good. Unfortunately, Mr Clarke had decided teaching was not for him, so this term we had Miss Green, who wasn't quite green enough to be drawn into discussing reproduction of any sort with us. Biology, however, was one of the few lessons where Danny and I were legitimately in class together, as we were in the same tutor group.

On that particular Friday we were supposed to be studying bugs I think, something small anyway (I wasn't paying much attention – the girls were playing netball again). Anyway, we were each given a magnifying glass. Danny, being curious as usual, soon worked out that by focussing the sun's rays he could burn things – set things on fire! He immediately began trying this out. He scorched neat little burn marks all around his biology exercise book. After watching him for a moment I grew bored and turned my attention once again to the girls outside. Watching boobs bouncing and long naked legs rising up to wobbling bums was far more interesting. Mistake!

A strong smell of burning bought me back from the realms of erotic fantasy. He'd done it again. My book was on fire. Frantically I grabbed it, bashed it on the desk to put the fire out, swiftly lifted the desk lid and shoved the charred book inside. Moments later my mind, (and my eyes), were back on the netball pitch.

SCREAM!!!

What? Oh, hell!

"What's going on? What's that smell of burning?" asked Miss Green, suspiciously.

Quickly I tried to cover up the smoke rising from the hole in the desk where in past times the ink well would have sat.

"It's Graham Bone, Miss."

"His desk's on fire, Miss."

Girls! Perfect in erotic fantasies, a complete pain in the ass in real life. The next thing I knew was Miss Green standing over me with a red face.

"Open - Up - That - Desk!" The words came out like bullets.

I opened it.

The smouldering remains of my biology exercise book suddenly burst into flames, setting the assorted jumble of rubbish hidden inside the desk on fire. Smoke billowed into the room. I leapt up, grabbed my duffle bag and began bashing the book. It just got worse. Flames leapt up, running around the inside of the desk, curling around the bag until that was on fire as well.

Miss Green fainted. She fell on a chair and then went sprawling on to the ground. Girls began to scream. Boys yelled with excitement. Danny jumped up and hit the fire bell.

"I've always wanted to do that," he said joyously.

"Well, you didn't have to set the school on fire to do it," I retorted, looking at the mayhem around us. Then I had an idea.

"Open the window," I yelled.

Danny rushed to the window, grabbed the handle and pushed it wide open. Playing the superhero I manfully picked up the flaming desk, rushed forward and flung it clean through the open window. Panic over.

Well, not *quite*. I think I might have got away with it if only the Headmaster had not been going past at that precise moment, almost running to see what idiot had set off the fire alarm and why. He wasn't expecting a flaming desk to come flying out of the window beside him, making him leap out of the way as it crashed onto the playground. He pounded, red faced and wheezing into the classroom, pausing only to gaze at the recumbent form of Miss Green, stretched out on the floor.

"Whose desk was that?" he yelled.

The girls pointed.

"You! Bone!" He grabbed me by the ear. "Come with me."

In vain I protested. "I can explain, Sir."

Six of the best – again.

On the way back to class with a throbbing backside I decided that the pain was almost worth it for the entertainment, at least we had livened things up for everyone.

Chapter 10

A New Friend

"Nick's broken his leg," announced Gary on the way into school.

"Nick who?" I asked.

"You know, Nick Taylor. He's in my class.

I still looked blank.

"That new lad. Dark, with black hair, you know him."

"Is he that quiet one?" put in Danny.

"Yeah," replied Gary. "He fell out of a tree I think, did something stupid anyway. He's got to be in plaster for three months."

"Cool."

"He's always by himself," added Gary. "But he seems OK."

"Let's find out what he's like then," said Danny, who always enjoyed meeting people and could talk to anyone.

We caught up with Nick at lunchtime. He was in the chemistry lab following his last lesson and was struggling to put his books in his bag while hanging onto his crutches.

"Grab him," yelled Gary.

Nick, hampered as he was by plaster cast, books and crutches, didn't stand a chance, especially against three of us. Danny opened a window and quick as a flash Gary and I shoved Nick feet first outside, hanging firmly onto his arms so he dangled above the flower beds. Not bullying you understand, we all hated bullies, no this was just to see how far he was willing to go for a laugh, to find out whether he would fit in.

"Bog off you lot," he yelled. "Mum'll kill me if I break the other leg."

"Give us an impression[12]," we cried, laughing. "Come on, an impression, you must know one."

Immediately he came back with "I'm free!" in a strangled voice, giving a passable take on Mr Humphries in 'Are You Being Served'[13].

"And another," I cried.

"Get off," he yelled. "I'm useless at impressions."

So were we, but we were not going to tell him that.

"Just one more," said Danny.

"Alright, I'm thinking," he muttered, then barked out. "Don't tell him, Pike!"

We fell about laughing and almost dropped him, his take on Captain Mainwaring from 'Dad's Army' was spot on.

"Not bad," spluttered Gary. "Should we let him in?"

We left him for a minute more, just to make the point. Then we hauled him back in. He'd passed the test. Having broken his leg 'doing something stupid' meant he was one of us. We had all injured ourselves before in the same way, so we had something in common.

"We'll come round to your house after school," offered Gary.

Nick nodded his head, rather warily I though, and made off smartish, well as fast as he could hobble with a plastered leg and a set of crutches.

Nick lived not far from Danny, but his family had only recently moved to Tadworth and we knew nothing about him. Most of us at De Burgh had been born on the Estate, or close by, and had lived there all our lives. It was rare that someone new came in, and if they did our mums and sisters usually had the low down on them. You know, the usual stuff, their family past and present, weight at birth plus any

---

[12] 'Who Do You Do' - a popular television programme in the 1970's, with a range of comedians giving impressions of celebrities.

[13] 'Are You Being Served' – a comedy sitcom about a department store, broadcast on BBC1 between 1972-1895

distinguishing marks, all within days of their arriving. It was odd that nothing was known about Nick or his family, and he was different, being quiet and almost secretive about his past, which of course made us *mighty* curious.

His house was one of the newer ones, built on the old horses' field, by the bluebell wood. It was basically the same as ours: lounge, dining room and kitchen on the ground floor, two bedrooms and a box room, plus a bathroom with separate toilet on the first floor, garden front and back with a brick built shed to side. His elder brother was tinkering with an old Morris Oxford in the road outside the house.

"Don't I know you?" he asked, wiping a smear of grease from his face with a dirty bit of cloth.

I looked at him closely for a moment, then realised who he was.

"Yeah," I said with a grin. "You sold my dad that Marina."

"How's it going?"

"Great, he's driving it all over the place. Took it down to Newhaven last weekend to do some fishing."

Cordial relations with the family established we were invited inside. The Corona[14] man had been around and the fridge was stocked with bottles of fizzy drinks. Nick poured us all glasses of Cream Soda and handed out packets of crisps, which we took into the back garden.

"Mum'll be home around five," said Nick's brother, giving him a warning look.

"We'll have this and go out," Nick assured him.

"Your mum give you trouble?" I asked.

Nick nodded gloomily.

"Mine's a pain in the neck too," said Danny. "Always tidying up, wanting the house kept

---

[14] Corona Soft Drinks Company – delivered fizzy drinks door to door from 1920's – 1980's, first by horse and cart then by lorry.

immaculate. You'd think we lived in a palace rather than a council house."

"Nah, she's not like that," said Nick. "She's... well, she's..."

We kept quiet and waited. Nick took a sip of his drink and studied his plaster cast.

"You don't have to tell us," said Gary suddenly, emptying the remaining crisp crumbs into his hand and then stuffing them into his mouth.

"Some things are your own business," I added. "Come on, let's finish these drinks and go over the heath for a bit."

It was a couple of weeks before Nick told us what the problem was. It turned out that his real dad was John McVicar, a well known armed robber who had been tagged "Public Enemy No. 1" by Scotland Yard[15]. He had been put inside while Nick was a baby. Nick's mum Edna had quickly divorced him, but she seemed to have a thing for bank robbers and had re-married a Paul Taylor, who had adopted Nick at a year old, but was now doing ten years for six banks and nine post offices (or that could have been nine banks and six post offices). Nick found this totally embarrassing, but the opposite was true for us, Nick was going up in our estimation all the time! His mum, Edna, had a really dark streak, and was definitely not one to cross. Nick would only sleep with a chair propped under the handle of his bedroom door as his mother had once stabbed him in his sleep for hitting his older sister, and he now lived in fear of both his sister and his mum. Danny and I, having sisters ourselves, could sympathise with anyone who had sister problems,

---

15 John McVicar was apprehended and given a 23-year jail sentence. He escaped from prison on several occasions. After his final re-arrest in 1970 he took an Open University degree in Sociology and was awarded a BSc first class. He was paroled in 1978 and his autobiography 'McVicar by Himself' was made into a film starring Roger Daltrey and Adam Faith. He went on to study for a postgraduate degree at the University of Leicester.

although his mum was truly terrifying. We all offered to help if we could.

We spent more and more time with Nick, and found him to be intelligent and resourceful. He was turning into a good friend to us all and had many fine qualities, but he struggled to make any other friends either at school or at youth club, something we were determined to rectify. The answer came when his mum took his sister away for the weekend to visit the prison, leaving Nick to look after his younger brother. As it was also Nick's birthday we decided this was the ideal time for Nick to have a party, meet more people and become popular. Nick was not so sure.

"Come on," I said. "Let's talk it over with Alan and Brenda."

We dragged him protesting around next-door. The neighbouring house was a shrine to the mighty 'ELVIS'. Every surface and every wall was covered with photographs and mementos to the King. Alan even sported an Elvis haircut, although not quite with Elvis's panache. Quickly I explained about the birthday and the proposed party.

"That's a good idea," said Alan, who was a friend of Nick's stepfather and had been concerned about how Nick was coping with him being inside.

Brenda was also a useful ally; Edna had upset her once too often. "We'll pick up the flack if anything goes wrong," she assured us.

We gave them all the money we had and they promised to supply the drink. We then went back to Danny's house and collected his new stereo system, and then got all our records together and went back to Nick's house. Soon we had everything set up, we had even put Christmas tree lights around the walls. We put the word out that the party would begin at six o'clock. Nick had never had a birthday party before, not in his entire fifteen years, so it was long overdue.

Friends began arriving with bottles of drink to suit all tastes. The house began to fill up, music blared out and the dancing began. Nick seemed to be enjoying himself and so was everyone else. The party spilled over into the garden, and the music bought more people over. Eventually all the decent drink had gone and we were left with a collection of cans and bottles that no-one wanted. It seemed a shame to waste anything alcoholic, so we poured everything into a Tupperware container and shook it up to make cocktails. The resulting brown liquid tasted disgusting, but everyone tried it and found it had the desired effect and got you drunk.

Some of the girls had made Nick a birthday cake with candles on it, which unfortunately started the trouble! Soon a food fight was in progress. Nick did his best to stop the house getting wrecked, but with fifty drunken teenagers and music pounding so loudly the walls seemed to vibrate, he had no chance.

"What am I going to do?" he yelled at me through the din.

Well, anything for a mate, we knew exactly what he needed. Within seconds he was locked in a bedroom with Rosie Wallis, who we knew he fancied, and a bottle of gin that was so disgusting it hadn't even made it to the cocktails.

"Let us out," yelled Nick, banging on the door.

"Not until you've drunk that gin," yelled back Gary, as we all creased up laughing.

Then we heard the window opening.

"They're trying to escape," cried Danny.

We all dashed downstairs and made our way through the throng to the back garden. Nick was busy pouring the gin onto the patio.

"You can't get out of it that way," I yelled. "Get back inside."

Gary picked up a clump of earth from the garden and chucked it at the window. It seemed a good idea, so Danny and I joined in. Unfortunately, one of us must have picked up a stone as well – that was when the glass got broken.

The police arrived at ten o'clock and told us to turn the music down. Someone, who shall remain nameless, peeing on them from an upstairs window was probably not a good idea. They came back again soon after eleven o'clock, this time with reinforcements. We were ready for them, with a garden hose pushed through the letter box to drench anyone approaching via the garden path, and bags of flour to drop from the upstairs windows. For some reason this seemed to antagonise them and soon a van with more police appeared. That was when the front door got smashed.

The police swept into the house and began to round us up. However, one look at us staggering around in various stages of inebriation and they decided that they didn't really want a lot of drunken teenagers in their nice clean nick.

"Come on you lot," said the Sergeant in charge. "Party's over. Off you go home."

Slowly everyone dispersed, at least the ones that could walk and were not being sick. That left just the passed out, one of which was Nick.

"We'll look after him," I said.

"And I think we'd better give him a hand with cleaning up," said Danny, surveying the mess.

The Sergeant gazed around at the piles of vomit, spilt drinks, broken glass and squashed birthday cake. He turned back to us and nodded. "I'll leave you to it then," he said.

We spent the remainder of the night sweeping, washing and cleaning up the mess, until by dawn we had the house looking normal again. Well, almost normal. My dad had a spare front door in his shed and Nick's neighbour was a carpenter and helped us take the smashed door down and replace it. There was some paint in the garden that was the same colour as the old door, and it took us no time to paint it and change the locks over. It was Sunday now, so there was no way to repair the broken window, so we cleared up the glass and hoped no-one would notice, at least not straight away.

We picked up Nick's younger brother who had spent the night at a friend's house. That just left Nick. He did not look good. There wasn't much we could do about that, so we left him hugging the toilet and went home to bed.

The whole of the following week all everyone talked about was Nick's party. From being Billy no-mates, he became the most popular boy in the school. He was popular with everyone. Well, everyone except his mum. She soon heard about the party, there was no way to keep it secret on our Estate.

"I blame it on those three new friends of yours," she yelled. "They're definitely a bad influence."

She was probably right.

Chapter 11

Derby Day

June was eagerly awaited on the Preston Hawe Estate – that was the month the Derby was run. What's so special about that, do I hear you ask? Well, the Derby dates back to 1780, and is a world renowned horse race run on the flat. Every year crowds flock to Epsom Downs to watch the race. The Queen and the Royal family usually arrive by train at Tattenham Corner station, and the hoi-polloi arrive in their droves by car, motorbike, coach, train, on foot or whatever brand of transport they can beg, borrow or steal. The entire area comes to a complete standstill as all attention is on The Race, unless you are a fourteen year old boy when attention is fixated on the fun fair and the attendant girls who will undoubtedly be in the vicinity.

Even more importantly, every year from De Burgh School's inception, the school had closed on Derby day, giving all the pupils a well deserved day off. Of course this was mainly so that the Headmaster and teachers could place their bets with the rest and enjoy a well earned break in the beer tent. However, in 1976 Mr. Mather, in his wisdom (following a nasty memo from County Hall about falling exam grades) decided that the school would stay open. A letter was sent out to all parents saying us kids would have to attend school and parents would have to answer if their particular kid failed to turn up.

This was war!

"What are we going to do?" I asked, as a group of us huddled in a corner of the playground during our morning break.

"My mum will make me come, even if she has to drag me to school," said Danny. "She's terrified of old Mather."

"My mum's the same," agreed Gary. "And dad will say if he has to go to work, them I have to go to school!"

Heads nodded all around. Everyone agreed we could not depend on our parents for help on this.

"So what are we going to do," I asked again.

Everyone looked glum, until Jackie piped up, "What if there was a bomb scare?"

"They'll know it's us," said Gary immediately. Every prank at school was blamed on us, goodness knows why!

"Not if it's the IRA[16]," said Jackie.

"We don't know anyone in the IRA," Danny protested.

"I do," said Jackie.

We looked at her in amazement. Jackie was usually quiet and well-behaved, the sort of girl who turned in her homework on time – now it seemed that she had hidden depths. It turned out that her elder sister had a boyfriend called Patrick who was Irish and worked on the roads.

"Are you sure he's in the IRA?" I asked.

"He brags about it when he's drunk," she said, "and he's always drunk."

Well, a bomb plot seemed a bit extreme, but this *was* war.

"OK," I said. "When can we see him?"

Later that afternoon we cycled around to Patrick's house, which was on the other side of the estate. It didn't look good, paint was peeling and there was a rusting old Moggie[17] up on blocks in the front garden, or what passed for a front garden. The weeds were knee high and a single pink rose struggled

---

[16] IRA – Irish Republican Army

[17] The Morris Minor car, affectionately known as 'Moggies'.

valiantly in one corner. We knocked on the front door. Then knocked again ...and again.

"There's no-one in," said Danny in disgust.

"But Jackie said he'd be in if we got here before the pubs opened[18]," Gary protested.

"Just a minute," I put in. "I can hear snoring."

We all listened. It was definitely snoring. We followed the noise around the side of the house.

The back garden was no better than the front, although the rose was yellow, and a row of wonky bean sticks at the rear proclaimed a long forgotten vegetable plot.

Lying spread-eagled among the long grass was the source of the snoring, wearing tattered jeans, a faded check shirt and sporting week old stubble.

"Do you think that's him?" I asked dubiously.

"Judging by the number of empty beer cans and that half bottle of whisky he's clutching it must be," surmised Gary, going over and giving him a kick on his foot.

The snoring stopped for a second, then increased in pitch.

Gary kicked the foot again, then leant over and gave him a shake on the arm, staggering backwards as an enormous alcoholic blast of fumes hit him.

"Bloody hell," he choked, "You could probably get drunk on just a whiff of his breath."

"Let's try yelling his name," I suggested. "Altogether, one, two, three."

"PATRICK"

That did it, well sort of. His eyes half opened and there was a muttered "F**k off!"

Gary bravely took a deep breath of fresh air, leant forward and gave him another good shake.

"Gerrof me." The eyes flickered again, and gradually Patrick heaved himself onto one elbow. "Woz

---

[18] In 1976 all pubs closed in the afternoon, their usual weekday opening hours being 11 – 2.30 for lunch, then in the evening from 6.00 – 10.30.

goin' on?" He flopped back onto the grass and for a moment I though he had passed out completely, but no, the eyes opened again and he gradually registered our existence and croaked "Oo a' you?"

"This is a waste of time," muttered Danny in exasperation.

"Let's at least give it a try," I said turning towards Patrick. "We're friends of Jackie's," I explained loudly, as though I was speaking to a particularly dumb three year old. "She sent us around to see you."

Patrick heaved himself upright with a huge belch, and then made his way unsteadily towards the house, carefully cradling the bottle of whisky, until finally subsiding onto the back step. We watched as he took a couple of long pulls on the bottle. He then produced a pouch of tobacco and rolled himself a ciggie, or at least we assumed it was a ciggie, it certainly wasn't the Old Holborn our dads used.

It took the rest of the afternoon to explain what we wanted, what with his drunken blur and us not understanding his broad Irish accent, but in the end it was agreed. Patrick would phone the school on Derby day and say he'd planted a bomb. The only problem was he wanted paying or he'd not do it.

Of course we didn't have any money, but then I had an idea. "What about a bottle of whisky?" I asked.

"Six," he demanded.

We whittled him down to four.

"Where are we going to get four bottles of whisky?" asked Danny as we cycled back to my house, knowing we certainly couldn't afford to buy it even if the off-license would sell it to us, and the only time our parents had strong liquor in the house (barring my mum's lethal homemade wine) was at Christmas, which was long gone.

"Mather's got whisky in his office," I answered. "There's six bottled hidden under his desk."

"How do you know that?" asked Gary.

"You remember the last time I got caned," I said, looking pointedly at Danny. My being caned for being a hero and saving the school from burning down still rankled.

The others nodded understandingly, not that it bothered them that I'd got the cane as we all got the cane on a regular basis anyway.

"Well, as I bent over I could see under Mather's desk, and there they were, hidden in a corner, six bottles."

"But how do we get hold of them?" asked Danny, seeing the flaw in my excellent plan. "You know he keeps his office locked."

"I've got an idea," I said confidently.

Danny's neighbour, Mrs. Brown, was a cleaner at the school and it was she who cleaned Mather's office. If we could distract her and get the key we could grab the whisky and make the deal – but how to distract her?

"She loves cake," said Danny thoughtfully and turned to Gary. "If you could get your mum to make one of her fantastic cakes, then we could give it to Mrs. Brown and grab the keys."

Gary though about it. "Yeah, good idea," he said slowly. "She found our cat in her shed last week and bought it back, that's worth a cake as a thank you. I bet my mum would go for that."

So it was agreed. The next day, after school had finished, we went back with the cake. Gary's mum was an amazing cook and the cake looked brilliant, a Victoria sandwich with a thick layer of strawberry jam and butter icing filling.

"What are you doing here?" demanded the Caretaker as we walked through the reception area.

Luckily Mrs Brown had told everyone about finding a cat in her shed, and they all thought it was nice we had made a cake for her. It could not have been timed better as she was cleaning Mather's office when we found her. She went off to find a knife so we could all have a slice of the cake with her and we were left alone. Quickly I dived under the desk. Yes, the bottles were there, but only four of them now, thank goodness we'd got Pat to agree to four bottles. Swiftly Gary opened the window and we dropped the bottles down under a bush outside, just as quickly shutting the window again. Then we stood around looking innocent.

Perhaps we overdid the innocent look, Mrs Brown peered at us a shade suspiciously when she came back, but a glance around the office showed her nothing was out of place. The cake was great, Gary's mum had done us proud and Mrs. Brown really appreciated the gesture, saying it was the best cake she had ever tasted.

We strolled casually out of school, then whipped around the corner, retrieved the bottles and took them around to Patrick – twenty year old single malt whisky, he was seriously impressed.

"I'll make the call in the morning," he promised. "I'll use a code that only the *real* IRA know and say we had heard the Queen is going to visit a school so we had planted bombs in all the local schools. They'll take that seriously."

On Derby day we went to school as normal and after registration, right on cue, the fire alarm began to clang. Swiftly the entire school was evacuated and the police and bomb squad called. It had worked! We were lined up in forms on the playing field and all waited confidently to be allowed home. And waited. And waited.

After an hour the teachers were let in to get some work for us. We could not believe it. They were not just keeping us at school; they were intending to make us work as well! This was low even for teachers and needed action. In minutes a fight was started, but was just as swiftly put down. It was beginning to look as if all our plans were for nothing, and then we were rescued by the girls. "Please Miss, I need to go to the toilet."

Gary quickly caught on and his hand shot up. "Sir, Sir, I need a shit Sir."

That was all it took. Half an hour later we were at the fair ground.

The fair had been visiting Epsom Downs probably for as long as the Derby had been run. Music blared out, the cry of "Roll up, roll up" punctuated the air and the aromas of fried onions, sausages and candy floss mingled enticingly. We had been coming to the fair since we were kids and all had our favourites, Gary loved the Dodgem cars although he preferred to bump rather than dodge, Danny liked the Whip and I loved the Dive Bomber (two rocket shaped cars on a long arm that rotated while the cars spun).

We knew that money fell out of people pockets as they tore around on the different rides and if you had sharp eyes you could find it in the grass. I was searching around the Dive Bomber for change when a rough looking man working the ride saw me.

"If you want to make some money get up here," he shouted, beckoning me to climb over the barrier.

"I'm Graham," I said, holding out my hand, but he ignored it and just showed me what to do to let the punters on and off the ride. This involved a thick leather belt which had to be pulled tight over their laps and through a hoop, then with the door shut you looped it back and pulled hard to keep the door from springing open while the ride was working. Watching Andy, the boy next to me on the stage, he could do it in seconds and it took me twice as long. I could see him getting annoyed as there was a long queue waiting to climb on, but I soon got the hang of it. The hardest part of the job was getting the people off and out of the gate as they staggered around looking drunk. To the left we had a sign saying 'Out to the Left Please', but they were too dizzy to see it.

I was really enjoying myself, but as the evening wore on more of the punters were getting drunk and being sick, and of course it was my job to get out the mop and bucket. However, the up side was that girls noticed me. It was like being a pop star up on the stage with the loud music playing and the girls actually hanging around to talk for a change. The food wasn't bad either, as the chap who owned the ride, I'd found out his name was Lenny, also owned the food stall next-door and gave me burgers and Coke. Loose change fell out in the cars and we grabbed it off the floor before letting the next punters in, and soon I had full pockets.

Danny and Gary made use of my new popularity and chatted to the girls who were hanging around. Lenny saw they were my friends and as it was getting late and things were slowing down he let them ride for free.

As I strapped them in I called "Give 'em a good one."

Lenny grinned and turned it up to full, giving them a ride to remember. The girls all started screaming and Gary went green. When we let them off they staggered around and had to be helped down. At least Gary waited until he got off before throwing up – although that ruined his chances with the girls.

By ten o'clock the fair was closing down.

"Help yourself to the unsold food," said Lenny's wife, making me a bun with six burgers in it and handing over a packet of slightly charred chips. As I began stuffing myself Lenny handed me a ten pound note.

"Come back tomorrow," he said.

Gary had gone home, but Danny had waited and helped my polish off the chips. Andy wanted us to go back to his caravan and play cards for money, but I was shattered, so we headed home.

At Tattenham Corner we met up with a couple of the girls who had been watching us. One of them had won a goldfish and had it in a plastic bag.

"I don't think I'll be allowed to keep it," she said doubtfully.

Danny, having a strong arm and accurate aim, had managed to win three coconuts and had shared them out with Gary and I.

"Here," I said, showing her the coconut. "I'll swap if you like."

She took the coconut gratefully, handing over the fish.

"We'll walk you home," I added.

The girls lived in a big house on the Burgh Heath road, about halfway down the hill. It looked like a fortress with a high brick wall topped with barbed wire all around it, and large wrought iron gates. We waited outside as they talked into the intercom. Eventually a large man opened the gate and showed them in, giving us a dirty look.

"Come back for tea tomorrow," called Felicity. "Four o'clock.'

"OK," I called, giving a wave.

"We're not really going are we?" asked Danny, as they disappeared up the long drive.

"Why not," I said. "They seem alright."

The next afternoon, we changed into our best clothes, I had flared denim jeans with a matching jacket and Danny had on the new tank top[19] his mum had knitted him. We got on our chopper bikes and rode around to the house. Talking into the intercom we explained that we had been invited for tea and were told to wait. Eventually the gate swung open and we were let in. It took ages to walk up the drive and the house looked massive, with steps leading up to a portico and loads of leaded light windows that seemed to frown down at us. The three bedroomed end of

---

[19] Tank top – knitted v-necked sleeveless pullover.

terrace I lived in would probably have fitted into the entrance hall that we just had a brief glimpse of when the butler opened the door. *He* was certainly frowning! We weren't allowed inside; just one glance had decided we were only suitable for the tradesman's entrance. He led us around the side of the house and through a gate into the rear garden.

The family were all seated outside at a wrought iron table on the terrace, the garden stretching out into the distance with an immaculate lawn, rose borders and a fountain. The two girls were dressed in spotless white dresses like a couple of angels. They looked happy to see us though, smiling in welcome. The same could not be said of their parents, who were staring at us as though we were something the cat had bought home.

Suddenly this did not seem such a good idea and I could feel myself squirming uncomfortably. Danny, however, seemed to find it hilarious. As the parents began their cross examination, he began to giggle, and of course that set me off. I began to see the funny side of the situation. Here were we, two kids from the local council estate, trying to fit in with the poshest family in the area. Their two beautiful daughters, just back from convent school, had met two boys from the fair ground. I bet they were shitting themselves with worry.

"Would you care to sit down," asked the mother with a wave of her elegant hand.

Two chairs had been placed between the parents, on the other side of the table from the girls. They were obviously intent on keeping their darlings as far from contamination as possible.

"Would you like tea?" asked the mother, reaching for a beautifully engraved silver tea pot.

This is better I though, as I gripped the delicate china tea cup and surveyed the cakes and sandwiches on the table. As long as I don't look at Danny and start giggling we should be alright.

Then the mother asked, "Do you go to the fair often?"

"I work there," I answered without thinking.

She looked at me as if I had admitted to being the anti-Christ. This was too much for Danny, who burst out laughing. Unfortunately he had just taken a slurp of tea, which now squirted out of his nose in two jets. Then to make it worse he proceeded to pour it back into his cup from the saucer and drank it! I tried to stop him, but by now we were both in hysterics. The poor girls did not know whether to laugh or cry. The father, who had not said a word since we had arrived, stood up slowly.

"I think," he said, looking as though he wanted to squash us underfoot, "you had better leave."

We were laughing so much by now that we were unable to speak, so just nodded and were shown off the premises by the butler, who looked even more glacial than the father.

Surprisingly enough we never saw the girls again, but the goldfish (christened Goldie) lived to the ripe old age of twenty-one. Not bad for a fair ground fish.

Chapter 12

Scalextric

June continued fair, getting warmer by each day and mum and dad decided to take advantage of the good weather to go away for the weekend.

"I'm trusting you to behave yourself," said mum, looking slightly harassed as she always did when taking a trip with my dad. There were bound to be arguments about her map reading skills.

"I'll keep an eye on him mum," Vivianne, my eldest sister, assured her, having been drafted in for just that purpose. I have no idea why my mother though I couldn't manage on my own (although elder sisters are always handy for cooking meals).

"Are you ready yet?" yelled dad from the front door. "You know I wanted to make an early start."

"I'm just telling the kids about the watering," mum yelled back, before turning to us and adding, "You will remember, won't you? I don't want my plants to die during this hot weather."

Dad's head appeared around the kitchen door. "I thought you'd already explained," he said. "Come on, or this weekend will be over before it's even started."

Eventually everything was loaded into the car and peace descended. Well, it descended for ten minutes. The time it took for me to get on the phone and give Gary and Danny the all clear.

"What are we going to do then?" asked Gary.

"We could watch the Grand Prix?" suggested Danny. The Le Mans twenty-four hour endurance Grand Prix was being staged that weekend, we had been talking about it all week.

I, however, had a better idea. I had been lying in bed thinking about how we could use the weekend and had come up with a plan. "No worry lads," I said. "I've got it all planned – we are going to stage our own Grand Prix. The entire twenty-four hours of it!"

"OK," said Danny, looking a bit dubious. "How do we do that?"

"We use our Scalextric."

"Brilliant!" said Gary, liking the idea immediately. "I've got plenty of track and I can borrow some from my brother as well. We can make it immense."

"I'll get my stuff as well," added Danny, following Gary to the door.

Soon our front room was piled with bags and boxes.

"What's going on here?" asked Vivianne, surveying the chaos.

My other sister, Hilary, had arrived and they both stood there, hands on hips, giving a frightening impression of my mother.

"We're going to have a Grand Prix," I explained reasonably.

"Not in here you're not," said Hilary. "I've got friends coming around."

"You can do it in the garden," suggested Viv. "Dad's got an extension lead in the shed, you could run it outside."

"Actually, that's not a bad idea," said Danny, having elder sisters he knew when it's useless to argue. "There's more room in the garden, we could make it bigger."

So into the garden we went, followed closely by our dog, Joe, who always wanted to be involved in anything we did.

It took us ages to lay down the track, as we tried to match the Le Mans circuit as closely as possible, but eventually we managed a four lane course, blocked in between the flower bed and vegetable garden, and avoiding the pond. We put up my two-man tent as a stop-pit, and also dragged out the black and white portable TV from my bedroom to watch the real race which was on all night on BBC2. Gary, who was really good at electronics, used his mum's knitting counters and linked them to the Scalextric as lap counters so we could count how many laps we did.

"What else do we need?" I asked, looking at the lay-out critically.

"We could mark the track with some colours," suggested Danny.

A quick search in my dad's shed unearthed some little tins of Humbrol paint left over from when he had his model railway. The selection wasn't vast, but I found tins of red, yellow, blue and green that actually had some paint in them.

"They'll do," said Gary, hunting through the jam jars of old brushes, trying to find one not solidified in crusty white spirit.

Carefully we painted coloured dots on the tracks and any cars that didn't match our beautiful colour scheme got a sticker with the correct colour. Word soon got around about what we were doing and people began to turn up, until soon the garden was humming. In the real race the amount of laps completed in twenty-four hours, from noon to noon, determined the winner. We wanted to do the same. We sorted out our friends into four teams, one for each of the four Scalextric lanes – red, yellow, blue and green. The TV was perched on one of mum's kitchen chairs, cars were in place, controllers at the ready. At twelve noon the klaxon on the TV sounded - the race was on!

Danny started for our team, the Reds, with a team of girls for the Greens, our new friend Nick for the Blues and Andrew from two doors down on the Yellows, four on each team to begin with. Competition was fierce, but as the afternoon wore on the hot sun made the track bend up on the ends, so speeds were up on the straights but down on the corners. We took it in turns, spending around half an hour driving before swapping over. James, our friend from Epsom College, came over and took a turn for the Blues, but eventually he had to catch the bus back to Epsom. Andrew's brother Paul turned up with Clive from next-door, both eager to put Yellows in the lead.

"I'm just going over to the shop for some more sweets," I told Gary as he took over from me.

"Back again?" remarked Mr. Patel, as I stepped into the shop. "This Grand Prix is great for business. How's Jasmine getting on?"

His daughter Jasmine was in my class at school, and was in the Green team.

"The girls are lagging behind," I told him as I paid for a quarter of chocolate éclairs and four bags of crisps.

"Here, Ashna" he called to his wife. "Come and watch the shop while I give our daughter a hand. We can't have the girls coming last."

His wife laughed and handed him a couple of bottles of lemonade. "I expect they will all be thirsty in this heat," she said.

Back in the garden things were hotting up with Nick's Blues in the lead, as Gary and Danny were busy fitting new brushes to our two Red Minis. Mr Patel took over from his daughter, the light of battle bright in his eye, and soon had the girls chasing first, with the Blues close behind, us Reds in third place, with the Yellows trailing by a few laps.

Our next-door neighbour Fred stuck his head over the wall to see what was going on. He worked nights on the Print[20] so had been asleep when we first started. At that moment half the track went dead.

"I'll come round," called Fred, and appeared a few minutes later with a screwdriver in his hand. "I'll soon sort this out." And he did. The race was back on and Fred joined the Yellow team as Andrew and Paul had been called home for their tea.

---

[20] Printing newspapers happened at night so the news was fresh for the following morning.

"Here, take over from me Jasmine," said Mr Patel. "I'm just going back to the shop for a moment."

Ten minutes later he reappeared laden down with supplies.

"I've closed the shop," he announced, handing out boxes of crisps, bottles of fizzy drinks, packets of sweets and a Tupperware box of samosas his wife had cooked. "This should keep us going for a bit."

"Thanks, Mr. Patel" I said, taking a couple of bottles of drink and heading for the fridge.

My sisters had been joined by the girls from next-door and they were all in the kitchen, making piles of food for their party, with the dog following their every move. They had already sorted the music and a pile of LPs and 45s[21] sat beside the record player. Viv's baby, Daniel, aged five months, was in his carrycot supposedly being looked after by his dad Melvin, who of course was more interested in the race. In fact most of my Scalextric track had been inherited from Mel, although my dad was also keen and had bought me the Minis.

"Are you coming in for your dinner, Fred?" yelled Pat from next-door.

"In a minute love," he yelled back, his eyes taking on the glazed look of a hardened racer, his finger pressed firmly on the controller taking the Yellow car speeding around the track.

Eventually his daughter Catrina bought his dinner around for him, but I think Joe ate most of it.

Silver Convention were blaring from the music centre, telling everyone to 'Get up and Boogie', as more of my sisters' friends arrived. A bar was set up in the kitchen, Party 7's[22] were piling up, and the girls had found a bottle of Advocaat left over from Christmas and were knocking up Snowballs[23]. As the night wore on

---

[21] LPs and 45s – vinyl long playing records and singles.

[22] Watney's Party 7 – Popular party drink in the 70's, seven pints of beer in one large can.

more of the boys left the party and came out into the garden, wanting to join in the race. Eventually my sisters and the rest of the girls gave up, turned off their music and joined us too. By now there were ten or more people to a team so everyone got fifteen minutes and the lap speeds increased. With our old camping Tilly lamps lighting up the track we raced into the night.

As some people left, more arrived bringing food and drink with them. We kept up with the real race on TV, but it was not as good as our Scalextric race, which was very close now with only ten laps between the teams and everyone trying their best for the lead.

By morning only about twenty people were left, a hard core of racers who had been up all night.

"Do you want breakfast?" called Viv, first up because the baby insisted on being fed.

We all nodded.

Hilary trailed tiredly down the stairs, looking for coffee and an aspirin. Eventually the heavenly smell of bacon floated out of the kitchen door, and plates piled with bacon, eggs, baked beans and fried bread appeared, closely followed by the dog.

By about ten o'clock people began drifting back to see who would win. The Yellow team had problems with their car, an excellent Sunbeam Alpine, race tuned, which had run all night but now needed brushes for the 'nth time and the wire had snapped so needed soldering. My Red team had the two Minis, and we kept swapping them over. In spite of their not being as fast as the others we were in the lead through consistency. Nick's Blues with F1 cars were fast, but kept crashing and the girls with the Green team had problems with their controllers and were way behind with their Jaguars.

Eleven o'clock came and the Greens and Yellows had caught up and tied for the lead, with Red and Blue

---

[23] Snowball – A cocktail drink.

just five and six laps behind. The neighbours' tabby cat kept running in and knocking the cars off the track, until Joe chased it up onto the shed roof. Then there came a swarm of yellow and black ladybirds, weird things we had never seen before, probably bought here by the unusual heat. They crawled over everything before settling for a feast on the aphids on mum's roses.

More people arrived, friends and neighbours, all keen to see who would win. We had been racing for almost twenty-four hours, but it all came down to the last few minutes.

Of course I had the controller for Red, pressing my finger down as hard as it would go, racing into the lead.

"Go for it," screamed Gary. "Go for it."

Nick with his Blue car was close behind me, almost neck and neck with Yellows, and Greens pushing him from behind.

"You can do it, Gra'." yelled Danny, leaping up and down.

Down to the last lap, total competitiveness gripped me. There was no way I was going to lose. I sent the car tearing up the straight. Win, win, I wished the car on, clenching my teeth with concentration. I am the Champion, I am the Champion. Pride of course comes before a fall. The car raced into the corner, much, much, much too fast. I looked in horror as the Mini went flying into the air and off the track, accompanied by screams of frustration from my team. In the grip of competition fever, Clive for the Yellows did the same, rolling his Sunbeam and taking out the Blues in the process. The girls with their Green Jaguar romped easily home. The entire garden erupted in cheers.

"For the winners," said Hilary, handing the girls a bottle of Brut cider. "Congratulations."

In time honoured fashion, the winners gave the bottle a good shake, well they were jumping up and down with excitement anyway, the cork popped and fizzy drink splattered us all. Which was ironic really as in the real race it was the girls on the podium who got soaked with champagne.

We were so busy enjoying ourselves that Jacky Ickx and Gijs van Lennep, winning the real race in their Porsche 936 went by barely noticed.

The local newspaper had somehow heard about what was going on in our garden and sent a photographer along. The following Thursday our photo appeared showing all of us with our cars - which took a bit of explaining when my parents saw it!

Chapter 13

The School Trip

Our nemesis, Mr. Watkins, Head of History, wasn't a bad old bloke, tall, thin with grey hair and a moustache, he had fought in WW2 and if you could get him chatting about the war and some real fighting he was really interesting, but that didn't happen often. It certainly wasn't happening on one particular day, as I sat in the far corner of the classroom idly drawing pictures of motorbikes on my history book. Mr Watkins was perched on the corner of his desk, wittering on about some place up north and yet another war, this one about red and white roses. I mean, what sort of war was that? How stupid can you get, fighting over some flowers. No wonder I was feeling totally bored, the really good stuff, like forms of torture and interesting ways of killing people, were always left out for fear of upsetting the girls. The only good thing about History was the trips, like the one to the Tower of London with all the swords, and the pikes with sharp spikes for impaling your enemies.

Feeling thoroughly fed up I swapped to trying to decipher the crude messages scratched on my desk. Suddenly my head jerked up.

"...castle, leaving on Friday, can you please collect your permission slips on the way out," said Mr. Watkins, pointing to a pile of paper on the corner of his desk. "The coach will leave immediately after assembly on Friday morning, please bring a packed lunch with you. Anyone without a signed permission slip will not be able to go."

I reached across the aisle and nudged Stuart. "Where did he say we're going?" I whispered.

"Bodiam."

"Uh! Where's that?"

"Bone, stop talking. I want no messing about on this trip, it's not a jolly, you'll be expected to take notes and I shall be setting homework when we return."

On Friday morning I finished my paper round and rushed back home. After putting my cycle back in the shed, I picked up the packed lunch mum had left on the kitchen table and stowed it in my duffle bag, along with a couple of cans of coke from the fridge. There was a moment of panic when I couldn't find the necessary permission slip, until I spotted it wedged between some plants on the windowsill. I carefully added it to the bag – there was no way I was missing a day off school!

Assembly seemed to drag. Mather swept onto the stage like an enormous black beetle in his mortarboard and gown, Miss Jennings attacked the piano for 'Holy, Holy, Holy', and I looked at the floor and opened my mouth occasionally to pretend I was singing. The only hymn I liked and joined in gustily was 'Lord dismiss us with thy blessing', sung on the last day of term!

Eventually the torture was over and we all rushed outside. Epsom Coaches, whose drivers must have been paid danger money, were once again providing the transport and their maroon and cream Bedford was waiting in the drive. Handing over our permission slips, Danny, Gary and I rushed for the back seat, as far from the teachers as possible.

The end of June was approaching and the temperature just kept going up. It had been 80°F for a week and the inside of the coach was stifling. We all pulled at the knot of our ties and undid the top button of our shirts. For once it was just too hot to mess about so we slouched in the back seat, eating the crisps from our packed lunch and passing around a can of Coke. By the time we reached Bodiam we were ready for some fun.

"Stay in your seats," yelled Watson. He did another quick head count, just in case any of us had managed to escape on the way down. “Boys you may remove your ties and blazers and leave them in the coach, but remember you are representing the school. Any misbehaviour with be punished, *severely* punished!” He seemed to be looking straight at us.

Eventually we were led in a crocodile towards the castle. The entrance looked alright, with slits for firing arrows and we could imagine pouring boiling oil onto our enemies heads, but inside it was falling down, just a load of old stones with a moat around it. We thought the tower looked interesting, but it had a rope across and a sign saying ‘No Entry’. Old Watkins was in his element. 14th Century, the 100 year war, then that War of the Roses again, King this, King that, he went on and on as though history was the greatest thing ever, darting questions at us if he thought we were slacking. My hand ached from writing, as I tried to take notes. Watkins was a stickler for homework and would expect an essay in book form when we got back. Eventually he got to the English Civil War, Cavaliers and Roundheads and decided we could have a break for lunch and led us back to the entrance where there was a large area of grass.

We all flopped down and immediately rummaged in our duffle bags for drinks. The sky was a bright cerulean blue and the sun continued to blaze down. It was so hot you could almost see the grass shrivelling.

“I bet it must be a hundred degrees now,” said Gary, gulping down an enormous swig of 7-Up.

“Look at the moat,” said Danny. “There’s hardly any water in it. I bet it’s usually right up to the top.”

“Yeah,” I agreed with a nod, looking at the trickle of mud coloured water topped with green algae. “You can see the brown line on the bottom of the castle wall.”

Our sandwiches were already beginning to curl around the edges, and the chocolate on the biscuits had melted and I had to lick it off the paper, I could see Danny and Gary doing the same.

"Get off," said Gary, flicking away a wasp.

We watched delighted as it buzzed over towards a bunch of girls who immediately leapt up and started screaming, giving us a good view of their knickers.

"What shall we do now?" I asked lazily, chucking an apple core into the moat.

"Let's ask if we can explore on our own," suggested Danny.

"Watson will never let us," I retorted.

"Let's ask him anyway," said Gary getting up. He ambled over to where Mr. Watson was having a quiet smoke with the couple of wet-behind-the-ears teachers he'd somehow bribed to help him keep us in order.

"Please sir," Gary knew how to grovel, he had an older brother. "Would it be OK if we went and explored on our own. We might have missed something while we were taking notes."

We were in luck; Watson must have been sipping from his 'secret' hip flask. "Alright," he waved his hand airily. "If the castle can withstand numerous wars in five hundred years, I'm sure three boys shouldn't cause a problem."

Quickly we made ourselves scarce before he changed his mind. Of course we made straight for the off-limits tower, jumped over the rope and headed up the spiral stairs to the top. Looking over the edge we could see the girls picnicking on the grass below next to the moat.

"Wouldn't it be funny if we pushed a stone over into the moat and splashed the girls with mud," said Gary, leaning over as far as he could.

"There's a loose one over here," called Danny, giving it a kick.

At the side of the tower, balanced on the parapet, was a large stone almost too big to move, but it was loose and with a bit of wiggling we managed to prise it out. We got it on its side, and then edged it around the battlements, until it lined up with the moat.

"After three," said Gary, and counted down.

On three we all kicked the stone as hard as we could. It went flying off the edge of the battlements, out into the air where it seemed to hover for a moment before crashing with a mighty THUD into the moat below.

The splash was not as outstanding as we had hoped as we only just got it into the water, the dirty mud completely missing the girls below, but it made an impressive noise which could be felt throughout the entire castle. Realising this would attract some very unwelcome attention we scat down the stairs as fast as we could.

As we jumped over the rope Watkins was waiting for us.

"What did you do up there?" he yelled.

"We only leant on it sir, honest, and it fell off," said Gary, trying hard not to laugh and looking red with the effort. Danny and I kept our mouths firmly closed, trying hard to stifle our giggles.

"It is not funny," he said, looking at us as though we were the thickest kids on the planet. "You should not have been up there. Can't you read the sign? Get into the coach immediately before someone comes. I'll deal with you three when we get back to school."

He rounded up the other kids and herded us all onto the coach, cutting the trip short before anyone official noticed the missing stone.

On the way home Watson came and sat on the back seat next to us.

"I want you to promise," he muttered fiercely, his voice low and extremely menacing, "that *nothing* untoward happened today. No mention of going up any tower, and definitely no mention of any falling rock. Do you understand? It was an unfortunate accident and you are to forget about it. On no account are you to mention it to anyone. Is that absolutely clear?"

We all nodded vigorously. Forgetting about it made perfect sense to us. The less anyone knew about our numerous activities the better. So we never did mention it to anyone. Until now! But you're not going to tell are you?

Chapter 14

Jumping

Graham with his Halford's Bronco Chopper

"I don't get history." said Gary when we got back to school. "Why don't they teach us something interesting like how the first motorbike was invented?"

Danny and I nodded enthusiastically, that would be more like it.

We all thought that the most important thing to happen in the whole of the Seventy's was that in July 1975 Evel Knievel jumped thirteen buses on his Harley Davidson motor bike. He was watched by eighty-thousand spectators inside Wembley Stadium. When he crashed, as he usually seemed to do, we watched him live on television announcing that he was retiring and would never jump again.[24] That left a gap in the market for a new daredevil that we all wanted to fill.

At the beginning of the show he would ride around on his Harley, lifting up the front wheel and revving the engine so flames came out of the exhaust. Then as he went faster his cape would fly out behind him and the Stars and Stripes on it would flap around which, to us, made him look like an American god. This was a skill we had to master.

"Hey," said Gary as we returned from our paper-round the next morning. "I've found the perfect place to practice our jumping."

"Where's that?" asked Danny

"Copley Way," he replied. "They just re-surface it."

Copley Way was a quiet, private road, which was as straight and flat as you could find, with the advantage of being blocked at one end so traffic was light.

"Let's get over there then," I said at once.

That Saturday football was forgotten and we spent all day cycling furiously along the road on our Chopper bikes, practicing wheelies again and again, until we could ride from one end of the road to the other with our front wheels in the air. Word soon got around about what we were up to. Andrew and Paul were the first to join us, swiftly followed by Terry and Nick, soon it seemed that half the Estate were having a go. By Sunday morning doing wheelies was old hat, so we started making jumps. There was a new house under construction and work had stopped for the weekend, so we borrowed a few bricks and a couple of scaffolding planks and made a ramp. Borrowing, *not* stealing – we had every intention of putting them back.

---

[24] Evel Knievel's retirement was short lived, he jumped further buses in 1976, finally retiring from major shows after a horrific accident involving a cameraman in 1980.

Practising continued until lunch (none of us were going to miss a Sunday roast), by which time we could clear six bodies laid side to side, if we got a really fast run up. There were a few casualties, but nothing serious, well not what we or Evel Knievel would call serious!

"I've been thinking," I said when we all met up again, stoked by our roast beef and Yorkshire pudding. "If we had a slope *after* the jump as well as before it we should be able to go further."

"Yeah," agreed Gary, with a nod. "We're good at the run up, but haven't got the power to go further on the flat. Where can we find a slope?"

"Over the 'Hills and Mountains'," I said.

The 'Hills and Mountains' was an area of Burgh Heath known to every kid on the Estate. It had been used for training in trench warfare in WW1 and by the Home Guard in WWII, and a century earlier for gravel extraction. It had been the scene of many of our games from Civil Defence to Kiss Chase. The area was riddled with dips and gullies, ideal for the death defying leaps we had in mind.

"Good idea," said Danny, getting on his bike. "Let's get over there."

Leaving the bricks and planks for a few of the younger kids we set off towards the heath. For once the 'Muddy Alley' was not ankle deep in mud and we bumped over the hard ridges of dried out puddles, our bikes feeling like bone-shakers. Out onto the heathland and the bracken was already chest high, but wilting in the continuing heat, and turning brown and crisp at the edges. We passed the pond, almost empty of water, the island in the centre marooned in baking mud. A moorhen with a couple of half-grown chicks paddled dejectedly around the willows. We had always been warned to stay away from the pond, (not that we took any notice), as it was rumoured to be bottomless – something the hot summer was beginning to disprove.

It didn't take long to reach a suitable area for jumping. Again and again we cycled furiously along the narrow tracks through the bracken, the sun hot on the back of our necks, sailing into the air to land in a gully or basin. One area in particular was just right for leaps, with a hill leading up and a long, fast, steep slope down the other side, ending in a dried gully making a lip that gave extra lift. It felt glorious as our bikes left the ground and shot into the air.

Gary was the first to try to do a loop, he might have been a bit overweight, but he was very strong and fit. He rode fast up the hill, went like the clappers down the slope, hit the lip and managed to get three-quarters of the way around before landing in the bushes, which probably saved his neck. His extra natural padding gave him an advantage when pursuing such extreme sports as looping a chopper bike!

"I'm next," yelled Danny, convinced that being small and skinny gave him a better chance.

He hurtled up the track, came over the hill, legs going like pistons, hit the lip and as he sailed into the air the bike flew upwards and twisted almost out from under him. Bike and rider landed hard, and then slew sideways in a tangled heap. "Sh*t! Sh*t! Sh*t!" he yelled, rolling around clutching his crutch while Gary and I collapsed in a heap laughing.

"You almost did it," I assured him when the swearing had stopped. "A bit more speed and you'd have gone right round."

"I'm going to have another go," he said, picking up his bike.

"No, I'm next," I said, desperately wanting to try, and convinced I could do it.

However, Gary had also sensed it was do-able. "It was my idea, so I'm going next."

"OK," I agreed. "But we need a soft landing."

Quickly we gathered together armfuls of bracken and heather and piled them at the bottom of the dip (which was probably part of an old gravel quarry).

Gary rode further back along the track this time, taking a much longer run up. We could see the muscles flexing in his legs, and his mouth set in grim determination as he flew past us. He hit the quarry lip, sailed into the air and did a complete loop, landing on his wheels. Unfortunately, bracken got stuck in his chain making him fall off, but he had done it, he had made the first loop.

"I've worked it out," he said excitedly. "You have to fling your head right back as far as it will go, so you're looking up at the sky, then the bike follows you around."

Finally it was my turn. "Right," I said. "I'll give it a go." I moved the bushes and bracken out of the way for a clear landing. I would have to do it first time or break my neck.

"Don't come running to me if you're a paraplegic," called Danny, cheerfully, trying to put me off. I was determined to do it even if it did kill me.

I took an even longer run up than Gary, peddling furiously and taking the slope as fast as I could, possibly a little too fast, as I hit the lip, flung my head back, saw the sky coming towards me, and did a complete loop, just like Gary had said. However, I over-rotated slightly and landed on my back wheel, but the feeling was brilliant, just like flying. Time seemed to slow down as I rotated around in the air with the whole world turning beneath me. Ground, sky, ground, and I had done a loop, without a safety net, as they say in the circus.

Before I had even stopped Gary and Danny were pedalling up the hill to try it. After a few goes it seemed easy and we started showing off, doing side flips and kick outs. On the way home we complimented each other. If Gary hadn't thought of it, and Danny not crashed proving we needed more speed, then Gary getting the trick of throwing his head back and doing it first proving it could be done, and then me perfecting it, it would never have happened. With team work we had pulled it off. It felt great – apart from the bruises and aches and Gary's snapped bike frame and my bent handle bars that is!

My poor old Chopper bike was looking decidedly dangerous with bits of sharp metal poking out where I'd been hitting it with stones to get it back into shape. Maybe I could ask for some new bits for it for my birthday, but I wasn't expecting much as dad was notoriously mean.

Chapter 15

A Birthday Treat

"It's your birthday on Saturday," said mum. "Fifteen at last. What do you want?"

This was a hard one to answer as there were lots of things I wanted, but none I expected to get. A Bultaco scramble bike or a Suzuki RM 125A would be great, but I knew they would be too expensive, and money was always tight in our household (most of it went on my dad's hobbies, there wasn't much left for mine). Toys had been long forgotten and I had all the clothes I needed, so it took me a while to decide.

"Can I have a day out with my friends in the car?" I asked finally. "But not fishing!"

My dad always wanted to take me fishing and he always insisted on leaving at the crack of dawn when any sensible person was still in bed. I had endured hours and hours on the river bank, keeping quiet so the fish would bite, which they rarely if ever seemed to do.

"OK," she said, looking worried. "I'll ask your father, but you know what he's like!"

Dad was a little shocked, but agreed to take me and my friends out for the day. Quickly, before he could change his mind, I rang up Gary and Danny and made the arrangements. Saturday, at my house, come around at 9 o'clock for a boy's day out.

On Saturday morning, waking at the crack of dawn for my paper-round, I stumbled sleepily down the stairs, and there in the hall was a brand new Raleigh Chopper. Brilliant! I could hardly believe it. After last weekends jumping my second-hand chopper bike was looking distinctly battered if not downright dangerous! It was a great present, and much, much more than I had expected, but would the boy's day out still be on? However, dad was true to his word and when Danny and Gary arrived he led us all out to the car. I climbed in looking cautiously for fishing gear, but there was none to be seen. Danny was disappointed as he loved fishing.

"So where are we going?" I asked.

"Wait and see," said Dad.

About an hour later we arrived – it was a Steam Fair. This was Dad's secret destination, and I should have guessed because the only thing Dad loved more than fishing was steam engines. It was actually a great idea as we all enjoyed looking at traction engines. The smell and power of them was fascinating, especially when they moved which made the ground shake and the sound of those large engines was almost musical. Dad had bought me a Mamod[25] model steam traction engine for my birthday the previous year, but had been disappointed when I blew it up racing it against Gary's steam roller of the same type (Gary's dad also being into steam, although he preferred trains).

Dad soon met up with some old friends and started chatting, so we wandered off on our own, the money from our paper rounds burning a hole in our pockets.

"Look, there's a fairground," said Danny, pointing to the other side of the arena.

We made our way through the crowds to have a look. All the rides were powered by steam; there were kiddie's roundabouts, colourful carousels with swings, Mary Poppins type galloping horses, and great steam organs piping out music. A go-kart track had been laid out on the grass but it had a huge queue of people waiting to go on, so we decided to give it a miss. Best of all was the Wall of Death, which instantly attracted our attention; we had never seen one before.

Debbie Smith was there with her dad Brian, who was also a big fan of steam. She had been dragged

---

[25] Mamod – A British toy manufacturer, founded in 1937, specialising in the manufacture of live steam models.

along, as she always was by her dad, who was listening to a very loud steam organ.

"Hello, lads," said Brian, recognising us from the times we had been around to their house, although we usually managed to keep out of his way. He didn't take kindly to anyone hanging around his daughters.

"Can I go with them, dad?" asked Debbie.

"OK, love," said Brian indulgently. "But behave yourselves," he added, giving us a look that threatened dire punishment to anyone who laid a finger on his princess, entirely wasted as Debbie could look after herself. In fact, there were some very rough looking lads wandering around giving us dirty looks, but we knew we were safe with Debbie – she would definitely sort them out if they started anything!

Outside the Wall of Death we could hear the motor bikes tearing around, to the accompaniment of lots of screaming. Painted on the outside were pictures of men riding no-handed, their bikes parallel to the ground.

"I've seen it before," said Debbie, nonchalantly. With a steam obsessive father she was a regular at these events.

"What happens inside?" asked Danny.

"Well," she said, giving him her well known 'all boys are morons' look. "They ride around the walls!"

We looked at each other, trying to imagine some kind of magic act where motorbikes could fly.

"It's the centrifugal force," explained Dad, who had come up behind us and heard us talking. "Come on," he added, "the next shows starting and we need to be at the front to get the best view."

He was obviously in a good mood for once and paid for us all to go in. Climbing the stairs we stood around the edge looking down into a large wooden barrel with motorbikes at the bottom. It soon filled up behind us as more and more people came in. As the motorbikes started revving up everyone pushed forward to look over the edge and see what was happening.

Debbie was squashed tight between Danny and Gary, who looked like they were thoroughly enjoying the experience!

With a great roar the bikes started off, whizzing around the wall, coming right up to the edge with only a wire to stop them coming out. Everyone moved back hurriedly. Riding the bikes there was a tough looking man in his early twenties, with long dark hair and tattoos, and a tall, slim, girl with long blond hair. An older, foreign looking man standing in the middle was commentating on the mic, introducing each new move and giving details about the bikes they were using. Swerving up and down, sometimes together, sometimes following each other, then crossing over at speed, they really put on a good show. Then the older man rode around on his vintage Indian motorbike. We had thought the younger couple were good, but he was something else, with unequalled style and riding no handed, right to the top. He was really talented, a true showman, and everyone applauded loudly. Then they all rode around together, very fast, and it was quite scary, the whole death wall shook and seemed to throb between our feet, as though the entire structure would fall apart at any moment.

When they eventually stopped everyone threw money down to them, as the riders looked up and waved.

Climbing down the stairs we felt disorientated, so we stopped outside to look at the bikes on show. They were selling t-shirts with pictures of the Wall of Death on them.

"Do you want one?" asked Dad. "Let's see if they have anything in your size. It's his birthday," he explained to the girl behind the stall. I noticed she was wearing a really cool leather jacket, with a skull and wings embroidered on it.

"Well, if it's your birthday," said the girl in an American accent. "How would you like to go in for a look around?"

Gary could not believe his luck, motorbikes were his obsession and he had been dying to get inside. We were shown through a small hatch that led into the bottom of the Wall. It looked much bigger on the inside and we all stood looking up, trying to imagine what it would be like to ride around the wall on motorbikes. The bottom edge was banked at 45°s so that the bikes could gain some momentum. We tried running around as fast as we could and managed to get a couple of steps onto the wall before falling back down. Then we took turns sitting on one of the bikes.

"I'd love to have a go," I said, gripping the handlebars, imagining myself whizzing around and doing all the amazing tricks. I was absolutely sure I could do it.

"I'd like to have a go no-handed," put in Debbie.

"You'll have to come back for a try-out when you're older," said the American girl. "We are always looking for girl riders as they are always getting hurt. It's not called the Wall of Death for no reason." She pulled up the leg of her jeans to reveal a mess of scars and broken bones. We were seriously impressed.

"Thanks for showing us around," I said, pleased at how well my birthday was turning out.

Outside again I tried on the small size t-shirt, it was a bit large for me.

"You'll grow into it," said Dad, getting his wallet out.

"It looks good on you," put in Debbie, so I decided to keep it.

"Would your girlfriend like one?" asked the girl, holding up another t-shirt with a stunning golden eagle on the front.

I could feel my face going red and stammered "She's not my..." But the girl just laughed and gave me a knowing look as Debbie scowled at me and Gary and Danny sniggered.

Debbie took the t-shirt and put it in her bag. "I'll try it on later," she said, as she paid the money. There was no way she was going to try it on in front of us, although that didn't stop us for hoping!

While Debbie sought out her dad, the rest of us went to look for some food. Grease burger and chips all round set us up for the remainder of the afternoon and we all went for a last look at the funfair. When we got to the go-karts the queue was gone.

"Do you want to have a go?" asked Dad, obviously feeling generous; he must have visited the beer tent with his friends.

We didn't need asking twice and raced over to the track before he could change his mind, jumping into the last three karts that were lined up at the start. Debbie strolled over with her dad and they leant against the barrier to watch. The bloke in charge showed us where the throttle and brake were (as if we didn't know!), then the flag dropped and we were off.

Being on the inside for the first bend we got into the lead and started battling between each other as the rest got left behind. Gary's kart seemed faster on the straight, but slid out more on the bends. Danny's kart looked unstable and he was struggling to keep it straight. Mine felt fast, but I could not get it past the others, what with Danny weaving and Gary pulling away on the straights.

After some laps the board was shown saying 'last lap' and the other two started barging about and pushing for the lead. As they got tangled up they ran wide on the last bend leaving a gap for me to shoot past. I'd done it, I'd won! As we all completed an extra lap to slow down everyone watching began clapping me. I felt great, James Hunt had better watch out, the next world champion was snapping at his heels!

As I got out of the kart I said, "Did you see Debbie waving?"

"No, we were too busy letting you win," said Danny, giving me a friendly punch on the arm.

"Yeah," agreed Gary. "Of course we *had* to let you win, because it's your birthday."

“Don’t listen to them,” said Debbie’s dad. “You looked like you were going to win from the start.

On the way home Danny asked if I had seen Debbie wearing the t-shirt. I hadn’t noticed, but I was glad she had something to remember the day by; we’d all had such a great time together. The best bit we all agreed was the Wall of Death.

Chapter 16

The Honda 90

Of course, after the Wall of Death we all wanted to ride a motorbike – but where could three young lads get hold of one? Gary's brother had a bike, but he certainly wouldn't let any of us ride it, if we so much laid a single finger on its gleaming chrome he would kill us. We would just have to wait – or would we?

"I'm feeding next-door's cat," announced Gary, looking pleased with himself.

"Are they paying you?" asked Danny immediately. We all knew that doing things for neighbours could be tricky, as our parents had a horrible habit of volunteering our services for nothing.

"No," said Gary, still looking smug.

"Well, what are you looking so cheerful about?" I asked.

"They've given me a key."

"So what?"

"Come round after school and I'll show you."

This had to be investigated, there was no way Gary should be so happy about feeding a cat. Admittedly it wasn't like looking after a dog that had to be taken for walks, or even worse a neighbours kid that talked non-stop, jumped all over you and had disgusting bodily functions that needed cleaning up. No, something was definitely going on, so after dumping our school books at home Danny and I walked over to Gary's house.

"Come on," he said, as he unlocked his neighbour's front door. He led us through the hall and into the kitchen, then took a key from a drawer and unlocked the back door. "Puss, puss, puss," he called. An enormous ginger Tom appeared and began winding its way among our legs, whining piteously as though it hadn't seen a square meal in months. Gary gave it a scratch behind the ear, then very slowly opened a cupboard door, took out a tin and put it on the draining board. The cat's whining when up a decibel.

"For goodness sake Gary," I pleaded, "Will you get on with it?"

Gary was determined to draw it out as long as possible, and the poor cat was beginning to think it was going to die of starvation, but eventually the food was in its bowl and the whining stopped.

"If you bought us all the way over here just to see you feed a cat you are dead," pronounced Danny.

Gary started to grin. "Come on," he said, leading the way down the garden path.

Leaning against the back fence, behind a row of blackcurrant bushes, was something covered in tarpaulin. Gary lifted the tarp with a flourish. Underneath was a beautiful little Honda 90, a bit rusty, covered in cobwebs, with a crack in the front mudguard and a large scratch along one of the leg guards.

"When did you find this?" I asked.

"Bill bought it for his missus," explained Gary. "The first time she rode it she had a crash and wouldn't get on it again. It's been here for a couple of years."

"We can't just take it," said Danny.

"No," agreed Gary. "But we could *borrow* it, just have a little go on it, and then put it back."

Danny and I nodded. No one would notice if we just borrowed it for a while, after all it wasn't being used.

It didn't take us long to get it cleaned up and oiled. We found a can of petrol in the neighbour's shed next to the lawnmower and soon had the bike revved up. There was an alleyway behind the houses, ideal for our first foray into the world of motorbike racing. Up and down the path we went, taking it in turns, wobbly at first, but getting better all the time. Avoiding the dustbins was a bit tricky, and the occasional cat, but the obstacles made it more fun.

"This is great," said Gary, always the first to take things a step further. "But, it would be even better if we took it over the 'Hills and Mountains', as long as we get it back in good condition."

"We can give it a good clean and put it back under the tarp when we get back," I suggested. "No-one will be any the wiser."

"Good idea," agreed Danny, looking at his watch. "But if I don't get home soon mum will be out looking for me. I'm well late for tea as it is and you know how she gets in a state."

We nodded. Danny's mum was a stickler for punctuality and tidiness and the last thing we wanted was to be found with the bike, any of our mums would definitely put a stop to that!

"Let's take it over there tomorrow after school," I suggested.

"OK," said Gary. "Just help me put it back."

The following evening we all met at Gary's house, our parents assumed we were going to the Youth Club, a regular evening event which caused no awkward questions. Parents have a peculiar knack of knowing when you are lying in reply to a direct question, better to avoid questions altogether!

"Have you fed that cat?" asked Gary's mum as we left the house.

"Just going around there now mum," replied Gary.

She looked at him suspiciously. "Well, don't let your friends in. Mrs. Brown wouldn't like strangers in her house while she's away."

"OK."

He hustled us out of the door quickly.

While Gary fed the cat Danny and I swiftly retrieved the bike from the back garden and wheeled it quietly along the alley. A few minutes later Gary joined us. We didn't want to invite any unwelcome attention, so we continued to push the bike through the Estate and onto the heath. The sun was shimmering through the silver birch trees, turning their bark a dazzling white. The air was buzzing with insects feeding on the rose bay willow herb, and small brown lizards skittered out of our way as we pushed the bike along the dusty track through the bracken.

It took about fifteen minutes to reach our favourite biking spot, where we had made the track for our chopper bikes. Of course Gary had first go, but we were soon taking it in turns to race around the track, throwing the bike around corners, up inclines, leaping over gullies, skidding on loose gravel, falling off and climbing on again. The more we practiced the better we got, it was great fun – until the Thomas lads turned up. There was Billy aged about twenty and his brother Warren a couple of year's younger, general layabouts and no-goods. Both of them a good six inches taller than us, with muscles developed at the boxing club, definitely not to be messed with. Anything that went missing on the Estate, the local Bobby knocked on their door first.

Warren stood, arms folded, in the middle of the track as Danny came belting around a bend, so he had to brake hard. Swerving to try and avoid him Dan ending up in a heap among the bracken and brambles. I helped him to his feet and wiped the blood from a deep scratch across his face.

"Not much good are ya!" retorted Billy, picking up the bike. "I'll show ya how it's done."

He revved up the bike, sending smoke shooting from the exhaust, and then shot off around the track sending a swirl of gravel into the air. Round and round he went, darting towards us every time he came close, sticking out his leg to try and kick us, laughing as we had to leap out of the way.

"Let's 'av a go," whined Warren each time he came past.

Eventually Billy got fed up and handed the bike over, giving Gary a good shove in the chest as he tried to intervene.

"Get out of the way, asshole," he smirked, as Warren revved up the engine again.

Warren got off to a wobbly start, but as the bike picked up speed he gained confidence, too much confidence. He came around the track like a bat out of hell, hit the lip of the gully we'd used in our Evel Knievel stunts, rose into the air, and came down with a crunch. The bike skidded out from under him, careered sideways on the loose gravel and ended up against a tree.

We stood looking at him, silently hoping the crash had killed him, but unfortunately not. He got unsteadily to his feet, shrugged his shoulders and said to his brother, "Let's get over to the pub then."

As he and Billy nonchalantly strolled off we stood and surveyed the wreck.

"Can it be fixed?" asked Danny, giving the bike a gentle kick with his toe. It didn't look hopeful, the front mudguard was now completely smashed, stuffing was coming out of the seat, several wires had come loose and it was bleeding oil.

"How on earth are we going to explain this?" asked Gary, looking at the bike in dismay. "I'm going to be in dead shit if the Browns come back and find their bike gone. They're sure to know it was me."

"Let's get it upright and see if it will start before we begin to panic" I said, grabbing hold of the handlebars and giving the bike a tug. "Here, hold onto it Gary while I fix some of these wires."

"I've got a pen-knife in my pocket," said Gary, handing over a beautiful Swiss Army knife, "and some string."

Neither Danny or I were surprised, Gary's pockets were always full of stuff that might be useful.

I used the screwdriver attachment on the pen-knife to reattach the trailing wires, and then tied them securely to the frame, climbed onto the seat and gave the kick start a jab, then another harder jab and wonder of wonders it started. We all grinned. The race was on again. As the evening wore on we roared around the track getting better and faster. Other friends came over and joined us and we took turns having a go, then we tried doing timed laps, making a competition of it, finding out who could do five laps of the course in the fastest time. Eventually the sky began to darken and we carefully hid the bike under some bushes and went home.

The following evening the exhaust fell off and the noise started attracting more attention. Then the throttle busted so it took two people to ride it, one to steer and one to pull the cable to make it go. This was so much fun that we decided to ride a bit further. Danny was steering and I was on the back pulling the cable. The bike was going well and we were flat out along the bridleway by the side of the locally called 'black' pond. Suddenly Danny shouted "Police!" and jumped off, leaving me on the back bouncing along with two policemen running up the path towards me waving and shouting "Stop!". I had no control over the direction I was travelling, so instinctively I pulled the cable as hard as I could, which seemed to work as the bike picked up speed. The policemen, realised their predicament, jumped out of the way. They were behind me now, so I lunged forward and got one hand on the handlebar, but it was no use as the speed I was travelling meant I had no chance of stopping. The bike went sideways up the bank to the pond and as I jumped off it flipped over, landing in the water with a hiss. It quickly disappeared down into the dark and slimy depths, among the reeds and leeches, nearly taking me with it.

Luckily I landed running and did not look back, just kept on going as fast as I could around the pond, up the old farm track and onto the Estate, only stopping exhausted when I reached the back of the shops. Danny and Gary had got there before me and we all stood, heads bowed, hands on knees, hearts hammering, trying to catch our breath.

"I thought we'd had it for sure," muttered Gary, leaning against the wall.

"Did you see that coppers face when you came flying towards him?" asked Danny.

We started to laugh, and then couldn't stop. We laughed until out stomachs ached.

"What are we going to do about the bike?" I asked, suddenly sobering up and becoming practical.

"Get some wood and prop up that tarpaulin," suggested Danny, "they'll never notice the difference.

So that is what we did. We crept into the neighbours back garden, propped some bits of wood under the tarp so that it looked like the bike was still under there, and then crept out. Then we sneaked back to spy on the police. They had got a grappling hook on a long length of rope and were trying to retrieve the bike from the pond. Unfortunately people had been throwing unwanted goods into the pond for generations. Out came a pram, bits of old mangle, a tyre, even an old scooter, but thankfully not the Honda 90. It turned out to be the perfect hiding place. Once again our skins were saved.

Gary's neighbours eventually returned from their holidays. They were delighted to find their cat well fed and gave Gary a couple of pounds for his trouble and a box of clotted cream fudge, which of course he had to share with his mates – delicious. I don't think they ever noticed that the bike was missing!

Chapter 17

Birch Bending

Burgh Heath

It wasn't only school that was boring in 1976, Sunday's were just as bad; at least they were in our house. Dad often spent the entire day fishing, getting up at the crack of dawn and not reappearing until the evening. This was a very cunning plan as it got him out of helping with the housework and squashed any ideas mum had about decorating. Mum liked baking and as she worked all week Sunday morning was usually spent in the kitchen producing a roast dinner, apple pie and a variety of cakes to last us through the week. She therefore thought that Sunday afternoon was her own, to relax in front of the telly watching old black and white films or, even worse, musicals.

Sometimes my sisters came over, but as my sister Hilary was now pregnant the talk was all about babies and there were some facts I really didn't want to know.

As soon as Sunday lunch was over I escaped the house, rounded up Danny and Gary and we all headed for our usual summer haunt, the Heath. We were quickly joined by other friends, all looking for something to liven up the dreary afternoon that stretched before us.

"What are we going to do?" I asked, idly picking up a stick and swiping the heads off the bracken.

"Why don't we do some birch bending?" suggested Danny, giving Gary a sly look.

Gary's face darkened and he began to scowl, birch bending was a sore subject.

"Good idea," I said immediately, always willing to stir up a mate. I gave Gary a slap on the back and his scowl deepened.

"Bog off," he muttered.

Perhaps I should explain about birch bending, as I think it was a purely local sport. I don't know who thought of it originally, (well, I do, but I won't dob a mate in), but it must have been the most stupid game ever invented. It was played between three and thirteen people (the more the better), and depending on the number involved a silver birch tree of suitable size to accommodate everyone playing was chosen. Then you all climbed to the top of the tree and started swinging it from side to side, bending it more with each swing to get it lower to the ground. When the tree bent so far that you could almost touch the ground, you would release the branch you were clinging to and jump off. However, being lads, everything had to have a competitive edge, so the aim of the game was to be the *last* to let go, otherwise you were a chicken and naturally you would be mocked accordingly.

A lot of the game involved tricking your fellow tree benders into letting go early. "This time, this time," we'd shout, or "next time, next time", pretending we were going to jump, lifting our hands up as if we were letting go and then grabbing back hold of the tree at the last minute. This was always accompanied by lots of shouting and whooping, and looking into each others eyes to see if we could tell how scared our opponents were and therefore more likely to let go.

Danny, Gary and myself were by far the most deranged and least likely to let go first, however the day before Gary had slipped and let go early, and of course had been mocked accordingly which he hated as he considered himself to be the most daring of all of us, which he probably was.

"Come on," said Danny. "Let's find a tree."

We trekked around the heathland, wandering along the dusty paths, stumbling through the bracken, jostling each other, bragging about how good we were and how rubbish everyone else was. A number of trees were examined before a suitable tree was finally found. A mature silver birch can grow to about ninety feet, and this one was getting on that way, probably about seventy feet high, with some sturdy branches low down making climbing up it fairly easy. There were about ten of us playing the game and we all scrambled up. Danny, who could climb anything, went first. Being quite small he could get really high into the tree canopy. Gary, determined to prove himself, swiftly followed him, and as he was quite sturdy the tree began to tilt to one side. Steve and Rich, two of our more foolhardy friends, climbed up selecting suitable branches to stand on, with me behind them, my feet on a strong branch with another in easy reach to cling to. Then the others following, getting as high up the tree as they could.

Hanging on tightly we began to swing the tree from side to side, slowly at first then, as we got into a rhythm, bending the top of the tree lower and lower. Gary was determined not to slip this time and wrapped some of the smaller, more flexible branches around his arms. Soon the tree was almost touching the ground.

"Next time, next time," I shouted, watching Danny grinning as the ground came towards us.

Suddenly we all let go – except for Gary. As we rolled into the bracken, Gary, hampered by the branches he had wrapped around his wrists, shot upwards, clinging on for dear life. Twang! With a noise like a shot from a gun the tree ricocheted back, the force tearing the branch from Gary's hand and sending him hurtling into space. We watched in horror as he travelled up into the sky almost as high again as the tree, spinning in a graceful arc, before landing with an almighty thud in a smaller tree about twenty yards away. As we ran towards him we could hear the shattering noise as he tumbled through the smaller branches of the tree and came to rest with an almighty 'thump' in the bracken beneath.

"Gary!" we yelled, as we trampled through the bracken like a herd of wild elephants desperate to see if he was still alive. Within seconds we were all huddled around his fallen body.

"Gary, mate, are you OK?" I asked stupidly.

A loud groan gave us hope. At least he was still alive.

Another pitiful moan and his eyes flicked open to see a circle of heads staring down at him.

"F*ck, that hurts."

We all burst out laughing with relief.

"Don't laugh at me you bastards, help me up. Ouch. No! Let me lie here."

"Where does it hurt?" I asked.

"Everywhere."

"Do you think you've broken anything?" asked Danny.

Gary gently eased himself into a sitting position and wriggled his feet, moved his legs, flexed his arms. "Ouch! I think it's just my shoulder."

We couldn't believe it, the jammy devil, whizzing through the air like that, falling through a tree and the only injury he had sustained was a dislocated shoulder! He was in pain though, and was looking a very pasty grey colour.

"How can we get it fixed?" asked Danny. "Anyone know a doctor?"

"I do," said Phil.

We all turned and stared at him.

"He's on my paper-round," he explained.

We all nodded. We all knew odd people from doing our paper-rounds. Apparently the chap was an ex-Army doctor called 'The Colonel' and lived in a large house on the edge of the heath. So, taking it in turns to clasp hands and make a seat, we carried Gary as carefully as we could across the heathland to the Colonel's house and knocked on the door. An elderly man, very stern looking, with short grey hair and an enormous moustache answered the door.

When we explained what had happened he burst out laughing.

"Come in," he said, ushering us into the kitchen. "I can fix it, but it's going to hurt like hell. You'll have to drink a glass of brandy first. OK."

Gary, in his confused state, would have agreed to anything, and nodded his head. "Happy to," he said, as he sank down onto a kitchen chair.

The Colonel went into the drawing room and returned with a large glass half filled with a golden liquid.

"Drink that," he said, handing over the glass.

Gary took a sip, grimaced, tilted back his head and drank the rest in one swift gulp. He then put the glass unsteadily down onto the table.

"Good," said the Colonel, with an approving nod. "Now this won't take a second."

And it didn't. One sharp twist and 'Pop', the shoulder was back in place. We'd never seen anything like it.

"Now that's going to hurt like hell for a while," said the Colonel. "But at your age it should heal fast, and it shouldn't give you any problem when you get older."

"Assuming you live that long," he added, wryly.

On the way home Gary's only concern was that his parent's should not find out.

"I'm swearing you all to secrecy," he said. "My parents must never know."

We all swore a solemn oath – we would never tell!

Chapter 18

An Unfortunate Accident

School ought to come with a government health warning. It is amazing that they let kids loose in a Science lab, especially with a teacher as wet in every way as Mr. Howlet, or Halibut as we called him. Actually he wasn't a bad teacher, but unfortunately his face was long and narrow, and if he looked straight at you his head seemed small, but if he turned sideways it was big, I mean really big – weird. Of course in his class we couldn't stop looking at him, pushing in the sides of our mouths with our fingers doing fish impressions. He also had a distinctive voice that was easy to copy – he didn't really stand a chance. If he had stuck to his usual subject, Geography, he would have probably been alright; however, one day our Chemistry teacher was off sick and some bright spark decided to send Halibut along as substitute.

Halibut had the unfortunate privilege of being Danny's form tutor and, as Danny was in trouble again Halibut had made the bad mistake of bringing him along too.

Gary and I were both in the Chemistry group and naturally we had taken our usual seats at the back of the class, as far from the teacher's beady eyes as possible. Danny hurried to the back to join us, dumping his bag of books down and perching on a wooden stool.

"What you doing here?" I asked, as soon as Halibut turned his back to start writing the day's experiment on the blackboard.

"Old Halibut wants to keep an eye on me," he replied, looking eagerly around the lab. "I've not been in here before, what's all this stuff for?"

Gary was keen to show off. "These are sinks," he explained, lifting up the wooden lid of the one in front of him. "There are four on each desk." He pointed along the row to the others. "And these are water taps and these are gas taps."

"Cool," said Danny, happy to be entertained.

"All right class," said Halibut, calling us all to attention, well some of us. "Mandy and James would you give out the Bunsen burners, please."

"What are these for?" asked Danny.

"You stick the rubber on here," I explained, showing how to attach it to the gas tap. "Then you turn on the tap and light the end. It's for heating up chemicals and stuff."

"Cool."

"DON'T turn on your Bunsen burners until I've explained exactly what I want you to do," Halibut's voice whined nasally down from the podium, where he stood safely behind the toughened glass.

Soon Halibut was droning on about chemical formulas and it wasn't long before I could see Danny glazing over. As the rest of the class sat taking notes because we were sure to be asked questions later, his fingers started roaming over the desk, exploring the possibilities of the water tap, then the gas tap and finally - the Bunsen burner. Swiftly he attached it to the gas tap, stuck the top of the Bunsen burner down the hole in the wooden cover over the sink and turned on the gas. Of course nothing happened. However, Danny, never having been in the lab before was totally unaware that the sinks were all connected by the overflow pipes (he knew nothing about plumbing either!). He also had no idea that gas is heavier than air, and that ignorance was about to become obvious. As we sat there the gas was slowly making its way along the overflow pipes and into the other sinks.

"Mr. Howlet" called Wendy from the end of our run of desks, putting up her hand. "Could you help me, please Sir, I can't get my Bunsen burner to light."

"Yes, of course," he replied, tripping down from the safety of the podium, delighted to be helpful. He took his lighter out of his trouser pocket, positioned it over Wendy's Bunsen burner and clicked.

BANG!

The explosion rocked the school, as the gas ignited and every wooden lid from every sink in the class was ejected high into the air.

The next thing I knew I was down on the floor in a complete daze. Lifting my aching head I saw Danny, Gary, Wendy and Mr. Howlet all lying at drunken angles among the carnage of school books, sink tops and overturned stools.

Physic's Jones, from the next lab rushed in. "Is everyone OK," he yelled, turning off the gas. Of course, being wise in the ways of labs and boys he knew immediately what had happened, and had probably done the same himself. "Everyone OUT," he shouted, helping to lift up old Halibut who looked more like a fish than every sprawled out on the floor. "Get yourselves down to the Hall and wait for me."

We left him opening the windows and all staggered down the stairs and into the main Hall. Minutes later Jones came in accompanied by the school Nurse.

"Sit down," barked Jones, who looked thoroughly pissed off. You could tell he refereed rugby in his spare time, the telling off he gave us was probably heard by the whole school. He followed it up with an entire class detention for that afternoon, to be spent doing laps of the school athletics track until he saw fit to let us go home.

"Hopefully, that will get rid of your excess energy, and give you ample time to reflect on your numerous shortcomings." He marched out leaving us to the ministrations of the Nurse.

It was soon discovered that none of us had suffered any serious damage to our hearing or to ourselves, although we milked it for all we were worth. Mr Howlet, however, did not get off so lightly, he lost most of his hair from the sides of his head which made him look like he'd had a Mohican haircut. Combined with his flat head everyone who saw him burst out laughing, the poor man never lived it down. Kids are so cruel!

Chapter 19

Joe and the Devil Worshippers

Joe

My dog Joe was the worst dog in the world. Of course I loved him, but he had the most annoying habits and was completely untrainable in every way. He was black with some brown splodges and white bits, a very waggy tail and droopy ears, definitely a mongrel of the Heinz fifty-seven variety, mainly collie, with a bit of spaniel and a lot of other things thrown in.

There were two really annoying things about Joe. The first was his fear of loud noises, which would turn him into a shivering wreck. If a car back fired, or a door slammed, he would try to climb into the broom cupboard, pulling everything out, shivering and whimpering for at least an hour. November the fifth was a nightmare.

His second and probably worse problem, exacerbated by my tight fisted dad refusing to pay to have him 'done', was his propensity for finding bitches. If a female dog was on heat in the area he would get out and run off, lying lovelorn outside her gate for days. No matter what incentive was offered to move he would refuse to budge. Biscuits, crisps, his favourite cheese, slices of succulent beef, all were looked at with distain. If you picked him up and carried him he would struggle and whine piteously, release your hold for a moment and he was off again. When locked in the house you only had to open the door a crack and he would be out, running as fast as he could no matter what you called him. He would stay away until a very annoyed neighbour would phone us to go fetch him, or on occasions the police would bring him home. Little Joe look-a-likes abounded on the Estate, and the owner's of pedigree dogs further afield often found to their horror that our scruffy mongrel had been their precious bitches' most favoured admirer.

"Graham," shouted mum, as I was lying on a deckchair in the back garden, with my feet cooling in the pond. "Joe's loose again. He pulled his lead right out of my hand. I've been calling and calling him. Can you see if you can find him?"

"Oh, mum, it's too hot."

"NOW!"

There are times when it's wise not to argue. I went looking.

No-one in our street had seen him, but someone at the flats had noticed a dog heading towards the heath trailing a lead. When I reached Burgh Heath a chap at the bus stop said he'd seen Joe run over the Brighton road and up the footpath to Alcock's Lane in Kingswood.

"Stupid dog could have got himself killed," I muttered to myself, as I waited for the traffic to clear on the very busy main road.

I hurried up Alcock Lane, called out to Joe. Eventually, about half way up, I heard whining coming from a thick clump of blackthorn.

I'm not going to get through that, I thought, looking at the dense prickles, I'll try to get around. I walked further up the lane trying to find a way in.

It's useless I decided after a few minutes, there's no way through these bushes. I walked back down the lane trying to decide what to do. Eventually I spotted a large chestnut tree towering above the blackthorn, the lowest branch was difficult to reach, but I scrambled up the link wire fencing and managed to heave myself up. It looked like there was a clearing in the centre of the bushes and I could just see Joe's tail, he was whining pitifully, obviously unable to move. I noticed that a path from the clearing led to the garden of a nearby house, so down I clambered, back into the alley.

I'll have to go and get him out, I decided, cursing the stupid mutt under my breath.

Eventually I reached the front of the house. It was quite posh looking, detached, and in a large private plot. I knocked at the front door. No answer. I knocked again. Still nothing. Joe's whining was getting louder and more frantic, even in the shade the temperature was in the eighty's, he'd bake to death if I didn't get him out. I could hear another dog barking from inside the house. Quickly I tried the side gate, it was locked, but the fencing beside it was loose and I managed to squeeze through. I ran along the side of the house, followed the path across the garden and into the clearing. Joe was in a sorry state; his lead was firmly attached to a branch in the blackthorn and his neck was sore where he had been pulling to free himself. As soon as I got him loose he began jumping up at me and licking my face.

I gave him a hug, holding firmly onto the lead.

"Keep still you stupid dog," I said, as I took a quick look around the clearing. It was then I noticed the strange symbols painted on the ground and a raised area to one side. I recognised it immediately – it was an altar. I'd stumbled upon the meeting place of a witches' coven. This must be where they carried out black magic. A shiver ran down my spine. I grabbed Joe and ran for the gate.

"Let's get out of here quick," I muttered to myself.

After taking Joe home and leaving him to the tender ministrations of my mum, I got out my bike and pelted around to Danny's house. By luck Gary had just arrived. Quickly I told them what I'd found.

"Let's get round there and have a look," said Danny immediately.

We rode back to Alcock's Lane as fast as we could. A large man was guarding the gate to the house now, so we went around the back and climbed up the tree again.

"Look," I whispered, pointing into the clearing below. "The marks of the devil!"

The others nodded seriously.

"Let's come back tonight when it's dark," suggested Gary quietly. "They might be sacrificing a virgin."

"Or dancing naked to the full moon," put in Danny, his eyes brightening in anticipation.

"If they resurrect the Devil we need to be ready with crosses to send him back to hell," I said.

The others nodded vigorously. We had all illicitly crept in through the emergency door at the local flea pit to see the Hammer House films. We knew exactly what to do to keep ourselves safe from witches, vampires and things that go bump in the night. We rode home to sort out our bibles and crosses, last used when we had all attended Sunday school.

"Try to remember the Lord's Prayer," said Danny, as we stopped outside his house. "If you say it they can't get you."

Unfortunately, although the Lord's Prayer was said every day in school assembly, we had made up so many funny renditions of it none of us remembered the real words that could save you from Hell. For one cold moment we all wished we had paid attention. Then Gary saved us.

"It's in the bible," he remembered, "at the front." So all those Sunday mornings in Church had not been wasted after all!

"A distraction would be useful," said Danny.

"I've got some jumping-jacks left over from last year's fireworks," offered Gary. "I could bring them."

That was sorted then. We agreed to meet later at Danny's, whose house was nearest to the heath.

At ten o'clock we were ready. In spite of the hot weather we were all wearing our parker coats with the hoods up and scarves over our faces, around our necks were our crosses and I had found a St. Christopher just to make doubly sure. In our pockets were our bibles. As we climbed up the chestnut tree we were ready to do battle with the Devil and save the Estate from the anti-Christ. We lay in wait for the Satanists to start their evil ceremony.

Weird music came from the house and we could hear cars arriving. As the evening wore on, darkness fell. I began to feel scared, very scared, and could see that Danny and Gary felt the same. We all feared for our mortal souls, being virgins we were all in equal danger of being drawn into Hell if we got caught. However, being good Christians (well, we'd been on the Sunday school trips to the seaside and Christmas parties in the Church Hall), it was our duty to protect our families and expose these evil doers for what they were.

At around midnight, just as we were considering the entire escapade a damp squib, the clouds cleared and a large full moon shone down. From our perch in the tree we had an excellent view of what was going on. The French windows at the rear of the house opened and people in hooded cloaks appeared. They were carrying candles that flickered and cast ghastly shadows on their faces. We watched in mounting horror as they walked down towards us in two lines. As they came into the clearing they formed a circle around the pentacle and the chanting ceased. A deathly silence descended. Gary, Danny and I collectively held our breath and clung tightly to the tree.

We watched, open mouthed, as a couple, both dressed completely in white, came out of the house. Hand in hand they walked slowly down the path and into the centre of the circle.

Then the chanting began.

We nearly fell out of the tree with fright.

Next they began ringing hand bells. This was puzzling. It was not quite what we had expected!

Finally another hooded figure came out of the house, bringing a small white poodle on a lead.

I nudged Gary. "That must be the sacrifice," I whispered.

We were almost wetting ourselves waiting for someone to produce a knife. Suddenly out of nowhere, my dog Joe appeared. He raced into the centre of the circle, totally ignoring all the hooded figures, made straight for the pretty white poodle and tried to mount her.

"You're not sacrificing my dog," I shouted, leaping to the ground.

Gary, thinking this was the sign, gave Danny a nudge. Within seconds they had lit their fire crackers and chucked them down into the circle. The Devil worshipers began to shout and jump around, followed by the crackers. Joe stopped mounting the poodle – the noise of fireworks was probably the only thing that would stop him - and he ran around in furious circles trying to find somewhere to hide from the noise. Grabbing the dog I made a run for the gate, but a large man stopped me.

"Don't you think you had better apologise," he shouted.

I stood there, clutching Joe and looking haunted. I'd been caught. I was going to be killed.

"Don't you realise you've ruined their wedding!"

Wedding, I though, confused. What wedding?

Feeling very sorry for myself I called Gary and Danny down from the tree. They eventually appeared, coming down the garden path, their crosses out in front of them like Vampire hunters.

It seemed the couple were holding a pagan wedding ceremony and we had ruined it. However, when we told them we were expecting the Devil to appear and showed them our bibles, they thought it was hilarious. Everyone started laughing. They assured us that Paganism was nothing to do with Satanism. Of course we didn't believe them, but then they showed us the crosses they were all wearing, so we decided they must be OK.

"Come and join us," said the bride with a smile. She looked really beautiful now we could see her clearly, her hair decorated with fresh wild flowers and her long white dress embroidered around the hem and sleeves.

Joe was shut firmly in someone's car, safely away from the poodle. Then we were each given a candle and stood in the circle. We joined in the singing, and watched as the couple said their vows and had their hands tied together with a white rope. Then we were given drinks of punch and told to help ourselves to food. The spread was amazing and we needed no encouragement to tuck in. Eventually we were given a lift home in a Triumph Stag, which made the night for us and Joe stuck his head out of the window and wagged his tail.

We all agreed later that if we ever got married we would definitely have a pagan ceremony out of doors, with lots and lots of food – but no dogs!

Chapter 20

The Bomb!

"Another scorcher," said weather man Michael Fish. "It will be dry, hot and sunny – again." July 1976 was shaping up to be the hottest on record and we were intent on making the most of it.

We set off early on our chopper bikes up the hill from Shelver's Way shops and cut through the footpath to Walton-on-the-Hill, along Chequer's Lane to the Boxhill road. We were following Gary, who had found a new track behind the caravan park down at the chalk pits at Brockham Quarry – a trip of over five miles, most of it uphill, on the hottest day of the year so far. It had been 85°F (30°C) when we left home and getting hotter all the time. We started peddling enthusiastically, but as the hills got steeper our enthusiasm waned. Luckily, as the water shortage had begun to bite the local Authorities had put in stand pipes and we stopped frequently to take a drink and rest for a moment.

Eventually we reached our destination. It was just as Gary had described it. The track ran around a large open cast chalk quarry, with a two hundred foot drop to the floor below.

"This looks great," I said, as we stood on the edge of the quarry and surveyed the area.

"You can ride around the top," explained Gary. "Or you can follow that track down to the bottom." He pointed to the narrow path that hugged the sides of the quarry, zigzagging down to lower levels, eventually leading to the quarry floor.

A sedate ride around the top - or a death defying plunge to the bottom? No contest really!

The track was much too narrow for us to ride three abreast, so Gary went first, as he had found the quarry, then Danny, with me bringing up the rear, but determined to overtake if the opportunity arose. We started off slowly, getting the feel of the track, gradually building up speed, our legs working like pistons. Going faster, and faster. The soft quarry edge a blur. The chalk dropping away to one side, sheer to the bottom. I could feel the adrenaline pumping through my veins. Then we realised that the chalk had stopped our brakes from working and the only way to slow down was to put our feet out. It was like being on a roller coaster, with death hovering beside us, willing us to loose concentration and plunge over the edge.

"Ye...sss!" we screamed as we came down the last decline and skidded sideways. Bikes tilting. Scraping. Rolling. Until we stopped in a heap. Laughing.

"That was brilliant," I spluttered, trying to get my breath back.

We sat in the dust, rubble and scrubby grass looking around us. There was a disused railway line with a narrow gauge track, a line of rusting trucks and a small diesel train that must have been used to transport the chalk. Everything was covered in white dust. Over to one side was a pile of rusting, smashed up old cars.

"I wonder what they're doing here," I muttered, picking up a bit of twisted metal and chucking it towards the nearest car. It bounced off the battered side door and slithered down into the grass.

"I know," replied Danny. "I remember my dad talking about it. They made a film here once, years ago, and the cars were pushed over the edge."

Looking up at the sheer chalk face we could all imagine the cars falling.

"It must have looked great as they crashed to the ground," said Gary, and we nodded in agreement, almost hearing the noise of smashing metal and glass, and the tremors of the earth as they hit the ground.

We'd brought a picnic with us and sat in the shade by the rusty trucks eating our curling sandwiches and drinking warm cans of 7Up. Jackdaws squawked and squabbled on the chalk ledges, and small blue butterflies flittered over the yellow flowers of the 'ladies-slipper' that had pushed up between the railway tracks. Eventually we decided to make our way home and began pushing our bikes back up the track. It was a long, steep climb and very hard work. Near the top we stopped for a breather on a wider section and sat on a rock. The sun was reflecting off the white chalk. I had never felt so hot. I pulled off my t-shirt and put it in my bag. Gary did the same.

"What are you doing?" I asked Danny, as he got up and started mooching about.

"Just looking around," he replied.

"He's mad," decided Gary. "It's too hot."

We watched as Danny began poking about some bushes at the side of the track. Suddenly he gave a shout.

"It's a bomb!"

"Great," muttered Gary, wiping the back of a dusty hand over his brow. "He thinks he's found a bomb. Can you be bothered to look?"

"No," I said, feeling the sweat trickling down between my shoulder blades. "It's too hot."

"Come over here," demanded Danny excitedly. "It's a *real* bomb!"

Gary and I looked at each other.

"I suppose we'd better have a look," I said eventually, "Just to shut him up."

"If it's a trick I'll kill him," muttered Gary, heaving himself to his feet.

"And I'll help you," I said.

We strolled slowly over to the bushes. Then we stopped, and stared. It was a bomb! He'd found a bloody bomb!

"What are we going to do with it?" asked Danny, looking pleased with himself.

"Let's chuck rocks at it," suggested Gary.

"Good idea," I agreed. "Let's see if we can make it go off."

We all grinned. Then we moved our bikes. Then we gathered up as many stones and rocks as we could. Once we had a decent pile of ammunition we moved as far back as we could and began taking it in turns to lob stones at the bomb. Again and again we took aim, and again and again we hit it. Soon the bomb was surrounded by debris as our missiles hit it and bounced off. But it didn't explode.

"It's a dud," said Danny in disgust.

"Let's turn it around so the point's sticking up," suggested Gary. "A direct hit on the tip should do the trick."

But who had the balls to turn it?

"Not me," said Danny. "I found it."

"Nor me," said Gary. "It was my idea to turn it."

That left muggings. "OK," I said. "But wait until I get out of the way before throwing any more stones." I knew exactly what the other two were like!

Before I could lose my nerve I jumped carefully down into the hole beside bomb. Hands trembling I lifted up the bomb and turned it upright. Then I got out fast and raced back to the others. Soon we were lobbing stones once again. A couple of direct hits on the tip confirmed what we had expected, the bomb was a dud.

"Let's try throwing it over the edge onto those cars," suggested Danny.

So we picked the bomb up, aimed it at the rusting cars below, and let go. It whistled on the way down and made a loud bang as it hit the bottom – but still it didn't explode.

"I'm going back down for it," said Danny.

"What for?"

"It's mine. I found it. I'm going to take it home."

"What do you want it for?"

"I'm gonna paint it and keep it in my bedroom. I'll use it to prop the door open."

"If your mum let's you," I said, knowing how house proud his mum was, making me take my shoes off every time I went around there.

"You can carry it," added Gary. "We're not helping you."

"Race you," shouted Danny, jumping on his bike.

That was a dirty trick. We all loved to race, but he had a head start so we had to take extra risks on the way back down to catch him. At the bottom we soon found the bomb and tied it to the saddle of Danny's bike. It just fitted and made the bike top heavy and hard to control.

"You'll never get that up the hill," Gary taunted. Which made Danny more determined that ever to lug it up in the sweltering heat. We had seen this madness in Danny before, when he set his mind to something his stubborn streak came out. He shocked us by pushing it all the way to the top, without complaining once. We could hardly believe it, he always moaned.

Riding back down Boxhill Road Danny's bike was so unstable it waggled all over the road and he kept falling off. We were getting heartily fed up with stopping to pick him up.

"Look," said Gary, pointing at a house at the side of the road. Above the door was a blue sign 'Police Station'. "Let's take it in," he said. "We might get a reward for it."

That seemed an excellent idea. Danny had cut his knee badly and getting rid of the bomb suddenly seemed a reasonable thing to do – especially if there might be some money in it.

We unstrapped the bomb, carried it into the police station, heaved it onto the desk and rang the bell.

A police constable appeared, looking hot and bored. Then he spotted our offering.

"What the bloody hell's that?" he spluttered, looking horrified.

"It's a bomb," we announced, looking pleased with ourselves.

"You f'ing idiots," he shouted. "Get out of here."

"It's OK," we said, trying to calm him down. "It's a dud." We began to explain what we'd done and watched as the colour drained from his face.

"You idiots, you idiots," he kept saying. "It could go off at any moment. I'll have to get the bomb squad. They'll have to disarm it. Go and wait by the road, I'll deal with you later. I'll have to evacuate the building. I'll have to call the army."

We decided we'd better leave. It didn't look as though we were going to get a reward.

We sat on our bikes by the road until the army trucks arrived and men in thick bomb disposal suits carried the bomb out to a field opposite the station. We watched as they covered it with a box and blew it up.

BANG!! The ground shook and the box flew up into the air.

"That was a good one," exclaimed the army disposal man. "Probably a mortar shell from the war, one of ours left over from practice. Did a lot of it around here," he added. "Picked most of them up, but must have missed that one.

"We threw rocks at it," said Gary.

"That was stupid. Go and look at the hole it's made. If it had gone off the shrapnel would have cut through you and ripped your arms and legs off."

We stood around the enormous hole and suddenly the day wasn't hot anymore, an icy chill had sprung up and was running right down our backs!

Feeling shocked and thoroughly chastened we apologised and promised never, ever to touch a bomb again.

The policeman's wife made us all cups of tea and handed out Bourbon biscuits. The policeman gave us each a leaflet about what to do if you find a bomb and told us he would be coming to our school to give a talk about it.

"You seem like good lads," he said kindly. "We'll take no further action. Now get on your way and don't go playing with bombs again."

On the way home we laughed about it, but in bed that night, with the temperature in the eighties, I could still feel that icy chill!

Chapter 21

Friends Old and New

Sitting in class, looking out of the window as usual, I was just wishing we had brought 'the bomb' into school instead of taking it to the police, when my delightful reverie was interrupted by a voice next to me.

"Hello, Graham. I've not seen you in a while."

Turning around the face was recognisable, but not the body! It was little Alfie, an old friend from infant's school, however he was not so little now, more like BIG Alfie. I remembered that when he was born his feet had pointed the wrong way, so he'd needed lots of operations to move them around. We had played together when he lived in the flat above his dad's butcher's shop across the road from where I lived, but when his parents had split up he had moved to Epsom with his mum to be near the hospital and I hadn't seen him for ages.

"Hello, mate," I said, shaking his hand. "How are your legs now?"

"Fine," he replied, sticking out a massive foot for inspection.

"Blimey! You've grown," I exclaimed, sounding like my granny.

He began to laugh. "Yeah, they gave me injections to build me up when I got worn out by all the operations. They make me strong but give me bad breath, so I chew gum all the time." He blew a bubble to punctuate the point.

"Are you back with your dad?" I asked.

"Only school days," Alfie explained. "At weekends I go home to Epsom with mum, there's a gym down there I go to. Dad has some weights still in the garage if you want to come over after school?"

"Sure," I replied. "Can Danny and Gary come too?"

"You still hang out with those two?"

"Of course, we're still best friends and now you're here the old team are back together again."

That afternoon we all met up at the garage behind the butcher's shop. His dad's van had been parked on the road outside and the entire garage had been converted into a gym, with a punch bag swinging in one corner and a bench for doing lifts. We were all expecting to do some weight training, but spent an exhausting couple of hours humping discs on and off a bar so Alfie could lift and squat with them.

It wasn't all bad though, his dad invited us to stay for tea and fried each of us a steak so large that it flopped over the edge of the plate. It took me ages to eat mine, Danny couldn't finish his and even Gary was full, but Alfie finished his in a few minutes and was ready for seconds. We'd never seen a meal disappear so fast.

"Let's go for a run," suggested Alfie, after we'd helped with the washing up.

That made us laugh because the last time we had all played together Alfie could not even walk unaided, all the time we had know him he had had crutches to get around on as his legs were always in plaster.

"What about a bike ride?" I suggested.

"I can't ride a bike," said Alfie. "Because of my legs I never learnt. I've only just started running."

It began to dawn on us how restricted Alfie's life had been.

"You three ride," he suggested easily. "I'll run with you."

So that was agreed. We decided to go to Epsom to see Alfie's mum. We went down to get our bikes while Alfie changed into his running shoes. We were just shutting the door to the garage when along came the Thomas brothers, Billy and Warren, sauntering around the back of the shops. Trouble - big trouble! Last seen wrecking the Honda 90 we'd borrowed.

Warren grabbed Danny by the arm and yanked him off his bike. "Where's the money you owe us," he snarled.

"I don't owe you any money," protested Danny.

"Oooh, 'e don't owe us any money," said Billy, grabbing Danny's other arm.

"Yes you eff'in well do," growled Warren. He reached down beneath the leg of his jeans and produced an evil looking knife. It glinted in the evening sunlight as he brought it up towards Danny's face. "Turn out your pockets."

This was looking nasty. None of us knew what to do. We were happy to wade in with our fists to help a mate, but that knife could be really dodgy.

Neither of the brothers saw Alfie come around the corner. He took in what was happening with a glance. His fist came out of nowhere and landed on Warren's chin. The knife clattered uselessly to the ground as the powerful right hook lifted Warren clean off his feet. He flew through the air and landed on the concrete drive – out cold. One look at his brother lying prostrate on the floor and Billy took to his heels.

"I hate those Thomas brothers," said Alfie. "They used to pick on me when I was little. Let's get 'im." He began to run, following Billy over the grass next to the shops.

Danny jumped on his bike. "Let's cut him off," he shouted. "Go round by the flats."

We caught up with Alfie just as he got to Billy Thomas, lifting him up with one hand against the end wall of the flats.

"Look he's wet himself," laughed Gary.

"Let him go Alfie," said Danny with a snigger. "He needs to have his nappy changed.

Alfie released his hand and Billy dropped to the floor in a puddle of wee.

"Tell your brother if either of you touch my mates again I'll rip your heads off," growled Alfie.

Billy nodded his head vigorously, tears running down his cheeks and mingling with the snot from his nose.

Looking at Billy blubbing like a baby I felt that justice had been served. "Let's go," I said.

As we got on our bikes again Alfie began to run. "Keep up," he shouted.

He really meant it too, going up hill we couldn't keep up with him. Going down the hill into Epsom he jumped on the back of Danny's chopper bike. The long seat was great for carrying two and they flew down the road. Soon we reached Alfie's mum's house, a large bungalow with a conservatory on the side containing every type of exercise equipment you could think of. It seemed his mum was a physiotherapist and she soon had us trying out all the different gear. After an hour's strenuous workout we swam in the heated swimming pool in the back garden and then lounged on the patio drinking fruit juice.

"This is great," I said, as I dived back into the pool.

"I can see why you enjoy staying here," said Gary, dabbling his feet in the water.

Floating on my back I could see the sky, clear blue above me. The garden was surrounded by bushes and flower borders, and in one corner was a large tree overhanging the fence to the neighbouring property.

"Have you climbed it yet?" I asked Alfie, waving a hand towards the tree.

"No, never," he replied.

We all looked at his as though he was mad.

"It's boys law," explained Danny. "If you have a tree in your garden you have to climb it."

"Let's do it now," said Gary.

"We can spy on your neighbours," added Danny with a grin.

"There are some girls that live behind us," said Alfie.

"Well, what are we waiting for?" I said.

We jumped out of the water, dried ourselves off, got dressed and headed for the tree. Soon we were hanging on the uppermost branches and looking out over Epsom. The view was great and you could see for miles. Alfie gave us the low-down on who lived in each of the houses around his. They sounded interesting people – especially the girls next-door!

"Look," said Gary. "You can see their underwear on the washing line."

Alfie moved further out along the branch to get a better view. CRACK! The branch snapped and Alfie disappeared.

"Wow! He must be heavy," exclaimed Danny. "Look he's snapped that thick branch."

There was a loud thump, followed by a groan and Alfie was lying spread-eagled on the grass.

We scrambled down the tree as fast as we could. Alfie's leg was sticking out at a strange angle. This was bad.

"Get his mum," I said. "It looks like that leg's broken."

"Not again," muttered Alfie.

The ambulance arrived and Alfie was carted off on a stretcher. We wished him well and promised to visit, well, it was all we could do, standing there feeling useless. His mum said the bones in his legs were still very weak from all the operations and he had been told not to climb trees. That made us feel bad, very bad. If we hadn't egged him on he wouldn't have been up there. His mum was really nice about it, which made us feel even worse.

"It's not your fault," she said. "You didn't know. Just try to visit him in hospital to cheer him up, because he gets very bored on his own."

We could do that, of course we could, he was a mate after all.

We got on our bikes and rode home. On the way back we all agreed it was not far to fall and he must have landed badly, but it was a real shame as we had all had so much fun together. We decided we must stay in touch with him, however long it took for his leg to mend.

What with Nick's mother still harping on about the damage to the house following the party, and now our friend Alfie out of action (just maybe because of us), we were somewhat cagy about inviting anyone else to join in our escapades. However, our good intentions didn't last long. Coming out of school a few days later we spotted a lad called Ian his face dripping with blood from a cut above his eyebrow.

"What's up with Ian?" I asked Danny, knowing they were in the same class.

"He messed up his dovetail joints in woodwork," Danny explained. "That old git Chambers gave him a clout around the head for not paying attention and that big ring he wears, you know, the one shaped like a skull." We nodded. "Well it caught Ian on the eye."

"Why didn't he send him to the nurse?" enquired Gary. "That cut looks bad."

"Oh, the bell went, so he just sent him home," Danny replied as we strolled towards the gates. "None of us could believe it," he added. "Ian's so quiet, he usually keeps his head down and manages to avoid trouble. That Chambers is a right bully."

We nodded in agreement. We'd all had Chambers for woodwork and had all been on the receiving end of his punishments at one time or another. He wasn't a teacher to hand out detentions; he was a great believer in a swift clip around the ear. You really knew when he hit you - your head seemed to buzz for ages.

As we watched Ian going through the school gates ahead of us a large man got out of a car and went up to him. The next thing we know the man goes to the boot of the car, lifts up the cover, extracts the jack handle and marches determinedly towards the school, with a face like thunder. Ian scuttled along behind him.

"Dad, dad," he yelled. "Don't lose your temper."

"Lose my temper, I'll eff'in kill him!"

"We've got to see this," I muttered to the others gleefully. "Come on."

We followed Ian and his dad back into school and along the corridor to the woodwork room. Mr Carley gave the door such a shove it almost came off its hinges. Chambers was sitting on his desk having a crafty smoke. He shot to his feet as the door slammed against the wall with a crack that seemed to vibrate through the entire school.

"Who are you? What do you want?" he stuttered. He didn't get a chance to say anything else. Ian's dad lifted the jack handle and brought it down hard. Chamber's lifted up his arm to defend himself. The jack landed with a sickening 'thud' and he sank to the ground gripping his elbow and screaming in agony. The colour drained from his face as he curled into a ball waiting for the next blow.

We huddled in the doorway and looked on goggle eyed.

"Let that be a lesson for you," shouted Mr Carley, towering above him with the jack still raised. "Keep your hands off my son or the next time I'll make you *really* sorry."

Leaving Chambers a shivering wreck on the floor, he turned and strode towards the door. We scuttled out of his way. He was certainly not someone to tangle with, especially with a jack in his hand. We were well impressed.

"Wow," said Danny, as we followed Ian and his dad along the corridor. "What do you think of that?"

"I think that boy needs a friend," stated Gary.

"Make that three," I said.

The following day we made a point of joining Ian's table at lunch break. Half an hour later we couldn't understand why we hadn't made friends with him before, he was a great lad. We soon found we all shared the same interests - motorbikes, cars, and girls with big tits. No! Forget the big tits, just *any* girl that was dim enough to show an interest in us, but most especially those that showed no interest in us whatsoever. We were obviously going to get along famously.

After school we rode back with Ian to his house in Chipstead. Ian's parents had split up some time before and he lived with just his father and brother. The house was a real eye-opener, definitely lived in only by men – there was a motorbike in every room! We thought this was paradise, especially Danny whose mum wouldn't even let him wear shoes in the house, let alone bring in a bit of greasy old bike.

"Come and see what I've got out in the shed," said Ian, leading us through the kitchen and out into the back garden.

"Wow!" we all exclaimed together. He had a bike, a *real* motorbike, of his own. It was a Bultaco 125 scramble bike. We gazed at it in envy.

"I ride it in school boy races as the weekend," he explained.

We helped him drag it out of the shed, and then watched as he started it up and rode it across the road into a field. He revved it up and wheelied it around, the front wheel high off the ground, waving with one hand as he steered with the other.

We knew he was showing off, but we didn't blame him, any one of us would have done the same if we could. We were really impressed, he rode so well and the bike was beautiful, well made and fast, it looked a handful, but Ian rode it as if it was just a bicycle. We gazed on amazed.

Soon his friend arrived on a Triumph Tiger Cub, another scramble bike - the afternoon was getting better and better.

Ian introduced him. “This is Gary Sandercock,” he said, “His family own the field.”

It turned out that Gary’s family owned not only the field, but all the land around. It was thanks to him that Ian had this brilliant place to practice.

“Have you got bikes?” he asked.

“Only our chopper’s,” I replied.

“You can use them down our wood if you like.”

“You’ve got a wood as well?” exclaimed Danny. This was great.

Gary nodded. It seemed his family not only owned fields, but also a wood as well, some people have all the luck. Grub Wood was two fields down and the two lads took us over and showed us the track we could use. It looked brilliant with the evening sunlight slanting through the trees and the track twisting and turning between the oak, ash and birch. We had a couple of practice runs, tearing around the narrow track, doing jumps and practicing *our* wheelies, before going back to the field to watch Gary and Ian. The lads had set up a jump next to a large oak tree and were taking turns riding over it, doing jumps that got higher and longer every time. Eventually Ian’s friend Gary landed badly, hitting his nuts on the tank. Ouch! We all winced at that, and it slowed him down a bit! However, Ian was getting more enthusiastic with new friends to impress and took a long run up, hitting the jump flat out. Unfortunately he hadn’t noticed the branch of the tree above him. Thump! He had jumped so high he’d hit his head.

“Just as well you had your helmet on,” I said, as we picked him up off the ground.

“Look at that,” said Danny.

The large dent to the top of the helmet was really impressive. Ian thought this hilarious and picked up his bike to have another go, but then realised he was running out of fuel so we walked back to his house with him.

"We'll see you at school tomorrow," promised Danny, as we thanked them for giving us such a good time.

On the way home we chatted about Ian.

"He's a bit wild," said Gary.

"That's rich coming from you," I retorted.

"No, he's right," put in Danny. "It's as though he's totally without fear, even more than us."

I didn't like to admit that there was anyone in the world more fearless than me, but I had to agree they were probably right.

"That Bultaco's something special," I said.

"It was bought for his older brother," explained Danny. "But there was a two year waiting list for it and when it finally arrived his brother was too old to ride it, so Ian inherited it."

"Lucky thing," said Gary.

We all agreed Ian was lucky to have such a great bike and somewhere so close to practice on it. He would surely be world champion one day.

"We're not doing too badly for new friends," said Danny.

"Bit of luck finding two with motorbikes," added Gary. "We're going to have some fun in Grub Wood."

"Good job Ian was wearing that helmet," I put in. "Or we'd have been up the hospital again. No wonder the casualty nurses all know our first names."

"I thought that was because of our stunning good looks and amazing personalities," said Danny, and we all started to laugh.

Chapter 22

The Day the Road Melted

Burgh Heath pond

As the days got longer the sun kept on shining. It had been getting hotter every day, no-one could sleep and everyone had their windows and doors open all the time trying to get some air into their houses. Getting up early in the morning for my paper round I found the seat of my chopper bike was already so hot I had to put a damp cloth on the saddle before I could ride it. Eventually we woke to find all the cars parked on the road had sunk almost to their axles in melted tarmac and were well and truly stuck.

"How am I going to get to work?" moaned dad, raking around furiously in the shed. "You've been in here again, haven't you? I've told you about touching my stuff."

“I was only looking for a spanner to mend my bike,” I protested. I couldn’t honestly see how anyone would notice anyway; dad’s shed was always stuffed to the gunnels with things that would ‘come in useful one day’.

“Well, get yourself over here and give me a hand with these planks. I’m going to be bloody late as it is and I’ve got an appointment over at Guildford at ten.”

Dad was Maintenance Manager South East for Unigate the big dairy with depots all over the country. His job covered an area from Essex and Kent, right over to Hampshire and even included the Isle of Wight. Travelling about in this heat was not making him happy.

We finally got out the scaffolding boards, last used when he decorated the hall and stairs (or more precisely mum did the paperhanging, dad just being on hand to offer criticism). We carried the boards out to the car, feeling the soles of our shoes sticking to the tar as we crossed the road. With the boards placed firmly against the front wheels of our Morris Marina dad got in and started her up. Into first gear, he let off the hand brake and gave it a go. Nothing. He tried again. The engine revved furiously. Nothing. He was collecting a crowd by now and the air was beginning to turn blue, but every swear word he could think of was not going to move that car.

“Language, Johnny,” mum put in helpfully. “There are kids present.”

I thought dad was going to explode.

Salvation came in the shape of Pete, a neighbour who lived across the street. As luck would have it he had driven his car off the road and onto his front lawn to do some minor repairs. His must have been the only car in the entire area that wasn’t stuck.

“Has anyone got some decent rope,” Pete asked. “If I drive along the footpath I might be able to tow you out.”

A rope was found and Pete spent the next hour towing everyone's cars out of the melted tarmac. Luckily the ground to the side of the path had baked solid so there was plenty of room for the car to drive along. He made a pretty penny too, as everyone was so delighted to be on the move they all chipped in with a handsome gratuity box as a thank you.

Unfortunately, the cars all left large dents in the road. We kids found that fascinating. If you stood on a cracked section you could feel it move about like pack ice moving on water, except it stank of road works and if you stayed in one place for too long you could feel the soles of your feet beginning to burn, even through your shoes.

Of course we had to have a go at riding our bikes on it. Our Raleigh Choppers had the advantage of wide tyres and if you lent back to keep the weight of the small front wheel it was possible to ride on the melted roads. It was hard work though, so we kept to the paths or rode on the grass which had gone brown and was dying off after weeks of no rain. The cracked earth turned to dust as you rode over it and flew up behind you, looking like smoke coming off the wheels.

At school no-one wanted to work it was just too hot. Windows stood open and at break times and lunch times we were allowed to sit on the grass, or what was left of it, the prefects and upper sixth bagging the best spots under the trees.

"Look," yelled Danny, pointing at the boundary fence.

"What?" I asked, bored.

"Look!"

Lazily I stopped harassing an ants' nest, propped myself up on one elbow and looked. It was a fire. The heath was on fire and it was coming towards the school.

We got up and started running towards the fence to watch it. Suddenly a bush on the boundary caught alight, sparks filled the air, smoke billowing and tiny flames running along the dry grass at the bottom of the fence.

"Get back, you idiots!" yelled a prefect.

We didn't need telling, we weren't *that* stupid, we were moving back fast.

In the distance we could hear the clanging bell of a fire engine. As we watched from the safety of the school playground a Green Goddess[26] arrived. They'd sent in the army.

We were swiftly ushered back into our classrooms and the windows were closed fast against the smoke and flying embers. We boiled. Friday afternoons were always dire, but this was definitely the worst. As school ended we rushed down to the heath to see what was going on, only to find a Green Goddess blocking the pathway.

"Why can't we get through?" Gary asked the very tired looking soldier on duty.

"It's too dangerous lad," he replied, rubbing his red ringed eyes. "The peat is burning underground and there's no water left to put it out."

"What about the pond?" I asked.

"Dried up," he said. "Completely dried up."

We pushed our bikes back to Danny's house which was of course nearest to the heath, and his mum made us all a cold drink.

"I can't believe the pond's dried up," said Danny, as we sat on his front lawn.

"Neither can I." agreed Gary. "Let's go around by the road, see if we can get to the pond and have a look."

"Good idea," I said. "Then we could go around to Debbie's, she might let us use her pool."

---

26 Green Goddess – the colloquial name for the green-painted Bedford RLHZ Self Propelled Pump, a fire engine originally used by the Auxiliary Fire Service (AFS) until they were disbanded in 1968, and then occasionally used by the British Army to provide additional fire cover in times of crisis.

The others looked at me knowingly and laughed.

We were exhausted by the time we reached Burgh Heath. The area looked like a battlefield with groups of firemen, helped by soldiers armed with beaters, some regulars, some Territorials, all working together to try and keep things under control. It looked like they were fighting a loosing battle.[27] They were far too busy to take much notice of us as we dodged around by the 'new' houses that had been built on the old school site. We left our bikes by a wall and hurried over to the pond. It was a very sorry sight, the island in the centre poking out of dry, cracked mud and the willows drooping wearily in the heat.

"What are *they* doing?" asked Gary pointing.

A group of people, some standing and some kneeling, were gathered in the empty pond. One man had a camera, another couple were taking measurements, a few men were scanning the ground with metal detectors and an elderly woman with a small trowel in her hand was digging around the base of the island.

We wandered over to have a look. Danny, always friendly, asked the woman what she was up to.

"We're from the local historical society," she explained. "This is the first time since 1911 that this pond has dried out, so it's giving us a chance to find out more about it." She put her hand in her pocket and pulled out a collection of small bags. "Look," she said, opening them up. Inside were fragments of pottery, rusty nails and even a few coins. "That one's a silver sixpence, probably been here since before the First World War."

One of the metal detectors began to beep loudly and we rushed over to see what had been found. Could it be treasure!

---

[27] It is estimated that during the summer of 1976 the Surrey fire brigade answered 11,000 fire related calls in 5 months.

"It's something big," said the man, waving his detector carefully over the ground. He knelt down and began probing with a screwdriver. "It's quite a way down," he added, sounding disappointed.

Another chap came over. "Here, let me have a go," he said. His metal detector was larger, it began beeping immediately and he started to twist a dial. "It's iron," he announced. "Definitely iron. Probably a bit of an old bed."[28]

We walked away in disgust. As we went back for our bikes I looked at the big old oak trees and remembered my grandfather telling me he had cycled down from London when he was my age and picnicked beneath those trees. They would have been old then, and would have seen this all before, but for us this drought was a once in a lifetime experience that had to be remembered for as long as possible.

We got on our bikes and rode around to Debbie's house.

"I'm giving Rachel one of those new afro perms," she said when she answered the door.

"Don't you let them in Debs," Rachel's horrified voice called from the kitchen. "I'm not having those boys seeing me in my curlers."

It wasn't our day. We could almost hear that beautiful, cool swimming pool mocking us as we rode away and we could certainly hear Debbie (as no doubt she intended), moaning to Rachel about boys in general and a certain trio in particular. We'd heard that all before.

"Look," said Gary as we cycled past the back of the shops. "Someone's dumped an old sofa."

Tipping was a blight in our beautiful part of the country, our parents were always moaning about it,

---

28 Four bombs were dropped on Burgh Heath during WW2, none of them exploded and only three of them were ever recovered. There is a theory, so far unproven, that the fourth bomb landed in the pond. Perhaps this was another lucky escape for our trio!

people just dumped rubbish and left it for the Council to remove or it got set alight on bonfire night. However, to us it held untold possibilities and we were always on the lookout for stuff that we could use. We left our bikes and went to investigate.

The antique shop on the Parade had closed down and there were a lot of bits and pieces, junk rather than antiques, left by the former owners. The sofa was enormous, a six-seater in red leather, probably from a pub. Of course we tried it for size.

"This is great," said Danny, bouncing up and down. "We could use this."

"Where are we going to put it?" asked Gary. "It's too far from my house. We'd never get it there."

"My mum would have a fit if I brought it home," added Danny.

They both looked at me expectantly.

"OK, back to my house it is. We can put it by my shed wall." Thank goodness my parents were tolerant of my 'finds', they were always bringing stuff home of their own.

"There's a table here as well," said Danny. "That might be useful." He pulled it out from under the rubbish. "And I can see an old pram," he added. "Perhaps we can put the sofa on that."

"Good idea."

Gary took one end of the sofa and I took the other and heaved it up, while Danny held the pram still, and soon the sofa was balanced precariously on top. We slung the small table onto the sofa. Then Gary held the sofa with one hand and his bike in the other, Danny pushed the pram and hung onto the middle, while I tried to balance the other end while holding onto the other two bikes. Of course the table kept slipping off, and we had to keep stopping to adjust the weight, and it didn't help that we had to go the long way round, but eventually we reached Acres Gardens. I lived in the end house on the corner and we propped the sofa against the back of our shed, looking out over a small green.

Borrowing my sister's saddle soap we set to work and soon had the sofa gleaming, the big red buttons coming up a treat.

"That looks really great," said Danny, standing back to appreciate our hard work. "We ought to sell it."

Gary looked horrified. "No," he said. "We should keep it. We can use it as a place to hang out."

I agreed with Gary, it would be great to have somewhere of our own to just sit in the sun and chat to our mates. Except for the youth club and the occasional church dance there wasn't a place to just be on our own, the sofa would fill that gap brilliantly.

"OK," said Danny, a bit miffed at missing out on the money, but it was two to one.

It was decided then, the sofa would stay. We cleaned up the table and put it in front of the sofa to hold our drinks or put our feet on, and added a couple of deck chairs. Soon people noticed and began to say hello and chat, they joined us on the sofa, or lounged in the deck chairs. In the evening we bought out some old Christmas lights and hung them from the shed roof. I got out my chess board and more people arrived. Mum made some sandwiches and dad gave us some money for cans of coke. Clive from next-door came around with some packets of crisps, and his sisters bought some more drinks. The air got cooler as night drew in and we played endless games of chess and set up a poker game for matchsticks. It was like an outside club that everyone in the area could enjoy. Eventually mum called time.

"See you tomorrow," called Gary.

"Come round to mine," said Danny. "Bring your bikes, I've thought of something to do."

"What?" I asked.

"Tell you tomorrow." Danny knew just how to wind us up!

Following our paper round the next morning we met up at Danny's house. It was only eight-thirty but already the sun was hot.

"Well, come on then, tell us."

"I thought we could ride over to Kingston," said Danny.

"In this heat," I protested. "You must be raving mad!"

"That's twenty miles away," joined in Gary. "Why would we want to do that?"

"Our next-door neighbour works for the Water Board," explained Danny. "He says the reservoir's dried up."

"Completely?"

"Completely."

This we had to see. Burgh Heath pond was small, but the reservoir was huge, it couldn't possibly be dry. We raided Dan's mother's fridge and got on our bikes. Actually it wasn't twenty miles, more like fifteen, as we cut across the Downs and took all the short-cuts we could think of. However, the heat made the ride seem longer and we kept hitting great clouds of midges, they got in our mouths and splattered our t-shirts. We were glad we'd brought some drinks.

When we reached the reservoir we hid our bikes, found the hole in the fence that we'd discovered on a previous expedition, and crept inside.

"It's gone," said Gary, as we stared down into the vast hole. "All that water, completely gone."

It was amazing, the huge old Victorian pumping house, built of red brick and with the sun glinting on its windows, stood on the edge of a hole – a very deep hole, with cracked mud at the bottom. From where we were standing we could not see a drop of water, not a single drop.

Sneaking around the perimeter we climbed down a large metal staircase and jumped onto the bottom of the pit. The dry mud had cracked like crazy paving without the cement, leaving valleys that in some places were almost chest high.

"Let's try to get to the centre," suggested Gary.

It was a strange, alien landscape at the bottom of the reservoir; it felt like being on a different planet where no-one had ever walked before. It was really hard going, some of the cracks we could jump over, others we just had to climb down and then up the other side. Eventually we decided to turn back. Climbing out, we walked around the side to where it was deeper, and found that there was still a little water, but not much, certainly not sufficient for all the thousands of people living in the area.

"Oi!" a voice shouted angrily. "What are you doing in here?" A man in navy overalls came striding towards us.

"We've come to have a look," we explained, standing our ground.

"You shouldn't be in here. It's private property."

"OK, we were only looking," protested Gary

"We'd heard it had all dried out," I added. "We wanted to see for ourselves."

"Everyone wants to have a bloody look at it," moaned the man. "We had a Government Minister here yesterday and he thinks if it doesn't rain soon we'll have to ration the water and turn off all the pumps."

He looked really worried and we realised what a difficult time it must be for him.

"We still have water in Tadworth, there are no standpipes" I said, trying to cheer him up.

"That's because you're on a spring down there," he explained. "But only on the Downs side because the chalk holds the water. The water table hasn't gone down much so there's still water underground, but not much, and it's hard to get at, so make the most of it. You could all be on stand pipes down there soon."

As we rode home across Epsom Downs the sun was so hot we stopped and bought cold drinks at The Hut. Remembering the sight of that empty reservoir we really savoured that first long, cold sip of coke. Then we propped our bikes against one of the wooden sides of the hut, lay down on the brown grass and gazed up at the sky.

"I've never seen sky that blue before," I said, lazily flicking an ant from my arm. "The blue seems to go on forever."

"They have skies that colour in Kansas," said Gary.

"How do you know?" asked Danny.

"Read it somewhere."

We nodded, it was a reasonable answer. Gary was always reading, wanting to know things.

Above us we could hear the song of a skylark as it climbed higher and higher into that amazing bright blue sky. In the distance came the whinny of a horse in the racing stables and the faint sound of one of the stable lads whistling cheerfully. It was so peaceful, looking up at that vast expanse of blue, with only the occasional white jet stream from a plane to break the breathtaking colour. It didn't seem possible on such a beautiful day that we were in the middle of a serious drought.

Riding home we were in sombre mood. Was the water really going to run out? Could we die? Was it that bad? As soon as we got home we started filling up containers just in case, and that evening, as friends and neighbours once more gathered at our new 'club' we spread the word – our water was drying up fast!

"With luck the school would have to shut," said Gary.

"No toilets, no school," added Danny suddenly cheering up.

We could only dream.

Chapter 23

Weird and Wonderful Teachers

De Burgh was a large school of over a thousand pupils, and being so big it was easy to pick and choose what lessons you went to. At the beginning of term you were given a weekly planner showing you which lessons you were supposed to attend, with correct times, classrooms, teachers etc. However, if you made up your own planner it confused the enemy completely, and left you free to come and go to whichever lesson you chose.

At break one day, towards the end of the summer term, we met up in the playground at our usual bench.

"We've got a brilliant new science master," said Gary enthusiastically.

Danny and I looked at him in horror; he was obviously sickening for something.

"No, it's true," protested Gary. "I've just had the best science lesson ever. This new teacher really knows his stuff, and better than that he makes it fun."

This needed looking into.

"Hey, Doyle," I said, calling a passing sixth-former. "Who's this new science teacher Gary's going on about?"

"Oh, that must be Professor Blake," Doyle explained. "He's a friend of Mather's from university. I think he's covering for Mr. Smyth.

"Smyth off sick again?" enquired Danny.

"Yeah." Doyle nodded and raised his eyebrows expressively.

We all grinned, everyone knew about Mr. Smyth's little drink problem. You could always mess about in his lessons after lunch.

"Let's join this new bloke's lesson this afternoon," I suggested. "Suss him out."

It was agreed. Unfortunately Gary couldn't skip woodwork to join us as his form teacher took that subject and would certainly ask questions if he was missing, so it would just be Danny and I.

As soon as the bell went we headed up the stairs to the science lab. We were surprised to see quite a queue waiting. It seemed that word had got about and we weren't the only kids wanting a look at this new teaching wonder. As more kids arrived the queue began to stretch back down the stairs, surely he wouldn't let us all in?

"Come in, come in," said the Professor when he arrived. "The more the merrier."

We'd never seen anything like it – a teacher who wanted to teach as many kids as possible. We all filed into the lab. The room was soon packed, with some kids sharing stools and other squashed at the back. We were all anxious to see what this teaching wonder was like.

He was a strange looking character, short and fat, but extremely well dressed, not like our usual bunch at all. He had on a suit with a silk waistcoat and a bow tie. His head looked upside down, with all the hair at the bottom and a completely bald pate on top. His eyes shone out from his shiny face, as did his smile, and he was so enthusiastic about everything he was like a kid in a toy shop. He hurried around getting all the equipment out, stuff we did not even know the school had, and then told us all about it in great detail. He was obviously very intelligent, but also slightly mad, which was great. His enthusiasm began to rub off on us and we all wanted to be involved with what he was doing.

Our favourite piece of equipment was the Van der Graaff Generator[29], which made static electricity and kept sparking across two spheres, a large one that

---

[29] Van de Graaff Generator – Invented by American physicist Robert J Van de Graaff in 1929.

was fixed and a small one that could be moved. The Professor demonstrated it by moving the small sphere in and out, which made a spark like lightening jump further and further. It was fascinating. Then for some reason the Professor turned and went over to another group and began explaining something to them.

"Sir! It's still going, sir," called Danny.

"With you in a minute," muttered the Professor distractedly. He carried on explaining to the other group.

"But it's still going."

"Um." He waved a hand towards us.

We could see the second sphere wasn't connected so the machine was still making static electricity.

Eventually he turned back to us, but the Generator was still charging up on his desk, which was raised up from the floor. Just as he got near a huge spark flew out, straight to his bald head which was now in line with the machine. BANG! He was hurled backwards onto the floor. This was not good. He looked dead.

"Get some help," I yelled, as I crawled around the back of the desk and unplugged the Generator.

Jenny ran next-door to the other lab and Chemistry Jones came rushing in. He managed to revive the Professor with some crystals, but the poor man still looked very unwell.

The last we saw of him he was being carted into an ambulance. He never returned to the school, which was a shame because he was a really first class teacher, and although we only had him for half a class he was remembered with great affection.

Teachers as a whole are a funny lot, you never know what you're going to get. Each year springs new surprises. In our first year at secondary school we had a French teacher called Miss Beatty, she was very strange and got confused by the smallest things. Teaching was not really her strong point and even us innocent eleven year olds soon realised we could play her up. We'd distract her with different topics of conversation. To our delight we discovered the subject of sex made her blush. Such joy! It's amazing how often our class wanted to talk about sex during our French lessons.

Miss Beatty went sick at the beginning of our second year and didn't come back, we all suspected that she had realised teaching was not for her and given up. Other French teachers came and went. We began to hope that we had finally discovered the knack of getting rid of them altogether.

In assembly one day Mr. Mather asked our class to stay behind.

"What have you been up to?" asked Danny as his class filed out.

"Search me," I muttered.

Eventually there was just our class left, and we shuffled from foot to foot waiting for the Sword of Damocles to fall.

"Come to the front all of you," said Mather, motioning us to move towards the stage.

We shuffled forward reluctantly.

"I, er, um," cough. For a moment Mather looked almost embarrassed. This was something new. We perked up slightly.

Mather adjusted his tie, fluffed out his gown and began again. "I've kept you here this morning to give you a talk about sex."

Not again. We'd done the sex thing in First Year Biology, the girls had been given a lesson in 'hygiene' and a booklet about sex in their Domestic Science class, the boys had been given a talk about contraception during Physical Education, and our Religious Education teacher had gone on about sex so often he'd almost succeeded in making the subject boring ("If there's anything you need to ask questions about come to me.") Now here was Mather visiting the subject again, if he'd only hand out some of the magazines we were sure he hid in his office we might be interested.

"With regard to sex, some people are, um, different," he said, addressing the back of the hall rather than us. "Um, there are men who, um, like men, and ladies um, who like ladies."

This was puzzling.

"What's he on about?" whispered Janice.

"He means pooftas," explained Mike, who had an elder brother.

The boys tittered and Janice continued to look puzzled, I could see some interesting questions for our next RE lesson.

Mather glared at us, and then continued in a rush. "There are also some men who could be ladies, and, um, some ladies who could be men."

We all looked at him astounded; he'd definitely lost the plot. He then began to ramble on about the Bible and God, so we started to muck about. However, he soon realised he'd lost control.

"Blake," he yelled, picking on a ginger kid he hated, just to restore the balance of power. "To my office immediately. The rest of you dismiss."

"What was that about?" asked Mike, as we watched Blake disappearing towards the head's office for another dose of the cane, Mather's favourite medicine.

"I've absolutely no idea," I said, feeling as bewildered as the rest of the class.

However, all was made plain later in the day when we were introduced to our new French teacher – MISTER Beatty. It seemed Miss Beatty had had a sex change and was now a man.

Remembering the fun we used to have with *Miss* Beatty we looked forward to the lesson with glee. We soon found that *Mr* Beatty was a completely different kettle of fish; you would certainly never believe he had ever been a woman. He made it abundantly clear that we were in his class to learn French, the language.

French kissing, French movies, French magazines, were no longer a subject for discussion. There would be no smutty tittering in his class.

"Get out your exercise books. Bone, hand out the text books. Turn to chapter seven, verbs." A steely glare swept the classroom. "Let's see how much progress you have made since I taught you last."

I could see my fake lesson planner would be needed once again! At least it would all soon be over as the summer holidays were almost with us.

Chapter 24

The Last Day of Term

Danny's elder sister had married a hippy called Tim. At night he played in a band, but by day he walked around in a daze saying "Peace, man" and smoking home-made cigarettes that smelt decidedly odd. People avoided him because of the way he looked and talked, but we liked him and so, when we saw him wandering around the school playing field, we went over to see what he was up to. He seemed to be picking things up from the ground and putting them in his pocket, or occasionally sniffing them. Strange!

"Hi, Tim, what are you doing?" asked Danny.

"Picking rooms, man," he replied, drifting over to another part of the field, his faded, multi-coloured kaftan drooping around his ankles.

We followed, still none the wiser.

"What are rooms?" asked Danny, catching hold of his sleeve so he wouldn't escape again.

"Mushrooms, man. Magic mushrooms." He began to drift away again, humming happily to himself.

We followed, determined to get to the bottom of this.

"What do you do with magic mushrooms, Tim?"

"Eat them, make tea, man," he mumbled, reaching down again. "These little rooms are magic, they make you happy.

This sounded interesting; mushrooms with magical properties. We ought to have some of those.

"Can you show us some?" I asked.

He took some little mushrooms out of his pocket to show us.

"Can we pick some for you?" asked Gary helpfully.

"Yeah man, but only the ones that look like this." He held one up for us to see. We examined it closely. It looked fairly ordinary to us, nothing magic that we could see, but if that's what Tim wanted then that's what Tim would get, and if they were especially magical we would save some for ourselves.

"OK," we said, and immediately set to work finding magic mushrooms. It was easy; they were growing all over the field. We soon had a pocket full each.

"What's going on here?" demanded Mr Greenway, an English master who'd drawn the short straw and was doing playground duty. He marched up to Tim. "This is school property, what are you doing here?"

"Chill man," said Tim lazily, still humming to himself and with a happy smile on his face.

"Get out of here. Bloody hippy stone-head."

"Peace man." Tim gave us a wave, and began to slowly walk towards the school gates, still humming happily.

"Don't talk to his type," warned Greenway, turning to us. "Get back to the playground. The bell will be going in a moment. Only tomorrow to get through and we'll all be free for six weeks." He seemed as pleased by the prospect as we did.

As we headed back into school Gary picked a couple of the little mushrooms out of his pocket. "What shall we do with these," he asked.

"Didn't Tim say you made tea with them?" I asked thoughtfully.

The others nodded.

"Well, teachers drink a lot of tea. They've got that tea urn in the staff room. I expect they could do with a bit of cheering up, they always look so depressed. They're always moaning and miserable. Why don't we come in early tomorrow morning and put the mushrooms in their tea urn? It's the last day and it might make them a bit happier."

"That's a good idea," said Gary enthusiastically.

Danny nodded. "They might even let us go home early."

The following morning we rushed around delivering our newspapers as fast as we could and as soon as we had finished we headed for the school. The car park was empty and the school deserted except for a few cleaners. We crept up the back stairs and along the corridor above the assembly hall. The staff room door was open. We took the lid off the tea urn and saw it was full of water. Quickly we dropped in a handful of mushrooms. They floated on top, so we pushed them down with a spoon, replaced the lid and hurried out.

We waited expectantly. By mid-morning break the only thing that had happened was that Geography Jones, who must have drunk a lot of tea, had gone home because he was not feeling well. Unfortunately he knocked a sign down as he drove out of the car park.

"What are we going to do?" asked Gary. "They don't seem happy at all."

"I've still got some mushrooms," I said. "Perhaps we didn't give them enough."

"Let's wait until after break and give them some more," suggested Danny. "We want them to be happy so we can go home."

Before going back to class we quickly went back to the staff room. While Gary kept watch, Danny and I threw the rest of the mushrooms into the urn and gave it a good stir.

Well, that certainly did the trick. The first clue that something strange was going on was after lunch. Miss Brown, the maths teacher, decided to take off all her clothes and dance around the playground naked. The second clue was that none of the other teachers seemed to notice! We stood and watched goggle eyed. Suddenly there was a rumpus from the sports block.

"Stay away from me. Stay away from me." Mr. Whitemoor dashed out of the gymnasium wielding a hockey stick. "I know you're going to kill me. Get out the way," he shouted, twirling the stick around his head. We followed him into the school, keeping a safe distance, "You can't get me, get back, get back." He seemed to be using the stick like a sword and slashing at imaginary foe. Eventually he spotted the broom cupboard, leapt inside and slammed the door. We decided he was probably safe in the cupboard and went back out to the playground.

SMASH!

A tile landed right beside us, shattering into little pieces.

"Run," I yelled, taking to my heels. The others followed close behind me. The playground was in complete bedlam, kids running in all directions.

"What's happening?" asked Danny as we reached the comparative safety of the tennis courts.

"Look!" Gary pointed up onto the roof of the sports block. Two teachers had climbed on the roof and were lifting tiles and chucking them down on anyone who came near.

Just then a domestic science teacher came wafting past, smiling happily to herself, she sat down on the steps and gently touched a dandelion with a look of wonder in her eyes, as if it was the first time she had seen one. Then more teachers appeared, wandering out of school, sitting on the grass, lying down under the trees, acting as though none of us kids were there. It was weird.

"I think we overdid it," said Gary.

"We need to get help," decided Danny. "Let's find Tim and ask him what to do."

We ran out of school and around to Tim's house. Luckily he was up and sitting outside on the doorstep. Quickly we explained what we had done.

"How many? How many?" he kept saying. "That's a weeks worth in one day. No-one has ever taken that many mushrooms before. It may not kill them, just make them mad." He paused and thought about it, then added, "Yes, probably just turn them insane. If you're lucky."

That was cheerful.

"Is there anything we can do?" I asked, rather frantically.

"Well," he said thoughtfully. "You could give them water. It might help to flush it through their systems. Possibly."

"We'd better try that," said Danny.

We ran back towards the school, wondering how we were going to get our teachers to drink lots of water. As we got close to the school gates who should we see in front of us but our arch enemies, the gang from Nork Park School. They had obviously come over for the end of term fight. As we ran down behind them the kids from our school came dashing out and the fight began. The drugged up teachers joined in as well, even Miss Brown who was still naked!

Eventually the police arrived and started arresting everyone, so we climbed up the nearest tree to watch it all and keep out of the way.

The Headmaster arrived back from his pub lunch, and ran around trying to stop people taking pictures. This was definitely something he did not want to get into the papers. But of course it did. The local rag ran the story as front page news. 'A spokesman for the school blamed the incident on the mushroom stroganoff that the teachers had all eaten for lunch, said the article. Fortunately, it continued, no-one was seriously injured and the six week holiday they will now have should assist their recuperation.'

The holidays had arrived!

Chapter 25

Streaking

"Six whole weeks," I said, sitting back comfortably on the red leather sofa. "What are we going to do?"

"I think I'm just going to sit out here and do nothing," replied Gary, putting his feet up on the table.

With school over, we had congregated at my house, sitting outside overlooking the green, although with the continued heat it was no longer green but decidedly brown. By way of celebration we had bought 99's from Mr. Whippy, our local ice-cream van. My dog Joe was lying in the shade under the table, his eyes mournfully assuring us that he was starving to death. I gave in first, broke off the end of my cornet, dipped it in the ice-cream and held it out. It disappeared in a flash. As I checked my fingers Joe turned up the offensive and dolefully put his head on Gary's feet.

"You've no chance there," said Danny with a grin. "It'll take a better dog than you to prise food from this greedy sod." He gave Gary a jab in the stomach.

"Hey, I almost lost my flake then," Gary protested. "And less of the greedy, I'm just a growing lad and need my food."

We all laughed, even Gary, and he broke off a piece of cornet and chucked it at Joe. It was great sitting in the sunshine with nothing to do. This is the life, I thought.

"We can't just sit here all afternoon," said Danny, tossing the last of his cornet to the dog.

"Why not?"

"We need to be thinking up a plan," Danny replied earnestly.

"I thought we were going to build some model aeroplanes and fly them over the Downs," said Gary. "I've got mine started already."

"Yes," I agreed. "I've spoken to my uncle and he's going to give me a hand."

My dad's best friend was Albert Briggs, European Champion in flying model aeroplanes, he'd even been filmed for Pathé News. Albert and his wife Ella had no children of their own so had taken on the role of surrogate Auntie and Uncle to my sisters and I.

"Well, you can come into Sutton with me tomorrow to get mine," said Danny. But that's not what I meant. We need a plan to meet that new girl. The one with the pink Capri."

"You're right," I agreed. "She's new to the Estate, she won't know anyone."

What I really meant was that no-one would have warned her! All the local girls had been well and truly warned about us by their mothers, and what their fathers had said about us probably shouldn't be written down. Of course, a stunningly attractive young lady with a Ford Capri was way out of our league, but that was not about to stop us.

"I've got an idea," said Gary. "We could streak[30]!"

"You're mad," I said. "Ever since you got chucked out of the changing rooms in front of the girls you've had a thing about running around naked."

Gary grinned. "Those girls noticed though," he said smugly.

We had to agree. Judging by the shrieks they had certainly noticed.

"How were you going to do it then?" I asked, always practical.

"Well, we could leave our bikes by those bushes opposite. One of us rings the bell. We hide behind the hedge, take our clothes off and as soon as she answers the door we run past waving. Then we get on our bikes and leg it, getting dressed on the way."

---

30 Streaking – Running naked in a public space. One of the first cases of streaking to hit the headlines was at the England/France game in 1974. The photograph won sport picture of the year.

"I suppose it could work," I said dubiously.

"I'm not sure it's a good idea at all," said Danny.

"Come on," urged Gary. "It'll be a laugh."

The problem was Danny and I both had sisters, and while Gary was thinking smiles of appreciation, we knew hysterical laughter and belittling comments about size were just as likely to be the result.

"Don't be chicken," he added.

Chicken! Us!

"OK then, let's do it. Now!" I thought that might call his bluff, but it didn't. Five minutes later we were hiding our bikes in the bushes.

Gary was the first to get undressed. Danny looked at me, I looked at him, we both looked at Gary and then fell about laughing. We couldn't help it. Gary standing in the middle of the Estate naked as the day he was born was just hysterical.

"Don't f'ing laugh," said Gary, looking totally pissed off.

That just made it worse, I was laughing so much my stomach was hurting.

"I'll get the bell,' spluttered Danny.

Seconds later the front door swung open, and out stepped this vision clad only in a short, black lacy negligee which left nothing to the imagination.

For a moment we all gawped. Then I shouted "Run Gary."

He was off. With a cheery wave at the startled girl, he dashed past and continued down the road. It happened so fast we just grabbed his clothes, leapt on our bikes and pedalled after him, the girl's horrified scream following us into the distance. Unfortunately, as we caught up with Gary a police car drove past heading in the other direction. It stopped. I don't think they could believe what they were seeing. Gary carried on past, legs pumping furiously, other bits jangling. We rode on past Gary. "Stop," he yelled. "Stop." But with the police behind us we just pedalled as fast as our chopper bikes would go. Gary was on his own.

Eventually we reached the Off Licence and beside it was Dog Shit Alley, which we knew was a safe escape route, so we waited there for Gary to catch us up. He was so out of breath he couldn't talk. Luckily he couldn't kick or punch us either, which is what he definitely wanted to do. He could hardly move, so we helped him get dressed. Then we started to laugh.

"Gary, mate, you were brilliant," I said, giving him a slap on the back.

"She's certainly going to remember you," added Danny. "Her face as you ran past!"

Gary pushed out his chest, beginning to feel like a hero. "We gave her a welcome to the Estate she won't forget."

He was probably right.

Chapter 26

Pot Holing

"Where's Danny?" I asked, as I skidded to a stop outside the newsagents.

"He's not back yet," Gary replied. "I suppose we'd better go and give him a hand."

Danny had the longest route on his paper-round and was often the last to finish so we usually ended up helping him. His route included the homes of three celebrities, (two famous footballers and a jockey), but he had been sworn to secrecy as to who or where. Of course we'd found out the name of one of the footballer's, but Danny was being annoyingly tight-lipped about the other one, and would only say the jockey was a 'red cheese' - intriguing.

We handed in our empty newspaper bags and climbed back onto our Chopper bikes. It was only eight o'clock but already the sun was high and we could feel the heat coming up off the pavement. It didn't take long to find Danny and complete his round.

"What are we going to do today?" Danny asked as we headed back to the newsagents.

"It's too hot to be busy," complained Gary. "I'm sticking to this bike already."

"Why don't we go pot holing?" I suggested. "It should be cooler underground."

The others eagerly agreed. Since we'd given up birch bending as too dangerous pot holing had become our latest craze. We had recently discovered that Epsom Downs was riddled with miles of underground tunnels, mostly dug out during WW1 and WW2. We had already explored the air-raid shelters on Ashey Road, but they led nowhere interesting. However, while indulging our passion for finding 'treasure' an exploration of a pile of rubbish off Burgh Heath Road had uncovered two large metal gates. They were set back in what looked like an old railway siding dug out of the chalk. The chains across the gates had already been broken, and we'd had a look inside and discovered an air-raid shelter with beds and toilets leading onto more tunnels. Unfortunately, without light we hadn't been able to see very much, now was our chance to thoroughly explore.

With Radio One blasting out C. W. McCall's 'Convoy', from Danny's transistor radio, we rode through the Estate yelling "Bear in the air," as a helicopter went over heading for Gatwick Airport. Freewheeling down hill to Tattenham Corner, we tore past the railway station and then onto the Downs. By the time we reached Burgh Heath Road the Wurzels were declaring "O'ive got a brand new combine 'arvester" with us joining in "Oo ar, Oo ar.".

Eventually we reached the quarry and carried our bikes over the piles of rubbish, rusty old cars, discarded furniture and even an ancient upright piano, to the hidden doors. The chain was still hanging loose, just as we'd left it, so we quickly pushed one of the doors open. It grated ominously. We slipped through and closed it carefully behind us; we didn't want anyone else prying about. Immediately the radio went dead and at the same time we were plunged into darkness.

"Turn on your lights," I said, leaning forward and feeling for my front headlamp.

Soon the thin light from our lamps was illuminating the walls. On our previous visit we had found a metal ladder which was hidden in the men's toilets which we had pushed down a hole to a lower level of much older tunnels. Some of these were made of brick, and they led off in all directions. We made for this now. Leaving our bikes at the top, we unhooked our front headlights and climbed gingerly down the ladder, testing each rung on the way. The lower tunnels were normally flooded, but with all the heat they had dried out completely.

"You go first Gary," I said when we reached the bottom. We had found on previous expeditions that Gary had an unbelievable sense of direction and so were quite happy to follow him, trusting he would instinctively know the way even if the ever-ready batteries on our bikes died.

We soon discovered that some of the tunnels had large wooden doors at the ends, which seemed to link up to the large local houses in the area. It was strange to come out into someone's cellar.

"Can you hear that?" asked Danny, as we stood among racks of dusty wine bottles.

Above us a man's posh voice was complaining, "Have you moved The Times, dear? I was doing the crossword." Then an equally posh woman's voice replied, "It's in the study, darling, where you left it."

We started to giggle.

"We'd better get out of here," I whispered urgently. "If we've caught they'll think we're burglars."

Hurriedly we closed the heavy door and re-traced our steps.

"This way," said Gary.

Minutes later we were through a large metal door and into a hospital ward. We were amazed to see rows of metal beds and cupboards full of medical supplies; there was even an operating theatre. The walls were all thick concrete, obviously bomb proof.

"Where's that light coming from?" asked Danny, looking up at the ceiling.

Above us we could see thin shafts of light shining down into the room, they seemed to be coming down through metal pipes.

"Where do the pipes come out?" I wondered, trying to think what could be above us.

"No idea," said Gary. "We'll have to investigate later."[31]

---

[31] Gary later worked out that some of the ornate cast iron Victorian lamp-posts in the streets above were hollow and were actually ventilation

We moved off down another tunnel. There was another metal door at the end of this one, with a broken hinge, and with a lot of pushing we opened it wide enough to squeeze through.

"Come on," said Gary, still leading the way. "There's some stairs here."

We followed him, our footsteps echoing on the concrete floor. Eventually we came out into what looked like an enormous, deep, swimming pool that instead of water was filled with old army trucks. We had never seen so many vehicles in one place, all abandoned and rusting – a scrap metal merchants dream! At the end of it was a large tube leading to two more, deep, empty tanks.

"It's Pluto," announced Gary exultantly.

Pluto (Pipe Line Under The Ocean) was built in WW2 to pump oil across the channel in pipes laid on the sea bed. On its way to the coast it needed a number of pumping stations, one of which was on the edge of Epsom Downs. We had always wanted to get into it, but it was protected by a mine field and two lots of barbed wire fences, defences against which even our ingenuity had failed – until now! We took the opportunity to thoroughly explore the inside of the building and around the holding tanks. It was fascinating, huge and really well made.

"Hey, look at this," called Danny.

He had found a round bricked-up hole, about six feet high. "These bricks are loose," he added, grabbing an iron bar and stabbing at the edge. Soon he'd made a hole, so Gary and I went over to help, pulling out the bricks until there was enough room to look inside. It was another tunnel and on the side someone had drawn a sign post saying 'Pluto' pointing back, and 'Dumbo' pointing down the tunnel.

"Go back and get the bikes so we can explore," I said. "I'll make this hole bigger."

---

shafts for the tunnels beneath.

"We left the bikes behind because they wouldn't fit down that small hole," complained Danny. "How are we going to get them through? There's not enough room."

I fished in my pocket and pulled out the dog bone spanner[32] I always carried. "Take off the handle bars," I suggested.

"That might work," agreed Gary. "We'll give it a try."

By the time they got back I had enlarged the hole so that there was enough room for us and our bikes to get through. The tunnel was enormous and seemed to go on for ages. It had pipes attached to the sides, but we could not see much more because it was so dark, our headlights only illuminating a small patch in front of us.

"We're going to run out of light soon," said Gary, who was still leading the way. "You two had better turn your headlamps off and just follow mine."

Eventually Gary's battery died, so I turned my light on and took over. It was scary being in the lead, going into the dark unknown, with occasional drips of water landing on your head, and with only a small beam of light. If there had been a hole in the floor we would have fallen down it, but luckily the road was smooth and flat. We must have travelled for at least five miles and the end was still not in sight when my light suddenly flickered and died.

Danny turned on his light – the last.

"What are we going to do?" I asked. "Shall we carry on or go back?"

"If we carry on and my light goes we'll be in deep shit," Danny stated bluntly. "We'll be stuck underground in the pitch dark."

"Well, there are rats down here," reasoned Gary (we could see the bright pinpricks of their eyes watching us), "so they must be coming from somewhere

---

32 Dog Bone Spanner – a double ended bicycle spanner.

because our end was bricked up. There must be an opening at the other end."

We decided to continue on in the hope of finding a way out. Then Danny's light began to dim. We could just about see the front wheel of his bike. It was too dangerous to ride, so we pushed our bikes into the darkness. Finally the light gave one last flicker and died. We were stuck deep underground, miles from the entrance, in a tunnel that was now so dark we could not even see each other.

"I don't like this," said Danny, his voice sounding shrill "We could die down here. There's no air, it's getting hard to breath."

We didn't tease him for sounding scared. He was only voicing what we were all thinking. Naturally we had told no-one where we were going, so no-one knew where we were. We could stumble around these old tunnels for weeks without food, water, light. We could die of starvation. Or go mad. We'd been reading 'Lord of the Flies' at school, was our friendship as solid as we thought?

Danny got out his lighter and sparked the flint, but it was out of fuel and only burnt the wick.

"Hold on," said Gary suddenly. "That radio tied on your saddle has a battery."

Relief! With Danny flicking his lighter we swapped the batteries over and carried on down the tunnel. We rode as fast as we could in the dim light, conscious now of the danger we were in. Our legs were aching and we were beginning to tire. The light began to dim again. We carried on in silence; it was all we could do. Then Gary gave a shout. "Stop! Look!"

High above us were two small rays of light. Attached to the wall was a ladder of rounded metal bars, leading towards the roof. Danny got off his bike and clambered agilely up. "There's a metal cover," he called down to us. "But it's too heavy for me to open."

Gary and I climbed up to give him a hand. The cover was solid and heavy, really heavy, but the thought of getting out of the tunnel spurred us on and eventually, with all three of us pushing for all we were worth, we managed to lift it and poke our heads up. Freedom at last! We stood balanced on the top rung of the ladder, squinting in the sunlight. Suddenly, above us was a terrible roaring noise, everything began to shake and then it went black.

"Ahgg!" we all screeched, clinging onto each other for dear life, as a blast of pressure tried to push us down the hole.

Then it went quiet again.

Cautiously we pushed the top of our heads out of the hole to see a large aeroplane taking off.

"We're at Gatwick!" exclaimed Gary. "We're at the end of the runway."

"How are we going to get out of here?" asked Danny, looking horrified.

"We'll have to make a run for the perimeter," I said. "Let's take the handlebars off the bikes again and get them up here."

We had to time it right because planes kept taking off and the thrust from their engines pushed us back. Eventually we got the bikes out. There was no time to put them together, we just dragged them over to the perimeter fence and collapsed there on the parched grass, panting. Eventually we got our breath back, reattach the handlebars and then began cycling along next to the security fence looking for a way out.

"Stop!" yelled a man, getting out of a truck and running over to us. "What are you doing in here?"

"We're lost," explained Danny, putting on his usual innocent act.

"How did you get in here, this is a restricted area," ranted the man. "You shouldn't be here, it's dangerous."

"We climbed over the fence to see the planes," said Danny, as if this would be an everyday excursion for us.

The man looked up at the twenty foot fence and then back to us. “You did?” he shook his head. “With your bikes?” He shook his head in disbelief. “Amazing. No-one’s ever done that before.” He looked up at the fence again. “Wait till I tell the others, you must be monkeys or something. Well, don’t do it again. It’s very dangerous with the planes taking off.”

He led us over to a gate set in the fence and let us out. “Do you want a drink?” he asked.

Did we? Water had never tasted that delicious.

We thanked the man appreciatively, got on our bikes and began the long ride home up Reigate Hill

“You know,” said Gary, as we slowly climbed the long hill. “It seemed flat in the tunnel, but now it’s really steep up this hill. We must have been travelling down in the tunnel.” He thought about it for a while, the added. “I bet it goes all the way down to the coast.”

We could see his little mind working as we pedalled on.

Eventually a smile lit his face. “I’ve had a great idea,” he said. “Let’s buy some more batteries and try again tomorrow.”

“No way!” yelled Danny and I in unison. We had definitely had enough of pot holing for one summer.

Chapter 27

Just Messing About

Marbles Way Pond, Tadworth

"Hi, Graham, do you want a hand?"

I looked up and saw Gary peddling towards me. "I'm glad to see you," I said as he pulled up beside me. "I really overslept this morning."

"Did you stay up after Danny and I went home?" he asked.

"Yeah, Clive and Andrew stopped by with a few of their mates. I think mum's getting a bit fed-up with having so many people hanging around. She was right miserable about me not getting up and muttering about the sofa having to go."

"There was quite a crowd of us out there last night," agreed Gary. "I thought your neighbours might complain."

"It's the neighbours that were out there," I said, dropping a newspaper through the next letterbox.

""Here, give me those," said Gary. "I'll finish off this street while you do down the lane."

With all the newspaper delivered we headed back to the Newsagents. Danny was already there waiting for us.

"I've finished my model," he said eagerly. "Shall we go over the Downs and fly them?"

"Good idea," I said. "Mine's ready too. What about you Gary."

It seemed that Gary had finished making his model aeroplane as well. With the weather being so warm and still it was an ideal time to try them out. An hour later we were on the Downs. We had each chosen to make different balsa wood models, Danny had a Vernon Champ and I had decided on a Keil Craft Cardinal, both of us had installed diesel engines. However, Gary had gone for a glow motor which needed a battery to start it. After much flicking and fiddling with the compression and needle valves we each managed a full engine run. The first flights were all crashes and needed repairs. Gary had the more methodical approach to this and his aeroplane was repaired first. We stood biting the balsa wood glue[33] off our fingers, and watched his Snipe Free Flight model climb almost out of sight before the fuel ran out and it dropped back down to earth, spiralling gently until it touched down onto the grass. This was exactly what we had been aiming for and with some help from Gary with trimming the models, Danny and I managed some short flights of our own.

The practicing went on all afternoon. Gary and I eventually managed longer flights but Danny's plane

---

[33] Health and Safety were unheard of in 1975, you couldn't make a balsa wood model without becoming encrusted with glue containing among other things arsenic and cyanide, and biting it off our fingers was the only way we ever found of removing it!

began to splutter and landed awkwardly. As he ran over the short turf to retrieve it a large black Labrador shot out from behind some bushes and grabbed the plane.

"Give that back," yelled Danny, giving chase.

Gary and I left our planes and joined in. The dog's owner began yelling as well. Of course the dog thought that a brilliant game, and wove around between us like a rugby forward, dodging between our legs, sending Gary tumbling. Then the dog's owner had the bright idea of distracting it with a ball. That did the trick. It dropped the plane and charged after the ball instead.

Luckily the plane wasn't too mangled and we managed to get it flying again. As the afternoon wore on I could feel the pangs of hunger making my stomach rumble, a good indication it was time to be making for home.

"Let's have one last run," I suggested. "Make it a race and see whose plane goes the furthest."

We filled up the planes with fuel and let them go together. Gary's circled around straight up overhead, Danny's hopped around just off the ground, but mine flew straight and true. We watched it disappearing into the distance.

"Go after it," yelled Gary.

I clambered onto my bike and started pedalling furiously, but the plane just kept on climbing up into the sky, the engine running strong. As it disappeared out of sight over the Grandstand the chain came off my bike and I ground to a halt.

"Well that's that then," I said, as Danny and Gary came to a stop beside me. "I don't suppose I'll see that again. We'd better go home."

Later that evening we gathered on the sofa again.

"It's a shame about your plane," said Danny. "It was amazing watching it disappear over the Grandstand. I bet it went on for miles."

"I'll have to make another one I suppose," I replied mournfully. "It's a bugger really, I'll have to save up some more money."

"Don't swear," said mum automatically, as she placed a tray with a jug of ice cold lemonade and a plate of sandwiches on the table in front of us. "And if you need money so badly you can mow the lawn."

The sandwiches disappeared swiftly and we made our escape!

"Let's see if anyone's up the pond," suggested Danny.

Marbles Way Pond, by the school, was a favourite meeting place for kids on the Estate. To one side was a large tree with a branch that stuck out over the water, great for making swings on.

"My brother put one of those ropes up there," observed Gary, as we gazed up at the vast tree. On the branch projecting over the water were the remains of at least three past swings.

"We could make another swing," suggested Danny.

"We'll need some decent rope then," said Gary. "Something strong enough to take our weight. We don't want to be falling into the pond."

We looked down at the water, or rather what was left of it. This pond had never been known to actually dry up completely, it was rumoured to be fed by an underground stream. However, it had shrunk considerably and now seemed more like an overgrown puddle, covered in green algae with scum around the edges. It did not look inviting and we certainly didn't want to end up in it – although the thought of one of our friends coming to a muddy end held a certain appeal!

"I know where we can get a rope," I said, suddenly having a 'light bulb' moment. "There's one in that old tree camp over the Heath."

Danny and Gary immediately knew the tree I meant. We had made tree camps on the lower branches of the old Elm when we were small, but some older boys had pulled them down and built themselves a larger tree house right near the top, where the trunk made a V-shape. Unfortunately, the branch below the camp had fallen off which made it impossible to reach and the camp was therefore long abandoned.

"How are we going to get up to it?" asked Danny.

"I've got a plan," I said. "Come on let's get back to my house."

Ten minutes later we were heading for the Heath. As soon as we reached the old Elm I jumped off my bike and began to climb. I had managed to find some six inch nails in my dad's shed and began to hammer them into the trunk of the tree, making a spiral staircase. I edged around the tree, hammering the nails in as I went, getting higher and higher.

"Go for it Gra'," yelled Gary. "You're getting close to the top."

"Another couple of nails should do it," added Danny.

At last I reached the old tree house. No-one had been up there for years and old comics Dandy, Beano, and the Eagle littered the floor. A copy of All Man, well thumbed, caught my eye and I stuffed it in my pocket, educational reading for later on. The camp was really well made and had real windows and a tiled roof. I remembered a row of old cottages near the pond had been pulled down to make way for new (expensive) houses, and to judge by the material used to build the tree house there must have been rich pickings. The view was amazing, I could see right across Epsom Downs on one side and over to Banstead on the other.

"Can you see the rope?" yelled Danny.

"Yeah, it's on a hook. I'll let it down so you can climb up."

A couple of minutes later Gary and Danny were up in the tree house with me.

"This is brilliant," said Gary, looking around. "It's so well made."

Fatal words! At that moment there was a momentous CRACK, as half the branch supporting it gave way.

"Get out!" I yelled, as the floor below us tilted and we slid towards the bottom corner. Grabbing onto anything we could to save ourselves, we watched in horror as half the tree house fell to the ground.

"That was a near miss," said Danny grimly, as we clung to the half that was still attached to the tree.

"Look it just crumbles," said Gary, crushing a piece of wood from the door in his hand.

"Get the rope and let's get out of here," I urged.

"No," said Gary. "We should get rid of it in case anyone else comes up here. We don't want any little kids getting killed."

"OK, let's smash it down."

Clinging on to the remaining branch we kicked at the rotten wood and sent it tumbling down to the ground below. It seemed such a shame to destroy such a beautifully made camp, but it was the right thing to do as the entire top of the tree seemed to be rotting[34]. We dropped the rope and climbed down, with me going last, using the claw of the hammer to remove each nail as I want.

We cycled slowly back to the pond, left our bikes propped against the school fence and walked over to the tree feeling pleased with ourselves. Now we had a rope, and what a rope – so thick you could hardly get your hand around it and so long it would be possible to go further out on the branch than anyone had ever done before. But who was going to climb out and tie it?

"Not me," protested Gary, looking at the green sludge.

"Nor me," I said. "I got the rope."

---

[34] Unbeknown to us we were witnessing the spread of Dutch Elm Disease that decimated our Elm trees and completely changed the look of the British countryside.

That left Danny. He didn't look particularly pleased. The tree was a climber's nightmare, a thick, slippery trunk and high up the one thick, tapering branch hanging over the pond, with no smaller branches from it to hold onto.

"We can give you a bunk up, and then you can walk along the top of the branch, with your hands out, like a tightrope walker," I advised. "We'll tie the rope around your waist and Gary and I will hold onto the end and pull you up if you fall."

Danny reluctantly agreed, climbed up onto my shoulders and shinned up the trunk to where the branch bent over and out across the pond. Tentatively he stood on the branch, stretched out his arms and began to shuffle carefully along, gritting his teeth and trying not to wobble. We could see he wasn't enjoying it.

"How am I going to get down," he cried suddenly, spotting a possible flaw in my plan.

"Just slide down the rope after you've tied it," I shouted, with all the confidence of one who had his own feet firmly on the ground.

It seemed to spur him on. He shot along the branch as though he'd got a firework up his backside, swiftly tied on the rope, and began to slide back down to the ground. A crowd had gathered to see what was going on, and his return to terra firma was greeted with much cheering and back slapping.

"Easy," he said nonchalantly, as he handed me the rope.

Someone found a large stick and we tied it to the end.

"I'm going first," declared Danny, taking hold of the stick.

Good, I thought, it'll probably break at the first go - rather him in the mud than me. It didn't break though, and Danny swung out over the pond further than anyone had ever gone before. After that we all had a go, then two at a time. It was great; you could swing out further with more weight. Then three of us climbed on, then four. How many would it take? Eight! No, eight and a small one. We started doing tricks, hanging on with our legs as someone swung us around, spinning by twisting the rope.

The whole day was spent swinging on the great swing over the pond, and no-one fell off and the rope did not break. It was a brilliant day and we all had a good time.

It lasted for about two weeks, and then someone from the Council took the swing down and put a sign up saying 'No Swings'. Of course we pulled up the sign and chucked it in the pond, but no-one else had a good piece of rope, so the swing couldn't be replaced.[35]

---

35 Over the years various attempts were made to replace the swing, but eventually some killjoy from Health and Safety cut the overhanging branch off.

Chapter 28

Miss Pink Capri

"There was a phone call for you," said my sister Vivianne, when I got home from my paper round.

"What are you doing here?" I asked suspiciously, mum was at work and Viv didn't usually call around if mum wasn't at home. Perhaps she had been sent to spy on me. Mum definitely didn't trust me at home on my own, goodness only knows why!

"Borrowing the washing machine, my spin-dryer's broken, and I've got hundreds of nappies to wash."

"Yuck!"

"Do you want to know about this phone call or not!"

"Yeah," I said lazily, more interested in the contents of the fridge.

"It was the railway station at Epsom. They've got your plane."

Well, that got my attention.

"Really?"

She grinned. "Yes, apparently it landed on their roof; someone went up and got it down for you. It's in their lost property department."

Immediately I was on the phone to Danny and Gary with the good news. Half an hour later we were cycling into Epsom.

"How did they know it was yours?" asked Danny.

"I put my name and address on it."

"That's a good idea," said Gary. "I'm going to do that to mine."

It didn't take us long to reach Epsom and a very helpful Guard showed us where the lost property office was. It cost me 20p, but it was worth it to get the plane back.

"It's hardly damaged at all," I said, after giving it a thorough examination.

"You were really lucky," observed Gary. "Fancy it going all that way. We'll have to get our planes out and have another go."

We got on our bikes and began the long climb up the hill towards the Downs and home. It was another cloudless day, and we were glad of the patches of shade thrown by the tall trees along the road. There wasn't a hint of breeze and the heat coming off of the tarmac shimmered and danced.

"Hey, look at that," called Danny, giving a piercing wolf-whistle.

We didn't need him to call our attention to it - we had already noticed! The young lady tripping down the hill in her platform shoes, breasts wobbling merrily in her low cut t-shirt, took one look at us with our tongues hanging out and stuck her nose in the air. It was the response we had come to expect from any female to our friendly overtures, so we waved and carried on cycling.

"Did you see the knockers on that!" exclaimed Danny, letting go of his handlebars and sticking his hands out in front of him, a happy grin on his face.

"That's all you think about!" shouted Gary, although I hadn't noticed him looking the other way.

Danny just carried on grinning. "I say, do you know what the gas man told me?" he said.

"What gas man?" I asked.

"You know - the one that's converting everyone."

Yes, we'd seen him about. All of our parents had received letters from the Gas Board saying they were sending someone around to convert our cookers, fires and other appliances to North Sea gas. There had been adverts on the TV, and it had been on the News, on the radio, in the papers. Yes, I think we'd got the message.

We carried on cycling over the Downs, past the Grandstand, heading around towards Tattenham Corner.

"Do you want to know what he said or not!" exclaimed Danny, eventually.

"Go on then, tell us."

"Well, he had to go into Miss Pink Capri's house to fix her gas fire, and in her sitting room was a full size picture of her," he paused for effect, then added. "Naked!"

"No!"

"Yes!"

We were all in agreement – this we had to see. The only problem was how?

The following morning Gary came rushing around to my house. "She's over at the swimming pool," he said, excitedly. "I saw her car there as I went past."

We rushed around trying to find trunks and towels, and then rode like the clappers over the field to the new swimming pool that had been built next to the Phoenix Youth Club. By the time we'd got changed and reached the edge of the pool quite a crowd had gathered. The Manager, lifeguards, cleaners, even the man come to fix the drinks machine, were lined up watching the show as Miss PC slowly and sensuously swam lengths. Danny's eyes nearly popped out of his head when she flipped over to do back stroke and her large breasts almost fell out of her miniscule pink bikini. He turned to us and said emphatically, "I *have* to see that photo."

Our chance came later that day when having strolling casually past her house about ten times we suddenly noticed her Pink Capri had a flat tyre. Knowing she would need help to change it we waited, and when she finally came out of her house we just happened to be walking past.

"Can we help you with that?" I asked politely, while Danny stood there with his mouth open.

"I've got an appointment," she said, looking anxiously at her watch. "Do you think you can fix it?"

"Of course," said Gary. "Do you have a spare?"

She just handed him the key. Looking in the boot we found the spare wheel and the jack, unfortunately we had never used one before, but that was not going to stop us. However, as we lifted the spare out we noticed it was flat.

"Shall I take it and get it repaired for you?" asked Danny, expecting her to be impressed, but she just said OK and went back to the house.

As soon as Danny had gone Gary and I tried jacking up the car and removing the wheel. It was hot work. Firstly the nuts were tight and as there was no oil in the boot, we had to jump up and down on the lever to loosen them. Then the jack was one of those that had to be cranked up by hand and it took ages.

Miss PC came out of the house to see how things were progressing. "Is there something wrong with your friend?" she asked. "The one who's gone off with the tyre. He keeps watching me."

"It's your car," explained Gary, with an amazing bit of quick thinking. "He loves Capri's. His dad's got one."

"We've never seen a pink one," I added.

"Oh, my Ex got it for me," she replied with a shrug.

Eventually Danny returned. "It just needed pumping up," he explained.

"Well, I must just make a phone call," said Miss PC, walking back to the house with a wiggle that had us panting.

Swiftly we put the tyre back on, tightened up the nuts and put the other tyre and jack back into the boot. She had left the front door open. This was our chance!

Danny put his head around the door and called out, "We've finished. Can we wash our hands, please?"

"Come in," she called back. "The sink's in the kitchen."

This was what we had been waiting for. Finally we were close to seeing the life-size photo. Danny's grin got bigger as we went in. All along the walls of the hallway and even in the kitchen were framed photographs of Miss PC. In each of them she was wearing a different and *very* revealing outfit. Saucy, my dad would have called them. Mum would have used a completely different word!

"Are you a model?" I asked, innocently, as she came into the kitchen while we were washing our hands.

"Oh, um, yeah. Something like that. Yeah, a model," she replied, a smile hovering on her lips.

We looked at each other wondering what she meant by 'something like that'?

"Do you have a towel?" asked Gary, holding dripping hands over the sink.

"In the bathroom," she replied, gesturing upstairs. "Help yourselves. I have to get changed to go out."

As we were drying our hands in the bathroom we were trying to work out how to get a look at the full length photo. Suddenly, in walks Miss PC. Stark naked! Calmly she goes to the airing cupboard and takes out some tiny, lacy items.

"Thanks for changing my tyre," she said casually "I haven't a clue about cars."

"That's alright," I squeaked.

"Happy to help," muttered Gary, one of his eyes developing a decided twitch.

Danny, for once, was stunned to silence.

We watched open mouthed as she stepped into a red g-string, pulling it up her long legs provocatively. Then she clipped on a matching bra, leaning forward so her breasts almost cascaded out, then pulling down the front to emphasise her cleavage.

"Does this colour suit me?" she asked, looked critically at herself in the full length mirror. She put her hands under her breasts, pushing them upwards and together, making them look even bigger. Almost as big as our eyes which were popping out of our heads.

“Looks good to me,” I blurted out, surprised I still had a voice.

“Red, um, really suits you,” added Danny, sounding as if his pants were strangling him.

“You’re really sweet,” she said, giving Danny a kiss on the cheek, then walking back to the phone, her bottom wiggling suggestively.

We let out a collective sigh and staggered to the front door, leaving her chatting to someone called Candy.

“See you later,” we called, as she waved us goodbye with a knowing smile.

“Do you think anyone with believe us?” I asked, as we walked back to my house.

“I don’t believe it myself,” replied Gary with a shake of his head.

“We never did get to see that photo,” I laughed.

“It doesn’t matter now,” said Danny, the happy grin still on his face.

“No,” I agreed. “I don’t suppose it does.”

Chapter 29

Disco

Even people who hated music went to discos in 1976. Abba's 'Dancing Queen' was number one again, and James's favourite 'Play That Funky Music White Boy' by Wild Cherry kept playing on Radio One. We had tried sneaking into the disco at the Surrey Yeoman (a pub at Burgh Heath) and even had a quick dance to Andrea True Connection (an American porn star) and K.C. and the Sunshine Band. However, the Manager had soon spotted us and we were out on our ear. The legal drinking age had been lowered to eighteen a couple of years previously. Although we might not have passed for twenty-one, we could have sworn we looked at least eighteen. Gary and I had even started to shave! (Just ignore my sisters comments about bum fluff, they know nothing.)

There was nothing else for it, once again we would have to make do with the Under 16's Disco, which was held on a Thursday night at the Phoenix Youth Club. The problem being of course that we knew all the girls who were likely to attend and even worse – they knew us!

We strolled in trying to look cool in our Levi flares and smelling of our dad's 'Denim Original'. Someone had drawn the curtains in a half-hearted attempt to make the club look dark and mysterious. The Bee Gee's were blaring out 'You Should Be Dancing', coloured lights were flashing, boys were lounging on one side of the hall and the girls were in the centre of the floor, dancing around their handbags, as usual. They flicked back their hair and pretended not to notice us, also as usual.

"Hey," muttered Danny. "Check that out!" He nodded in the direction of the D.J.

Clustered around the turntables were a small group of girls, giggling and chatting up Harold as he changed the records. The girls were all wearing the latest gear, make-up heavy on the eye-liner, and a liberal dousing of Avon perfume.

"Don't recognise them," remarked Gary, giving them the once over with approval.

"Might be in with a chance there," I said, optimistically.

We sauntered over to the makeshift bar and placed our usual order – three cans of coke and three packets of crisps (the youth club was 'dry', much to everyone's disgust). Then we casually walked around the room, gradually nearing our quarry, greeting friends, chatting noisily and generally showing off on the way, just to ensure we were noticed. Finally we reached the turntables.

Harold, who had been watching our progress with amusement, knew exactly
what we were after. "This is Pam, Karen and Claire. Visiting us from Kingswood." The girls turned and looked us over. They didn't seem very impressed, but that had never stopped us before.

"Do you a fancy a drink?" I asked, master of the chat up line.

The one called Pam took pity, or perhaps she was just thirsty. "Yes, please. I'll have a 7Up."

The other two decided to have the same, they must have realised the choice was limited. That limited choice might also have been why they settled for us that evening. I've no idea what they put in 7Up in the Seventies, but it seemed to work, or possibly it was our scintillating wit! Anyway, by the time the disco ended at ten-thirty we had made a date for the following Saturday night. We said we'd take them to the Eclipse Nightclub above the Midday Sun Pub, near Woodmanstern. The problem was that the pub was down Outwood Lane, through Chipstead and in the middle of nowhere and therefore really difficult to get to. No, I lie, that was not the problem. The *real* problem was that Gary had told them we had a car and would pick them up from Kingswood. We now had two days to get a car and learn to drive.

"I know where we can get a car," Gary assured us on the way home. It seemed his brother Chris had a mate who needed to get rid of a car that had been left in his front garden. He thought we might get it for ten quid.

The following morning, having clubbed together all our available cash, we went around to view it. The car turned out to be a wreck of a Mark 2 Jag, possibly red under the dirt, with bushes growing through the floor, up on bricks, with no wheels attached. John, who was selling it, assured us it had run three years ago and its owner Paul (detained at her Majesties pleasure - nine years left of a sentence for armed robbery) would be glad to be rid of it, and so would John's mum! The wheels were in the shed and had good tyres.

After a bit of negotiation we struck a deal - £10 plus we tidy up the garden. It was definitely the agreement to tidy up the garden that swung it. After paying the money we borrowed a saw and cut away the bushes from the inside, put on the wheels, borrowed a foot pump to fill the tyres with air, and pushed the car off the bricks. The saw came in handy again to cut some wood to cover up the large holes in the floor. Then we opened the bonnet and found the battery was missing.

"We've got a spare in our garage," said Danny, coming to the rescue.

While Danny cycled off to fetch the battery and some petrol, Gary and I pushed the car onto the road. We then made good our promise on the garden. All those years of enforced gardening, as punishment for various misdeeds, suddenly turned into valuable experience. We'd never get jobs as landscape gardeners but it looked reasonably tidy, good enough anyway to satisfy John's mum, who was standing in the doorway giving instructions.

Finally, Danny arrived and we fitted the battery and filled the two fuel tanks. I jumped in, adjusted the seat, and pushed the button marked 'Start'. Nothing!

"Try putting it in neutral," suggested John.

Of course I had no idea how the car, an automatic, worked. My dad had only ever owned vehicles with a manual gearbox. There was no way I was going to show my ignorance though. I fiddled with every knob and moved every lever within reach until the one behind the steering wheel made a red bar line up with an 'N', which I assumed was for neutral. This did the trick and pushing the start button now caused a lot of noise, and a great deal of smoke shot out of the exhaust.

"Pump on the throttle," said John, and by a process of elimination I realised the small pedal did help if pressed down. The car now had flames shooting out and smoke pouring from underneath. After a bit of revving the flames died down and the smoke turned a less poisonous shade of grey.

"Get in," I yelled.

Of course the doors were corroded shut, so Danny and Gary climbed in through the windows. Concerned that John might change his mind (his mum clearly having decided to ignore our ages in her joy of finally getting rid of the eyesore from her lawn), I swiftly moved the lever again, and the letter 'R' showed up. Just as I was wondering what this meant the car leapt backwards towards the neighbour's fence.

"Use the brake," Gary shouted.

"Where is it?"

"That's the handbrake and that big pedal is the footbrake."

"Which one should I use?"

"The pedal of course. Now put it into drive and let's go."

Slowly we jerked away, waving goodbye to John and happily ignoring his worried frown. We had wheels!

I turned the car into Merland Rise and drove up to the car park outside Banstead Football Club. We'd already discovered there was an empty garage there and we'd planned to keep the car in it, safely out of sight. Finding some oil and tools in the boot we freed up the car doors and then set about cleaning. An hour later and a lot of elbow grease and it looked like a car again – a very smart red Jag.

Gary's brother pulled in and offered to give us some driving tips, so we took turns driving around the empty car park and soon discovered that although Gary was the youngest of us, he had a natural aptitude. It was decided - he would drive the Jag to the Eclipse the following day. We pushed the car into the garage and went home.

The next morning, after our paper-rounds, we all got paid, so we forked out for some more petrol, and then went home to get ready. Trying to look older in tank tops, flares and platform shoes, we rang the girls and arranged to meet at Claire's, who lived above a Pub on the way. Soon we were pulling up outside the Pigeon Pair[36], it seemed Claire's father was the proprietor.

"Come in," he said, playing the jovial host. "Claire, take them upstairs, I'll bring them up some drinks. Three pints of best bitter, OK boys?"

We nodded enthusiastically and then followed Claire up the stairs to the family's very comfortable lounge, where the two other girls were already waiting. I noticed they were all drinking fancy cocktails decorated with fruit and pink paper umbrellas, and hoped fervently that they weren't expecting expensive drinks from us. Dad had generously given me a fiver to go out with, and I had what was left of my paper-round money, but that wouldn't go far if they wanted fancy drinks. I crossed my fingers and hoped they'd go Dutch.

---

36 Now called The Kingswood Arms

"Lovely car," said Claire's dad, as he handed out the drinks. "I used to have a Jag just like that when I was in the police force."

I cast a quick glance in Gary's direction; he was drinking fast and studying the carpet.

"Yeah," added Claire proudly. "Dad was a Chief Superintendent before he got shot in the leg and had to retire."

Another glance at Gary. I'd never seen a drink disappear so fast!

"I think we'd better be going," he said, hastily putting his empty glass back on the tray. "We want to be able to get a table."

His herding of the girls was masterly for a fourteen year old with no sisters. He had those girls finish their drinks, grab their handbags and down the stairs to the car in five minutes flat!

Arriving outside the Eclipse Nightclub we parked in the car park and let the girls go in first as they looked older in their tube tops and spandex, although we had worked out by now that they were probably the same age as us.

"Have you finished your homework?" asked the bouncer as we approached the door.

"Nice car," added his partner. "Can you reach the pedals?"

But they let us in as we had the girls with us and had the money to pay – just!

The music was deafening, a glitter ball on the ceiling rotated, bouncing beams of flickering white light around, and all along the walls the mirrors were surrounded by flashing coloured lights. Up on the stage the DJ was busy, surrounded by massive speakers and banks of more flashing lights pulsating to the beat of the music. We mingled with the crowd, weaving around knots of people, and gradually made our way to the bar. Thankfully the girls were happy with halves of cider. The barmaid looked at us closely, but allowed us a pint of bitter each. We wandered around the room enjoying the atmosphere, pausing to watch the dancers. Suddenly, a voice we recognised called our names. It was Debbie with her sister Angie who looked fantastic in a lurex jumpsuit that clung to her body, emphasising her curves in way that got Danny's pulse racing. Didn't do my pulse any harm either.

"How did you get here?" asked Debbie.

Swiftly we explained about meeting the girls and getting the Jag.

"You must be mad," she retorted. "If you get caught you'll get locked up."

"We know." We assured her with a grin

Once again 'You Should Be Dancing' by the Bee Gees started playing and Angie dragged us all onto the dance floor. We were having a great time, flinging ourselves around, gyrating to the music, legs and arms jerking in all directions. The beer had gone to our heads and we were convinced that everyone was watching us in admiration.

"Angie's been invited to a party," said Debbie eventually, when we had danced ourselves to a standstill. "If you give us a lift you can come too."

This was too good a chance to miss and the girls were up for it. We all clambered into the Jag, Gary driving, Angie on my lap in the front and the other five squashed into the back. Angie pointed the way and we followed her friends who were in a little green sports car. Gary had to drive fast to keep up with them, weaving down the country lanes, as we tore through the Surrey countryside in the dark. The party was at a large country house, a marquee had been set up as a bar, and a band were playing next to the swimming pool in the garden. The girls were soon sipping Babychams and Camparis, while we found a Watney's Party Seven and passed it around between us until it was empty.

"Show us your dance moves," I shouted to Gary, pushing Pam in his direction.

Unfortunately, he was a little unsteady on his feet by now and not expecting a girl to be flung at him. He staggered backwards, arms flailing. Splash! We could hardly pull him out of the pool for giggling. It was unfortunate that fat girl got wet, well soaked; but there was no need for her to swear like that. Of course Debbie took exception, no-one swears at her friends, although I must admit punching the girl cold was a bit excessive. That was when we got asked to leave. Pity really, it had been a good party up until then.

Danny, who'd spent more time chatting up the girls than drinking, did a great job navigating his way home. As we came down the hill over the bridge at Kingswood the engine cut out.

"We're out of petrol," said Danny, immediately realising what the problem was. So we rolled the car around and parked it in the station car park. Then we all tumbled out of the car and escorted the girls over the road to Claire's, promising we'd give them a ring.

Laughing and joking we began the long walk home. The *very* long walk home. By the time we'd staggered over the heath the night sky was beginning to lighten and we were starting to sober up and regret the night's excesses.

The bright light of day had us nursing colossal hangovers, but we all got up to do our paper-rounds. Why do people want Sunday newspapers? They ought to be banned. Danny had actually remembered to bring a can of petrol with him, so, papers delivered we sauntered over to Kingswood station to retrieve the Jag.

"Where is it?" asked Gary, looking at the empty space.

"Some buggers pinched it," Danny replied in disgust.

"Probably for the best," I said fatalistically, and the others agreed. It had been fun though.

So that was the end of our driving, well, for the time being anyway.

Chapter 30

Dustmen

Getting up early for our paper rounds we soon got to know the other early risers in the area. Milkmen, postmen, district nurses, midwives, doctors, everyone gave us a cheery wave, everyone that is except the dustmen. They were a surly lot, always in a rush, swearing at anyone who got in their way, and hating all kids without exception. Of course collecting rubbish was a smelly job; rotting veg, putrid meat, decaying fish and the occasional dead cat caused an indescribable stink even in cold weather. I suppose it was understandable if they were grumpy at times, however, the hot weather of 1976 did nothing to improve their temper. Usually we kept well out of their way.

It was said around the Estate that the dustman would throw anything in their truck. Anything you put in the bin or even close to it would be chucked into the back of the dust cart and crushed. Broken chairs, wonky ironing boards, rusting prams, if left in the vicinity of a dustbin would vanish as if by magic, never to be seen again. This of course was usually most helpful and grateful householders, spared the trouble of fly-tipping Gran's old bed, could be relied upon for a large Christmas box when the festive season arrived. However, occasionally things went wrong.

"Look," said Danny, as we rounded the corner of the flats. "There's Charlie Scott. He looks really pissed off. I wonder what's up with him."

We pedalled over to see what the trouble was. Charlie lived just around the corner from me and was a year younger, but we got on well. His dad was the local caretaker, a useful chap to know, and everyone liked him.

"What's the matter, Charlie?" I asked, as we came to a stop in front of him.

"It's the dustmen," he explained angrily. "They've taken my chopper bike. I've only had it a couple of weeks."

"Where did you leave it?" asked Danny.

"By the bins," Charlie replied. "I was looking for my dad. I only left it for a second."

"Where are they now?" asked Gary.

"Round the corner by the washing lines."

"Let's go."

We rode furiously along the path beside the flats, Charlie running behind us. Skidding around the corner we saw the dustcart parked in the cul-de-sac, the wheels of Charlie's bike poking out of the back.

"Oi! Stop!" yelled Gary, as we skid to a halt beside the truck.

"You've picked up a bike by mistake," I shouted to the driver, jumping off my bike and clambering up the back of the truck. The others followed me as we all tried to reach the bike and pull it out.

"Get the f**k out of there!"

Suddenly three burly dustmen, muscles bulging under their grubby singlets, appeared from the back of the flats. In a flash they grabbed hold of us and chucked us onto the grass as easily as if we had been bags of rubbish.

"Keep your hands off that truck."

"But you've got my bike," protested Charlie, scrambling up. "You've thrown it in the back."

"It's too late now," laughed the dustman, reaching into the cab and pressing a button.

With a horrible grating noise the truck's enormous claws chomped down on Charlie's beautiful bike. We looked on in horror as the terrible machine began to work, snapping and crunching, grinding metal, smashing the frame and handlebars, the wheels and pedals. Finally we heard the bike's tyres pop and then there was silence. The monster machine had swallowed the bike completely.

"That was Charlie's bike," shouted Danny furiously. "It wasn't rubbish. You're only supposed to pick up rubbish."

"It looked like rubbish to us," sneered one of the dustmen giving a cruel laugh. He grabbed hold of Danny's handlebars. "There's some more rubbish here." He turned to his mates. "Shall we chuck this one in too?"

Gary turned and shoved him angrily, much to the amusement of the other men.

"Leave 'em," shouted the driver, sticking his head out of the cab. "We've got to get a move on, we're late."

The men all jumped into the truck and it sped off to the next block of flats, leaving us staring angrily behind.

Poor Charlie, his eyes were glistening with tears. I put my hand on his shoulder. "Don't worry," I said. "We'll get 'em back for this."

"Let's go and find your dad," suggested Danny. "We'll tell him what happened."

It didn't take long to find Mr Scott; he was on the top floor of the flats mending a broken door. Quickly we explained how the dustmen had taken the bike and chucked it in their truck.

"Bloody dustmen, I'm always having trouble with them. You wouldn't believe the amount of litter they leave behind in the bin areas." He turned to Charlie. "I'm sorry son, there's no way I can get you another bike, not right away, they're too expensive."

"It's not fair," said Charlie, kicking angrily against the metal banisters. "They had no business taking my bike, they must have known it wasn't rubbish. How can I play with my mates if I haven't got a bike?"

"I'll try and get you a new one for Christmas," said Mr Scott. "I know it's a long time to wait, but you know how short money is."

Charlie nodded miserably. No-one on the Estate had any money, we all knew that. It was just the way things were.

"It's those dustmen's fault," said Gary angrily. We nodded. We were all feeling sorry for Charlie, losing a bike like that, it didn't bear thinking about. We all relied on our bicycles to do our paper rounds and to get into town. Tadworth was miles from anywhere, and there was nothing to do in the village except the occasional Church dance and the Phoenix youth club. No bike meant no fun.

"They're nothing but trouble," agreed Mr Scott. "They only half do a job because they're always in such a rush. They want to get finished by lunchtime so they can all go down the pub for the afternoon."

So they all wanted to go to the pub, did they? Well, that gave me an idea.

"Come on lads," I said, giving Danny a nudge. "We'd better leave Mr Scott to get on."

Danny caught on immediately. "Yeah, we'd better let you get on with that door."

He rounded up Gary and Charlie and we all tramped down the stairs. Picking up our bikes we pushed them around to the back of the washing area and held a council of war.

"What's your idea then Gra'?" asked Danny, having a good look around to make sure no-one could overhear us.

"The dustmen will be collecting around at the new Estate next," I explained, keeping my voice low. "If we hide behind that grass bank up there we could chuck a load of turfs at them and then, when the driver gets out, Charlie can get the keys to the truck and run off with them. They'll be so busy trying to get us they won't notice."

Gary grinned widely, he loved a good fight. "Good idea. We can jump on our bikes and be off before they can catch us."

"I like it," agreed Danny. "That'll slow them down and keep them out of the pub. Serve 'em right."

Charlie nodded. He was so upset at having to watch his bike being crushed that he would probably have agreed to anything. So it was unanimous. We hurried around to the dustbin area behind the new flats, where the dustcart would have to turn. We knew it was tight and the truck would need three goes to turn it around, giving us plenty of time to attack. Quickly we climbed up the grass bank and set about pulling up clumps of earth and grass, making a pile of ammunition to throw.

"Go and hide behind those bushes Charlie," I said, pointing to some low growing hawthorn and elder trees. "We'll give you a sign when it's time to go."

Charlie ran off and tucked himself behind the bushes. Some of the smaller kids had made a camp there and added extra branches so he was well camouflaged.

"They're coming," whispered Danny urgently.

Swiftly we ducked down behind the bank and waited.

"I need the toilet," called Charlie nervously.

"Well, go behind the bush then," Gary called back, keeping his voice low. "But be quick, they're nearly here."

"I hope he's not going to let us down," whispered Danny. "It could spoil the whole plan."

"No, he's a good kid," I said quietly. "He'll keep his nerve."

At that moment the big truck rumbled into the narrow cul-de-sac, the three dustmen jumped out and headed towards the dustbins.

"Now!" I yelled.

We all began chucking clods of earth as hard as we could. Danny got one of them in the face (he always had a good arm). The man must have swallowed some mud as he bent over and began to cough and splutter.

The other two soon realised what was happening and ran towards us.

"Quick!" I shouted. "Run!"

We shot off down the field, taking the remaining turfs with us, chucking them as we pedalled. We expected them to give up, but one young dustman just kept coming.

"Split up," I yelled, and we all scattered.

Luckily the bloke made the mistake of following Danny and we knew he'd never catch him. Cutting back through the trees we made our way to the new flats. Ahead of us we could see Charlie running towards the shops.

"Charlie, stop," shouted Gary.

"Have you got the key?" I asked as we caught up with him.

Charlie leant against a lamppost holding his side and fighting for breath, he seemed to be shaking with fright.

"They're not coming," I reassured him. "Just get your breath back."

Charlie took a big, shuddering breath, then fished in his pocket and held something out. The key! It glinted in the sunshine, the big brass plate attached to it swinging like a pendulum.

"He's done it," laughed Gary, triumphantly. "He's bloody gone and done it."

"Well done," I said, patting him on the back.

"The d...door got stuck," he stammered as he got his breath back. "I couldn't get out. I had to jump out of the window."

"Well done!" I said again and laughed. "Now, let's get back and see what they're doing."

Back at the truck the air was blue. The men were swearing and shouting at each other. One of them was blaming the driver for getting out of the cab. The driver was blaming the others for not catching us. The young bloke was sitting on the ground holding his side and cursing fluently. It was brilliant.

“What do we do now?” asked Gary, when we had retreated to a safe distance.

“It’s up to Charlie,” I said. “It’s his key now. Do you want to keep it, drop it down a drain, or even give it back to them? You decide.”

“Let me talk to my dad,” he replied. “He’ll know what to do.”

Well, I wasn’t sure this was a good idea, or how his dad would react when he found out what we had been up to, but if that was what Charlie wanted we’d all back him up.

On the way back we met up with Danny who was full of himself having cycled until the dustman got out of breath and had then chucked more turfs at him.

“It was great fun,” he said with a big grin. “We should do this more often.”

As I thought, Charlie’s dad was not amused.

“That was a stupid thing to do,” he said (typical adult). “You could have got hurt. I’ll take the key and go and sort it out.”

Ten minutes later he was back and grinning. Holding out his hand he showed us a large wad of notes.

“I made ‘em pay to get the key back,” he said. “They knew they’d lose their jobs if the bosses found out, so they’ve all chipped in to buy Charlie a new bike!”

So everything turned out OK in the end, but we kept well away from the dustmen after that - although we did nod now if we passed them, as a sign of mutual respect. They might not be as fast as us, but they had some mighty muscles.

Chapter 31

Helping an Old Friend

"Is there any more drink mum?" asked Danny, holding open the fridge door.

"No there isn't," said Mrs. Haste crossly. "That's six bottles you've drunk already this week. I'll be glad when you go back to school. I don't know why you're all hanging about here, getting in my way while I'm trying to get the cleaning done."

"We've got nothing to do," complained Danny.

"I can soon find you something!"

Gary and I edged towards the back door nervously, we knew the kind of things a mother would find us to do, and they were certain to be nothing that we would enjoy.

"And it'll occupy you two as well," said Mrs. Haste, blocking our escape.

Caught! Mums, they do it every time. We stood awaiting our fate.

"That friend of yours is still in hospital and Mrs. Cooper up the road was saying it's his birthday today. Why don't you go and visit him."

"What friend?" asked Danny suspiciously.

"You know - the one that broke his leg."

"Alfie?"

"Yes, that's the one. It must be boring stuck in hospital. I expect he could do with cheering up."

Well, that wasn't too bad. In fact when we thought about it that was a really good idea, especially as it was probably our fault he was in the hospital, although we tried to gloss over that.

Mrs Haste picked a bunch of flowers from the garden for us to take and we stopped at the shops and bought him a suitably rude birthday card and a bunch of grapes. It was good to be out on our bikes and the steep hill down to Epsom was ideal for a race. As we swept into the hospital gates Gary was first, but only because he had gone up on the pavement to overtake the cars at the lights.

"Hi, Alfie," we called, bursting through the doors of the ward and earning a black look from the nurse.

"Don't worry Janice, they're friends of mine," he said breezily.

"First name terms with the nurses, eh?" I said with a wink.

"Friends of my mum," he explained, grinning. "I know 'em all now." Alfie's mother was a physiotherapist and worked at the hospital.

We dumped our gifts on the bed. Unfortunately the race hadn't done our carefully chosen presents much good, the grapes were squashed, the flowers looked battered and the card was bent, but even so Alfie looked pleased to see us. His family had been to visit earlier in the day, but we could fill him in on all the local gossip, tell him what had been going on while he was off the scene. We were soon messing about and Alfie was laughing and getting louder and louder. I think the nurses must have given him some extra medication he was so full of himself, and with us to egg him on he was getting a little over the top. Eventually he laughed so much he had to make a dash for the toilets.

"Hey, his charts are on the end of the bed," said Danny, picking them up.

"Let's have a look," said Gary, peering over Dan's shoulder. "There's a picture of his leg here."

"Where?" I had a quick look too. "Hey, I've got an idea, have you got a pen?"

Quickly I drew a dotted line across the picture of Alfie's leg.

"You do Latin, Gary," I said. "How do you spell 'Cut here' in Latin then?"

He thought for a moment. "Hic something, um... hic amputare, I think. Something like that anyway," said Gary.

Swiftly I scrawled it on the notes, trying to imitate a doctor's spidery writing, and added an arrow to the dotted line.

When Alfie returned from the bog we all stood with straight faces at the end of his bed.

"How the leg, Alfie?" we asked.

"Fine," he replied cheerfully. "Should be getting out soon."

"Oh, really?" we said, trying not to laugh. "Let's look at your notes shall we."

Picking them up, we passed them between ourselves and then dolefully shook our heads.

"It looks bad," I said in a serious tone, and Alfie's face dropped.

"You can read Latin, Gary," said Danny, handing him the notes. "What does that say?"

Gary looked at the notes and frowned. "It says 'cut here'." He passed the notes to Alfie with the picture of his leg with the dots across the knee and my scrawling next to it.

"Sorry Alfie," I whispered, staring at the ground. "It looks like they want to cut it off."

"Yeah, sorry mate," added Danny and Gary, both biting their lips and keeping their heads bowed.

Poor Alfie's eyes were nearly popping out of his head as he looked at his chart. There in front of him was his leg which had caused him so much pain being broken and reset to get his foot pointing the right way, only to be cut off below the knee while he was in his prime. He shrank down in the bed, looking as if someone had kicked him. A nurse came over and tried to comfort him.

"Have you had some bad news, Alfie?" she asked sympathetically. "Is it a girlfriend?"

"No. They want to cut my leg off," he choked out, trying not to cry. He held out the notes.

The nurse looked at them and immediately realised what we had done. Scowling as us she said angrily, "I think your mates have some explaining to do."

All three of us burst out laughing. Danny was laughing so much he fell to the ground hugging his stomach. Even Alfie saw the funny side of it and we all ended up with tears of laughter running down our faces. The nurse went off shaking her head.

"I knew there'd be trouble if we all got together," said Alfie, and he was right.

Eventually, we wished him a happy fifteenth birthday and promised we'd visit again, then rode home trying not to fall off our bikes as we kept remembering and laughing.

"You lot back again," said Mrs. Haste, as we came into her kitchen. "Did you see your friend?"

"Yes," we said and began to laugh.

Mrs. Haste eyed us suspiciously. "I hope you didn't do anything to upset him?"

"Oh, mum, of course we didn't," Danny answered, trying that innocent look we all knew. "I think we really cheered him up."

"I hope so," said Mrs. Haste, not at all convinced. "Well, I expect you're all thirsty, riding back from Epsom in this heat. The Corona man's been, there's a bottle of cream soda in the fridge, but only one glass each!"

We took our glasses of cold drink out into the garden before Danny's mum asked any more awkward questions. I don't know why our mothers had such difficulty in believing us when we told them we hadn't been up to anything.

"I'm just going for a pee," said Danny, disappearing back into the house.

Minutes later he came bursting out of the back door with a big grin on his face.

"Hey," he whispered excitedly, looking over his shoulder to make sure his mum wasn't listening. "You'll never guess what."

“What?” asked Gary.

Danny giggled.

“Come on Dan, stop messing about,” I said. “Tell us what it is.”

Danny was obviously bursting to tell us anyway.

“Esther and Debbie are in the garden sunbathing.”

“So?”

“Topless!”

Now this was news. Esther, Debbie and their elder sister lived two doors down from Danny. All three girls were older than us, tall, blond, with enormous ...! (Well, you get the picture.) This we had to see.

“Let’s go up to your bedroom and have a look,” said Gary eagerly.

“Not likely,” protested Danny. “Mum would kill me if she caught us doing that.”

This was regrettably true. Mrs Haste would certainly not be pleased if she caught us hanging out of a bedroom window ogling her neighbour’s daughters, and it wouldn’t only be Danny in trouble as she was sure to complain to our mum’s too. We sat dejectedly in the garden, just yards from where those stunningly beautiful girls were exposing themselves to the warm sunshine. We couldn’t get as much as a glimpse. We needed a plan.

“I know,” whispered Danny. “What if we climb up that tree by the garages and climb along the fence?”

We knew exactly what tree he meant. None of us had climbed it before. It was a strong tree that looked like a round tent, more of a giant bush than a tree. You’d have thought we would have learnt our lesson having just come from seeing Alfie in the hospital, but our brains held only one thought – girls. Quickly we let ourselves out of the side gate, carefully avoiding Danny’s mum, and ran around to the block of garages.

What we hadn’t realised was how prickly the tree was, with long, nasty spines on every branch. We burrowed under the lower branches to reach the trunk and then tried to fight our way up its winding, twisted centre. It was too painful for me, so I climbed back out. Gary did not last much longer and crawled out after me. Danny, however, was possessed, the promise of even a glimpse of naked flesh kept him fighting his way to the top, bearing unimaginable pain from the deadly spikes that stabbed and tore at his skin. My arms and legs were bleeding and so were Gary's, but Danny's head was poking out of the top of the tree now and we could see him climbing out onto the six foot high wooden fence to get a better view. Just as he got his two feet onto the fence something went wrong.

"Agh...!" CRASH! Thump!

That's when the screaming started - ear shattering screaming, followed by screeching, and the sort of swearing that would make a navvy blush. It was amazing the words those two girls knew!

Gary and I ran around to the side gate and knocked on it. Mrs Beasley answered and let us into the garden where Danny was lying flat on his back in a rose bush.

Gary saved the day. "Sorry, Mrs. B. we were trying to get our kite. It got stuck in the tree and Danny must have slipped."

Hurriedly we made our apologies and carried Dan out, watched by the girls, not naked but in miniscule bikinis. In spite of being dazed and having numerous injuries Danny's face wore the most enormous grin, but we never talked about it again. Danny had suffered enough and narrowly avoided upsetting his neighbours, which we all knew on our Estate was not wise!

Chapter 32

Neighbours

Mum at Acres Gardens

There is a saying that begins 'You can't choose your family ...', but it is equally true that you can't choose your neighbours. In Acres Gardens we were extremely lucky with ours. Next-door to us were Pat and Fred Wentworth, a lovely couple, laid back, easy going, and we got on well with them and their seven children. Next to them were the Dobson's, another great family, their son Andrew was a good friend who, with his younger brother Paul, could be relied upon to join in any scheme Danny, Gary and I thought up! Pat and Fred threw brilliant parties and we were always invited and, as apart from their son Clive they had six daughters, these occasions were eagerly anticipated. Altogether our street was a happy one, and on the few occasions there was friction it was easily sorted, like the old sofa outside our house. At first it had been fun, but soon the sofa began to get tatty and mum got fed-up with so many people hanging around our back gate, then the neighbours began to complain about the noise, so we moved it to outside the Phoenix Youth Club – problem sorted. (Well, moved anyway. The sofa was soon set on fire and disappeared completely!).

Danny, however, was not so fortunate. His immediate neighbours were fine, upstanding, law abiding citizens - but up the road lived the Brown's. Now, don't get me wrong, the Brown's were also a fine family, Mr Brown was always decorating and busy in the house and garden – but they were different, definitely different. The problem was they were all hot tempered, and this led to lots (and lots) of arguments. The entire road soon knew when another row exploded. Suddenly the air was blue with insults being traded at full volume. Gary, Danny and I were friends with the younger son Kenny, and at any visit to his home we had to be fully prepared for a quick exit as china smashed around our ears and physical violence erupted. We thought them totally mad, very entertaining, but definitely a little bit scary!

"Do you want to come around tomorrow night?" asked Kenny, one Thursday as we were sitting, bored at the under-sixteen disco. "I thought we could have a late night poker game."

"Seems a good idea," I said, lazily swigging from a can of warm Cola.

"Well, there's not much going on here," put in Danny, looking around at the half a dozen people who had bothered to turn up. "Why don't we have it tonight?"

"Chris is home tonight," explained Kenny. "It'll be better tomorrow, he's going out."

We could never understand why Kenny seemed so scared of his older brother Christopher. To us it seemed that Chris was the only sane one among them; he always appeared laid-back and easy going. We all liked him as he was always friendly and besides he rode a Honda 750 as a dispatch rider in London, which of course swung it for us. He was big and very strong, and we knew that like any elder brother he'd give Kenny a whack if he got out of line, so assumed that was the problem.

Friday evening we all went around to Kenny's. His father had built an amazing patio at the back of their house so, as the weather was still baking hot, we decided to take the poker game into the garden. Dad had bought a case of Mackesons[37] home, and I'd managed to smuggle half a dozen bottles out. With a cold beer each the game began. By ten o'clock the sky was only just beginning to darken and Kenny's dad made a great show of putting on the new lights for us. We were playing for money, not big stakes, but enough to add some excitement to the game. We all had other jobs beside our paper-rounds. I cleaned toilets at the Legal and General (Insurance company), went grass cutting, washed up at the Happy Eater and did a bit of caddying. Gary delivered drugs for the local Chemist shop, Danny caddied and also helped serve fish and chips from the van that came around and Kenny helped the milkman. So we all had money in our pockets, and were intent on winning more off our friends if we could.

Late in the night our game was interrupted by the sound of a motorbike.

"That must be Chris coming home," said Kenny.

"Let's go and see that bike," said Gary, getting up quickly.

---

[37] Mackeson - a milk stout first brewed by Mackeson's Brewery, Kent in 1907. Whitbread acquired the brand in 1929.

Danny and I followed him outside, keen to see Chris and his Honda, while Kenny trailed along behind us. As we emerged from the house we could see Chris was not looking his usual sunny self.

"Oh, oh," said Kenny, turning swiftly. "I'd better get my dad."

"What's up, Chris?" I asked, innocently. Big mistake!

"That pillock, that's what's up," he shouted, pointing to his garage. Mr Basil, neighbour from hell, and all time pain in the neck, had parked his new Ford Cortina blocking the Brown's garage doors so Chris couldn't put his prized motorbike away.

At that moment Mr Brown came running out of the house. "You and that bloody bike. You're always causing trouble. I was fast asleep, and I don't need you waking me up."

This was not the line to take. Chris, already agitated, looked like he was going to explode. He threw his helmet down and marched across the road to Mr Basil's house and gave the front door a mighty kick shouting, "Move your f**king car!"

A window shot open and Mr Basil poked his head out. "Piss off!"

Chris did not say another word, he just ran over to the new car and climbed up onto the roof. Jump - Bang! Jump - Bang! The night echoed with the noise of size ten motorbike boots stamping down upon metal. Soon the car roof was covered in dents.

Gary, Danny and I stood transfixed – here was a side of Chris we had never even imagined. No wonder Kenny tried not to upset him!

For a second we thought that would be enough, but no, we watched with horror as Chris jumped down from the car and seized a garden fork that had been left carelessly in one of the borders. At that moment Mr Basil made the mistake of opening his front door. With a roar Chris chucked the fork at him. We all hated old Basil, but I'll say this for him, he was quick. He dodged back into the house as the fork embedded itself in the door.

As Kevin and his dad rushed indoors to phone the police Chris yanked the fork out of the door and returned to the car. Methodically he circled the vehicle jabbing fiercely with the fork, stabbing it through the boot, then one by one the windows. Glass was flying everywhere, cutting his face and hands, making him more and more angry. Screaming and kicking, he ranted and raved, poking holes in every panel, swearing as his hands dripped with blood, stopping only to walk over to the Basil's house and scream obscenities.

Be-bah, be-bah, blue lights flashing the police arrived. They didn't get out.

By now all the neighbours were outside, the men had pulled on their trousers, women were arrayed in fetching and not so fetching dressing gowns. It was a shock to see Mrs Bailey in a racy black negligee, and Rosie Walker didn't look half so sexy in her rollers. We all looked on as Chris carried out his ruthless destruction.

Standing on the bonnet he pierced the dashboard and must have hit the electrics. A collective "Oh!" went up as sparks lit up the night. Then the fire started.

One of the policemen plucked up enough courage to get out of his car. "Come on lad," he called nervously. "You've made your point. Better get down before you get blown up."

Chris totally ignored him. Still mad with rage he pulled the burning back seat out and threw it at the Basil's front door. "Come out you bastard," he yelled.

This polite request was ignored.

I nudged Danny and pointed. Mr Basil was watching proceedings from an upstairs window.

"Wonder if he's enjoying the show?" Danny whispered delightedly. He'd had many a run in with Mr Basil.

Just them Mrs Brown came running out with a bottle of pills and dashed over to the police. "Give him his medication," she called urgently.

Seeing his pills Chris walked over, grabbed a handful and threw them down his throat. The change was almost instant. Instead of a raging maniac, back came our usual Chris, calm and quiet. We couldn't believe it. The police put him into their car and we watch as they drove him away.

As soon as the car disappeared around the corner Mr Basil came out to survey the damage. Just as he reached it - BANG! The car exploded, lifting right off the ground. Mr Basil went rolling across the garden as the car turned upside down, landing with a THUD on the path. Smoke filled the air, but the explosion had put out the fire.

Seeing a gap we quickly pushed Chris's bike into his garage, placed his helmet carefully on the saddle and shut the door.

Job done.

"Where will they take him?" I asked feeling concerned.

"Cane Hill," Kenny replied.

We stared at him in horror. I could feel the hair on the back of my neck stand up. Built in the Victorian period, Cane Hill[38], near Coulsdon was a huge mental asylum. Gary had made us ride past it on one of our numerous expeditions and it looked truly frightening. Stories abounded at school of the evil experiments the doctors did there, drilling into people's brains, sticking metal plates inside their heads, and performing frontal lobotomies to cure madness, but the experiments rarely worked and often made things

---

[38] Cane Hill, Coulsdon, Surrey, built in 1881 as the Third Surrey County Lunatic Asylum, was gradually run down following the Mental Health Act (1983) which emphasised 'care in the community'. The building was demolished in Feb 2008, leaving just the Chapel, Administration building and Water Tower.

worse. Then there was the electric shock treatment, which turned people epileptic and made them run around screaming. Horrible!

We had seen a mental patient when we had visited Alfie in Epsom District Hospital, and the man had needed two large orderlies handcuffed to him at all times, even though he was in a straight jacket. The man had two deep dents in his forehead, one on either side – they proved the stories were true.

"I hope they don't lobotomise your brother," said Danny, with some concern.

"No, don't worry," replied Kenny. "They just give them drugs now. Anyway they're trying to close the place down."

"What about all the dangerous patients?" I exclaimed.

"You can't let people like that out," Gary said, appalled.

"They're OK when they have their medication," Kenny assured us.

We weren't so convinced. Surely a patient as violent as Chris had just been wouldn't ever be safe to walk around on their own, no matter how many drugs they were given. What about when they forgot to take their medication, or forgot to collect them from the chemist, or just lost them, or didn't take the right amount. What then? No, that wasn't right. No-one would allow that – would they?

After all the excitement we carried on with the poker game, Kenny was winning and keen to keep playing late into the night.

Chapter 33

Golf

The following morning I was feeling tired and fed-up, so went around to Gary's house. Soon I was sitting at his kitchen table, mindlessly eating baked beans on toast, which Gary's mum thought cured everything. It should have cheered me up, but it didn't.

"I think I'm going to have to stop this poker lark," I said mournfully. "Kenny cleaned me out last night."

"You're just miserable because you crashed your plane yesterday," said Gary.

That's the trouble with mates, they know you too well.

"That engine's buggered," I complained, felling sorry for myself.

"Didn't you get paid your paper-round money?" asked his brother Chris.

"It's not enough. I'm going to have to earn some more."

Chris put a glass of ice cold orange juice in front of me. "Drink this, you'll feel better."

"It's alright for you," I protested. "You've got a full-time job. You can afford new engines whenever you like. Some of us have to exist on a pittance."

"Don't give me that," said Chris. "You've got loads of little jobs on the go. You should be rolling in it."

"He was," laughed Gary. "Until he drank all those Mackesons of his dad's and was so sozzled he didn't know what he was betting on."

"Serves you right," said Chris grinning. "Does diddums have a sore head then?"

"Shut up," I said sourly. "No, I haven't got a sore head. Some of us can hold our drink."

At this Gary and Chris both fell about laughing.

"Stop taking the piss and think of something. This is serious. I need a new engine for the plane, and dad made me pay for the bloody Mackesons, so I've only got," I fished around in my pocket, "one pound twenty-four pence."

"Well, I do know they're looking for caddies out at Walton," suggested Chris.

I groaned. Caddying, spending an entire day lugging a set of golf clubs around in the hope of getting a financial reward at the end of it, was not my favourite way of making money. I could never understand the appeal of golf, hitting a ball around obstacles just to get it down a hole seemed a stupid sport to me, but there were no end of people who seemed to enjoy it.

"There's no-one collecting balls out there either," added Chris. "You might make a bit extra on that."

He was right, it was amazing how many balls got lost on a golf course, and if you found them and they weren't too damaged the club would buy them back at a rate of five pence each It might be worth going over there.

"I'll come with you," said Gary. "It'll be something to do."

"You just heard Auntie Jean's coming over this afternoon," said Chris knowingly.

Gary laughed and dashed for the door. "I'll leave you to entertain her then," he yelled as we made a swift getaway.

It didn't take long to cycle over to Walton-on-the-Hill, and we joined the queue of other hopeful caddies standing outside the Club House waiting to be chosen. Unfortunately, it was Eli who did the choosing, a really creepy man with a limp, who it was wise not to cross. A little Hitler, he enjoyed his moment of power, so if you wanted to be chosen you had to suck up to him. Unfortunately, I wasn't very good at sucking up, which usually meant he would only employ me as a last resort, and that Saturday was no exception.

"So, it's little dog's bone and his side kick is it," said Eli loudly, making sure everyone could hear his clever repartee. "I don't for one moment think we'll have need of your services today."

It didn't seem a good beginning. Undaunted, Gary and I went looking for golf balls instead. Having taken a few people around the course we knew just where to look, and soon had a reasonable collection of balls to exchange so made our way back to the clubhouse. Luckily Eli was no-where in sight, but a couple of players were just getting their clubs out of their car.

"Do you need caddies?" I asked hopefully.

"You caddied before?" asked the larger of the two suspiciously. He had an American accent and was wearing an extraordinary collection of brightly coloured clothing; a buttercup yellow t-shirt, tartan trousers, tartan socks and even a tartan cap. We weren't going to let it put us off though; it was well known that Americans all had money.

"Yes," said Gary quickly. "We're regulars. We know the course well."

The other bloke was struggling to get his golf bag out of the car, so I went over and gave him a hand.

"You really know the course?" he whispered hopefully.

I nodded.

"I'm sure these boys will be helpful, Horace," he said loudly to his partner. "We don't want to be carrying our own bags in this heat."

Horace was already mopping his forehead with a large handkerchief.

"It certainly is hot, Jack," he said and hurriedly passed his bag over to Gary.

After they had signed in at the clubhouse Gary and I showed them to the first tee. It swiftly became apparent that the game was to be a business round, with Horace calling the shots. It was also swiftly apparent that Jack did not have a clue how to play and was trying hard not to let on. Luckily Gary and I had done quite a bit of caddying and had at least an idea of how the course should be played, and which clubs players normally used for which holes.

Trying to give Jack a helping hand I kept passing him the clubs I would generally be asked for by more experienced players, but he kept getting in the rough and was soon way behind. There was one hole on the course that no-one could do. It was stuck up like an island with bunkers all around it and you had to get past a line of trees to even see it. By the time we reached it Gary and I were really pissed off with the American who insisted he didn't need any advice from amateurs, and marched around the course as if he owned it. He smoked one large cigar after another, and they stank like an old bonfire.

Of course Horace teed off first, and as instructed Gary offered no advice. We watched the ball as it flew into the air and landed easily at the end of the line of trees. Horace wasn't waiting for his partner but began striding towards his ball with Gary trundling along behind him.

John took out an iron and began setting up his shot, trying to emulate Horace. He hadn't a hope in hell.

Oh, for pities sake, I thought, if you hit it that way you'll hit a tree and it will probably ricochet and kill us. Quickly I butted in

"If you give it a wack over there mate," I said, full of the technical terms. "You might get it on the green with this." And I handed him a wedge.

"Do you think so?" he said uncertainly.

"It's worth a try," I replied, shrugging my shoulders.

He obviously thought he had nothing to lose, so had a go. It was a good shot, the best he'd played so far. The ball cleared the trees and disappeared in the direction of the green. We hurried after the ball, fighting through the brambles following a short-cut I knew, and came out in sight of the hole, where his ball lay close to the flag.

We could see Gary and Horace in the distance, so stood on the green and waited.

"How did you get it there?" exclaimed Horace, in disbelief. "This will put you level if you sink it."

Luckily, Jack kept his nerve and tapped the ball into the hole. He then continued to ask my advice. I had caddied for some good players, so I told him what they did and it seemed to work as he won the next two holes. By the time we got back to the clubhouse Horace was in a foul mood, he paid Gary and strode off towards the bar. Jack, however, looked as though he had thoroughly enjoyed his game; he shook my hand and gave me a tenner.

As we walked back to our bikes Gary was fuming. "Look what that miserly bastard's paid me," he spluttered, holding out his hand. "A pound! One f**king pound!"

"We'll get him back," I said angrily. "We'll fix his car. Come on."

We hurried over to Horace's car and began to stuff mud up his exhaust pipe.

"That'll teach him not to be so tight," I said.

Unfortunately, Eli came around the corner and spotted us.

"You little bugger's," he roared, giving chase as we hopped swiftly on our bikes. "Get out of here and don't come back."

That was the end of our caddying careers.

On the way home we stopped at the shop and I bought Gary a cola and some sweets out of my ten pounds to cheer him up.

"Golf's a mugs game anyway," I said later, as we sat in my garden. "Hitting a little ball about - where's the excitement in that?"

"Boring," agreed Gary. "Not a sport for real men, like racing motorbikes."

"Or Formula One," I added. "That's real entertainment. Where someone could have an accident or get killed. That's a sport that takes real skill."

"No-one dies playing golf," said Gary sagely.

We sat back in the sunshine dreaming of being racing champions.

"Evel Knieval's what you call a real sportsman," said Gary, pretending to rev up a bike, jumping buses in his head.

"And Barry Sheen," I said, grabbing imaginary handlebars and roaring around a track.

"And James Hunt," said Gary, switching to a steering wheel and putting his foot down.

"Even Graham Hill[39]," I added.

Gary looked at me. "He's a bit old," he said doubtfully.

"He was good in his day," I asserted. "My dad met him once at a party before I was born. Dad reckoned he was a real man, and any son he had should be like him, so when I was born he called me Graham. He wanted me to grow up and be a Formula One legend."

"It's a good ambition for a son," agreed Gary, steering into a bend and through the chequered flag. "Champion!"

"Formula One driver's are always surrounded by beautiful girls," I added, looking across at Gary. I could see he was deep in thought.

After a minute he nodded and grinned, "Yeah!"

---

[39] The legendary Graham Hill had very sadly died in a plane crash on 29 November 1975.

Chapter 34

Vicars and Bunny Girls

As the summer wore on it became increasingly obvious that the local girls were avoiding us, and avoiding me in particular. We decided to hold a meeting at my house to discuss tactics.

"Have you heard," said Danny, eager to turn the knife as a good friend should. "Debbie Smith is going out with Pete Michaelson!"

"Not that wimp!" exclaimed Gary in disgust. "What does she see in him?"

"He's useless," I said indignantly. "He lives right outside the school gates and still can't get to school on time. You'd have thought she could find someone better than that."

Naturally Danny and Gary both knew I fancied Debbie, we all did, she was the best looking girl around. Hearing she had chosen to go out with Pete Michaelson instead of one of us was a severe blow.

"The problem is we've got a bit of a name," said Gary. "Girl's mums don't like us."

"Their dad's don't like us either," added Danny.

This was depressingly true. You only had to overhear the mums gossiping at the shops to know it was quite clear that they had told their daughters to have nothing to do with us. According to them we were Trouble with a capital T. Of course it was understandable that their dads didn't trust us, they had been fifteen themselves and knew exactly what our dirty little minds where thinking when we were eyeing up their daughters!

Now I wouldn't want you to get the idea that we were short of female company, on the contrary we were outnumbered, what with the Wentworth girls next-door to me, and the Dobson girls next-door to them, not to mention all their friends. Then there were the girls around the corner who had been stalking me and making my life a misery since before infant's school. They went around in a group and were never to be trusted, calling out names and giggling. Oh, yes, we knew all the local girls - the trouble was they all knew us!

"We're going to have to start looking further afield for talent," decided Gary.

"My sister said there's a new Youth Club at Banstead," said Danny. "Why don't we give it a go?"

"When's it on?" I asked.

"Thursdays."

It was decided. The following Thursday evening we all cycled over to Banstead. The club was held in the village hall, on much the same lines as our local club. There was a pool table, and table-tennis, groups of tables and chairs, and somewhere to get cold drinks, sweets and crisps. It didn't take us long to make some news friends, there were some kids from Nork Park School and some that had come over on the bus from Epsom.

"There's a disco on at the weekend," said one of the organisers as we were leaving. "You're welcome to come along."

Saturday saw us dressed to impress and liberally splattered with our dad's Old Spice aftershave. As soon as we walked into the hall we saw them, three girls sitting at a table together, talking animatedly, all flicking their hair and flashing their eyes. They looked better dressed than the other girls there, with carefully applied make-up and expensive hairdos – they were obviously meant for us. Danny was particularly smitten and determined to chat them up.

Casually observing them from the opposite side of the room, we plotted our cool and sophisticated approach. Waiting until they all went together to the toilets we waited a couple of minutes and then pushed Danny in after them and held the door shut.

“This should do the trick,” laughed Gary. “He’ll get to know them now!”

After much screaming and shouting Steve, who ran the club, made us let him out. Poor Danny had taken a beating but had some important news.

“You’ll never guess,” he whispered, as we huddled in a corner. “The one with the nose was adjusting her dress.” He paused for effect. “She was wearing stockings and suspenders!”

“Wow!” I exclaimed. “A real suspender belt.”

“What colour?” asked Gary.

“Red!”

This just got better, we had to find out more about these girls.

“Who was holding the door?” demanded one of the girls angrily as they came marching out of the ‘Ladies’ together.

This was great, at last some girls with a bit of fight in them. Quickly, we introduced ourselves. We soon found out that the one in stockings was called Tracy and she was easily the most outspoken. I thought that Janet was the prettiest, with big eyes and a nice smile. Jackie had lots of hair and was smart and quick witted, she had an answer for anything we said to her. Soon we realised that they were the female version of ourselves, having got bored with the boys in Epsom they were looking further afield. It was clear we were all going to get along, and even if they weren’t interested in us they had friends who might be.

“Do you want to come to a party next Saturday?” asked Tracey, towards the end of the evening.

“Whereabouts?” I asked.

“In Epsom. A friend of ours is having a party to celebrate his birthday. He missed his actual birthday because he was in hospital having his leg repaired after falling out of a tree,” explained Jackie.

This sounded familiar.

“Is he a big lad?” asked Gary.

"Yes," answered Janet. "You ought to come. His house has a swimming pool."

"That sounds like Alfie," said Danny.

"His name is Alfie," said Jackie, looking surprised. "Do you know him?"

"Only since infants," I said. "We're good mates."

"Well, the party's fancy dress and the theme is to be vicars and bunny girls," explained Tracey. "Meet us at Janet's house, that's the garden centre at Drift Bridge. If you get there after lunch we can all get ready together, and then we can walk to Alfie's after."

This sounded great to me as I was sure Janet liked me. We couldn't wait for Saturday when we would see them again. We walked them back to the bus stop and saw them off on the bus back to Epsom.

"I can't wait to see Tracy dressed as a bunny girl," said Danny, laughing. "Trust Alfie to think of that one."

"He's got good taste, I'll give him that," said Gary.

The following Friday afternoon Danny and I went to Sutton to get stuff for our costumes. Gary had other ideas as black didn't suit him. By the evening we had our costumes worked out ready for Saturday night.

As we arrived at Gary's on Saturday afternoon, both in our vicar's fancy dress costumes, we were shocked to find Gary dressed in full, red Cardinal's robes. His mother, a brilliant seamstress, had been busy.

"Bless you my son," he said solemnly, touching us on our heads.

We cracked up. This was going to be brilliant.

"Do you want a lift?" asked his brother Chris, eager to show off his new Morris van.

It was a bit embarrassing arriving at the garden centre dressed as clergy, and of course the girl's weren't ready.

"We had a sleep-over," said Janet, as if that explained it.

We were shown into her living room and waited, and waited. Eventually we decided to make a start on the cider we'd brought with us.

"That looks good," said Jackie, coming back into the room still in her dressing gown. She grabbed one of the bottles for the girls and disappeared.

We continued to wait, and wait. Two hours we'd been there. We drank the last bottle. At last Jackie came back, still wearing the dressing gown.

"What's going on?" Danny asked. "You've been ages."

"It's the costumes we hired," explained Jackie. "They're too revealing. There's no way that Janet or I will wear them, although Tracy says she's going to wear hers. We just don't know what else to wear."

"Let me try on one of the bunny outfits," said Danny boldly. I knew I shouldn't have let him have that last bottle of cider, the stuff always goes to his head.

We followed Jackie upstairs and Danny took the outfit into the bathroom and put it on, then pranced out into the hall pretending to be a model, mincing up and down and giving us all a twirl.

"You look really good," said Janet.

Well, I wasn't having that.

"Why don't we do a swap?" I suggested. "Danny and I'll go to the party as bunny girls, and you and Jackie can wear our vicar's outfits."

This seemed a good compromise and possibly the only way we would all get to the party. Luckily the girls thought it would be hilarious and a good chance to show us boys what it really takes for a girl to get ready, with full body hair removal and a make-over. I was beginning to regret I'd suggested it.

The next few hours were spent being totally humiliated, I don't know how girls put up with waxing, Danny and I had tears in our eyes, and it wasn't helped by Gary falling about laughing. However, the end result was two convincing bunny girls, complete with fishnet tights, and furry ears and tails. The girls had managed to find a couple of blond wigs for us; even our best friends would not recognise us.

Alfie's face was a picture when he opened the door to us. We took the party by storm. Gary blessed everyone and baptised them with beer, much to the annoyance of Alfie's mum. She had invited some student nurses back from the Hospital to keep order, but was having trouble controlling them as they ware partying like there was no tomorrow. They were still in their uniforms and making things worse by teaching us drinking games. This went badly for Janet and Jackie who kept losing and having to drink loads, with inevitable consequences.

Danny and I were thoroughly enjoying ourselves, as the girls loved our new look, even after we got thrown into the pool by Alfie, which made our make-up run and our tails soggy.

"This is great," yelled Dan, making his sock filled boobs jiggle, much to the delight of the girls on either arm. "We should have dressed up like this before."

"Don't you drip water all over my carpet," shouted Alfie's mum.

We recognised that tone from home and hurried up to the bathroom to do our best to clean up. Two of the nurses helpfully redid our make-up, although our false eyelashes were past repair.

Tracy was waiting for me at the foot of the stairs. "I think you should walk Janet and Jackie home," she said, looking concerned. "I don't think they're well at all."

She was right. Completely sloshed the pair of them.

"I'm never playing drinking games again," vowed Jackie, as I tried to steer her in a straight line.

"Mum's going to kill me. Mum's going to kill me," muttered Janet over and over again, holding firmly onto my other arm.

However, the long walk home helped, they were at least upright when I left them at Janet's house, and Janet had been sober (or drunk) enough to give me a proper kiss. I headed back to the party feeling very smug, until the reality of the situation sunk in – I had to walk back to Epsom from Drift Bridge on my own, along narrow roads, late at night, dressed as a bunny girl! Removing my high-heel shoes I began to run, ducking quickly into the hedge whenever I heard a car. I was almost half way there when, on a particularly tight and narrow bend with nowhere to hide, a car slowed down. Looking over my shoulder my heart sank – it was the police!

"You OK luv?" asked a concerned voice through the open window.

"Fine," I answered, in the highest pitched voice I could muster.

"Do you want a lift?"

What the hell, I thought, pulling the wig over my face and jumping into the back of the car as fast as possible.

"Where to?" asked the two young coppers.

"A party at the end of Ashey Road," I squeaked.

"Are there more bunny girls there?" one asked.

"Yes, and nurses," I squeaked again, trying not to laugh.

"Sounds like we'll have to see you in when we get there," said one with a lecherous grin.

It was too much. I burst out laughing, which of course completely gave the game away.

"You're a bloke," the younger one spluttered as the car skidded to a halt. "Get out you pervert!"

He jumped out of the car, wrenched open the door and dragged me onto the ground. I couldn't stop laughing, and I don't think it was helping matters. Luckily a group including some bunny girls and nurses were walking back from the party and ran over to help me. The two constables looked on open mouthed as the girls picked me up and started to re-do my make-up.

As soon as the police drove off the girls sneaked me into the student nurses quarters. I don't remember much after that, well nothing after the strip poker. I think I must have passed out. I woke up the following morning inside an ambulance, which was a bit worrying, until I realised the nurses had kindly arranged for it to take me home. Apparently they though me walking around Epsom in a bunny outfit might cause some comment!

Later in the day we all met up outside the shops.

"It went really well last night," said Danny.

"You were right Gary," I said. "It was worth looking further afield. We should do that more often."

Chapter 35

The Brighton Trip

Paper rounds finished and money in our pockets, we were standing outside the newsagents wondering what to do with the rest of the day.

"Let's do something different," said Danny. "Mum thinks this weather won't last, we've already had some rumbles of thunder."

We all looked up at the clear blue sky, already without a cloud in sight, and couldn't believe that the summer would ever really end.

"Why don't we cycle down to Brighton," suggested Gary.

"That's fifty miles," said Danny doubtfully. "It's hot already.

Brighton sounded a good idea to me. "We could stop at Earlswood Lakes," I said. "If we do the trip in two stages it won't seem so far."

So it was agreed, we'd meet back at Danny's house in half an hour. I went home to raid the fridge and found my sister Hilary was sitting in the kitchen moaning about the heat.

"You'll feel better when the baby's born," mum assured her.

"Well, I wish it would arrive now," she said. "I'm fed up with the waiting and I hardly slept last night with the baby kicking so much, I just couldn't get comfortable."

"Only another couple of weeks," said mum. "And maybe it will come early, first babies often do."

Looking at the size of Hilary I could imagine the baby arriving at any moment. I hurriedly packed up a picnic of sandwiches, crisps and drink, eager to make my escape. When talk turned to babies it was definitely time to make myself scarce.

"See you later, mum," I called, opening the back door.

"Hey, where are going?" asked mum.

"Gatwick," I answered. It wasn't really a lie, I wanted to stop at Gatwick and watch the planes. Mums worry if you tell them the truth, it's really a kindness not to upset them.

"Alright, just don't get into any trouble."

As if!

Quickly I got my bike out before there were any more questions, and soon Danny, Gary and I were on our way, crossing the heath and picking up the A217. The road was already busy with Saturday traffic as we passed through Lower Kingswood. Danny had been right about the heat and it was a relief to freewheel down the hill into Reigate. The town was heaving with shoppers and we wove our way around cars and buses, onto the pavement and off again, narrowly missing pedestrians gawping in shop windows. Why do people do that - just stand there getting in the way? Idiots! We careered down the Woodhatch road until we reached Earlswood Common[40].

"Let's take a boat out," suggested Danny.

"Good idea," I said. "It should be cool on the water."

We rode our bikes down the dusty track, watching tiny cream and brown lizards scuttling out of our way. All around us were areas of blackened and charred heathland where fires had burnt away the gorse, and the air still smelt of wood smoke. It was quiet, almost eerie.

---

[40] Earlswood Common is a nature reserve, now partly used by the golf club. There are two large lakes, the lower one has a concrete bottom and was used in WWI to test the ability of primitive tanks to cross flooded landscapes. The upper lake, a popular picnic destination, has a tea kiosk and boats for hire. I once got lost by the lakes – four times in one day! Mum refused to take me back there again, she said her nerves wouldn't stand it.

"Wow!" said Gary as we reached the lake. There was hardly any water left, certainly not enough to take out a canoe.

"The fire brigade had to use water from the lake on the fire," explained the man at the kiosk. "I thought I was going to lose the shop and the canoes. The fire took hold so quickly, everything was tinder dry. The heat was unbelievable."

We stared at the scorched earth around the wooden building and realised how close he must have been to losing his livelihood.

It must be exciting to be a fireman I though, imagining myself battling the flames, holding a hose while gallons of water flowed through it, beating the fire back, saving property and human life. The HERO!

"You having a cornet or a lolly?" asked Danny, interrupting my glorious daydream.

"A lolly might be cooler," advised Gary.

"Yeah, what lollies have you got?"

"Fab, Zoom, Captain Rainbow or I've got Smash in Lemonade or Raspberry."

We settled for a Zoom each and stood licking them, standing in the bit of shade by the kiosk. The lollies melted faster that we could eat them, dribbling down our chins and over our fingers. Soon we were surrounded by a cloud of flies and then the attack began. Wasps - loads of them.

"Let's get on to Gatwick," I said.

It was depressing to see the glorious heathland looking so desolate, covered in grey ash and the shrivelled remains of gorse and trees. The few remaining ducks were sitting disconsolately by the edge of the near empty lake, their usually glossy plumage tatty and covered in dust. The wasps were the last straw. So far it hadn't been the fun day we had imagined.

It didn't take long to reach the Airport, and the car park attendant let us leave our bikes by his shed.

First we went to the café and bought some 7Up and then found ourselves a good view point.

"What's that?" I asked, as Gary took a book out of his rucksack.

"It's a new book," he explained. "Dad got it for me, it only came out this year."

It was a 'Spotter's Guide to Airline Movement', listing the different aircraft that might be seen at Gatwick.

"Cool!" I said, looking at it enviously, I liked aircraft almost as much as motorbikes.

Of course we knew a lot of the aircraft types already, we could all spot a DC-8 or a Boeing 747, but Danny was delighted when we saw a Dan-Air Comet taxi onto the runway and take-off.

We didn't stay long though; we wanted to press on to Brighton. There was even more traffic on the road. It was the start of the Bank Holiday weekend and it seemed we weren't the only ones heading for the coast. As we got closer to Brighton we joined a long line of cars almost at a standstill. Bouncing up onto the pavement we tore past them, laughing at their fuming faces, as they ground to a complete halt and we went dashing by, through the park and down the hill into the town.

We hardly noticed the Royal Pavilion, carrying on down the Old Steine towards the sea front, cruising past the Aquarium to the Pier. The pebble beach was heaving with people, all making the most of the glorious weather. We nudged each other as we eyed up the girls in their miniscule bikinis, this was more like it. Madeira Drive was lined with Mods each with their scooter, we wandered along the road admiring Vespas and Lambrettas, many with banks of lights attached. Brighton and Hove Albion must have been playing at home as the place was thronged with football supporters, and a large group of skinheads, already drunk, were shouting and offering to fight anyone. The police were out in force, lining the road and trying to keep the different groups separate.

More football supporters were falling out of the pubs and ready for trouble. The skinheads were being steadily rounded up by the police, hit smartly over their heads with truncheons and slung in the back of vans.

"Let's go down to the beach and have our lunch," suggested Gary, thinking of his stomach as usual.

"Good idea," I said, jumping down onto the pebbles, the cycle ride had made us all hungry.

We managed to find a space under the pier and sat on the stones to eat our sandwiches. There was so much going on. There was music from a concert in the distance and the promenade was getting even busier, with people arriving all the time. The tide was going out and the beach was packed, the deckchair attendant was doing a roaring trade. Kids were getting lost and dogs were making the most of any picnic they could invite themselves to. It seemed as if everyone had decided to travel to Brighton that day.

"Let's see if we can get onto the pier," said Danny, when the sandwiches and crisps had disappeared.

As we dragged our chopper bikes up the steps we bumped into a group of Bikers, not Rockers (the Mod and Rocker thing had been over in the Sixties), these were just real motorbike enthusiasts. They had some brilliant bikes and seemed happy to chat with us as soon as they realised we were as mad about bikes as they were.

"Hey, you kids ought to make yourself scarce," said one of them suddenly.

We looked at him confused.

"Things are kicking off," agreed his mate. "Get away now!"

Turning we saw what he meant and ran, lifting up our bikes, crunching over the pebbles, past screaming girls until we reached the relative safety of the pier. Ducking under the large metal structure, we flung ourselves down on the pebbles. Lying flat out, trying to catch our breath, we looked around at sheer bedlam.

It seemed surreal, while up above us music played, in front of us the beach had turned into a battleground. A policeman seemed to have been cut off from the others and was blowing his whistle. Bottles started flying through the air. A gang of Mods jumped down onto the beach and began throwing stones back at the people who were throwing the bottles. Some of the stones hit the motorbikes and with a roar the Bikers waded into the fray. Kids were screaming, girls were screaming, parents were screaming. People were running everywhere. It was like a war zone and we were in the middle of it. We pulled our bikes further under the pier, in case someone decided to use them as weapons, and kept our heads low.

The carnage carried on for most of the afternoon. It must have been around five o'clock when we finally ventured out. A car had been set on fire and there was blood on the path, but amazingly most people seemed to be carrying on like nothing had happened.

"Do you think this is normal for down here?" asked Gary with a shake of his head.

"Must be," said Danny.

"Yeah, it must be," I agreed.

"Let's get some chips," said Gary, which seemed an excellent idea.

Sitting on the sea wall tucking into hot, greasy chips with lashings of salt and vinegar, we tried to make sense of the violence we had witnessed that afternoon.

"I think the Skinheads started it," said Danny.

"Might have been," Gary replied, waving his hand in the air, trying to protect his chips from marauding seagulls. "They're always fighting over football," he added, "And the bikers joined in because their bikes were getting damaged, and so were the Mods scooters."

Danny and I nodded and then swiftly ducked as another gull swooped in low.

"What I can't understand," I said, "is why the Mods fight the Bikers? It's not like they don't all ride bikes. Even if scooters do have small wheels they're still bikes and the ones with all the mirrors and lights look really cool."

"It's because the Mods dress smart," replied Gary sagely.

"You can't keep clean riding a motorbike," added Danny.

That was a fact we had found out for ourselves. All of our clothes had rents and tears in from our escapades on the PuchMaxi and the Honda 90, not to mention the tree climbing, birch bending, pot holing, football and just generally falling off our bikes. Looking at each other it was plain that, in spite of our mothers' best efforts, the summer had taken its toll on our clothing and we were definitely leaning towards the Bikers more than the Mods.

"That fighting was really mad," I said, pointing to the blood on the path which had dried out and left a dark red stain. "The heat's not helping," I added, feeling the sun burning my arms and my t-shirt sticking to me."

"The Unions don't help either," said Danny. "Making everyone go on strike for more pay."

Danny's dad worked in the print and we knew he was off work again and it was causing problems at home.

"The Government should sort it out," I declared, aping my father.

"My dad says it's all the Government's fault," agreed Danny. "He reckons they shouldn't be letting all those foreigners in, taking our jobs."

"Not where we live," pointed out Gary. "There's no problem with foreigners on our Estate."

That was true, the only foreigners we knew, like the Patel's at the shop and our friend James and his sister, fitted in well and never caused problems. James had been over quite a few times during the summer, playing football or beating me at chess, and he always seemed to fit in. No-one cared that he was a Prince, as long as he could score goals, and he was equally happy to be in a place where no-one was lobbing bombs at him.

We finished up our chips and began the long ride home. We had a lot to think about. It seemed the hot weather wasn't only causing destruction in the countryside, but just a spark might cause the entire country to explode into violence. It wasn't a good thought to accompany us on our journey home.

Crossing Burgh Heath we could smell the acrid stench of burning peat as once again the fire fighters battled to beat back another fire. Smoke drifted across the path as dense as fog, making us cough and our eyes sting.

As we swung into Marbles Way we all heaved a sigh of relieve.

"It's good to be back on our Estate, where nothing ever happens," said Danny.

Gary and I agreed. Preston Hawe might be boring, but it was safe.

Chapter 36

The Cannon

"Only another week," said my mother with a smile on her face, "and you'll be back at school."

"What!" My head jerked up and my toast stopped, suspended in mid-air.

"A week. Just seven more days, and you will be back at school."

Did she need to say it with that joyful tone in her voice? I stared at her in dismay. "Where's the summer gone?" I asked. "I thought we had ages yet before we had to go back."

"Well, you'd better make the most of what's left. Now I'm off to work. Please try to remember to pick those loganberries for me. I want to make some jam when I get home."

I picked up another slice of toast and spread it liberally with butter and jam. How could the summer have just disappeared? Mum was right we ought to make the most of the few days left. Quickly I ate another couple of slices of toast and jam, dumped my plate and mug in the sink and hurried around to Danny's house.

"We've only got a week left," I said urgently, when Danny opened the door.

"What are you talking about?" Danny looked at me as if I were mad.

"This time next week we'll be back at school!"

His face dropped. "Let's go round to Gary's, we need a plan."

Soon all three of us were sitting in Gary's back garden, tucking into bacon sarnies, washed down with tea. No-one ever went hungry in the Johnson household, Gary's mum saw to that.

“So, what are we going to do?” asked Danny. “I don’t want to go back to school.”

“Neither do I,” said Gary. “This summer’s been the best. I don’t want it to end.”

“Life stinks,” I said, and the others nodded in agreement.

“Let’s at least finish making our racing track,” said Gary. “We could do that before the summer ends.”

We had been working on a racing track around the ‘Hills and Mountains’, putting in ramps and banking up the corners so that we could go faster. It was coming on well, but we were sure we could improve it.

“Come on then,” I said, giving him a shove. “Bet I get there first!”

We ran to our chopper bikes, pushing and shoving each other, and then raced through the heath, our wheels sending up clouds of dust which puffed out behind us like wood smoke in the still, hot air.

“I think we should work at making the far corner better,” said Danny. “Make the surface smooth and bank it up so we can swerve into it really fast.”

It seemed an excellent idea. Soon we were all working hard. We found some dry wood to put around the corner as a base. Then began digging into the soft peaty soil and carrying it to the corner, covering up the wood, making a solid curve.

“Hey, what’s this,” called Danny, digging furiously.

We went over to see what he had found. Sticking out of the ground was the end of a metal pipe.

“Let’s dig it out and see how long it is,” I said. The heath was littered with Victorian rubbish dumps and we often found interesting stuff.

It took a while to dig around it, but eventually we got it out. The pipe was about a yard long and six inches in diameter, capped at one end and really heavy.

“That would be perfect for making a cannon,” said Danny, his eyes sparkling.

“We could blow up the school,” I said, immediately seeing possibilities.

Gary nodded enthusiastically, game for anything as usual.

We balanced the pipe across two of our bikes and carefully wheeled it back to Danny’s. His mum was at work and his dad was on the picket line so we had the back garden, and more importantly the tool shed, to ourselves. We got a bucket of water and gave the pipe a good clean.

“We’ll need to make a hole in it for the fuse,” said Gary.

Danny went into the shed and got out his dad’s drill. The metal was really hard, and we broke three drill bits before we managed to make a decent hole. Then we used up all the sandpaper we could find making the inside of the pipe as smooth as we could. By now a group of our friends had joined us, all keen to help.

“What are we going to fire?” I asked.

“I’ve got some ball-bearings at home,” said Colin. “I’ll go and fetch them.”

“There are plenty of nails in the shed,” said Danny.

“What about gunpowder?” asked Gary.

“I’ve got a couple of fireworks left from last year,” piped up David.

We looked at him in surprise.

“I thought they might come in handy for something,” he said.

Well, that made sense, they would.

Someone had some paraffin, so we used that to make the fuse. Eventually everything was set. We hoisted the pipe up onto an old set of pram wheels and took it back over to the heath. Eagerly we set it up where there was a break in the school fence, aiming it carefully towards the school, lit the fuse, hid behind the trees and -

BANG! WHOOSH!

The pram wheels shot backwards and the nuts, bolts and nails trickled out onto the floor.

"Well, that was bloody useless," said Gary, looking at the smoking pipe in disgust.

"No, it works," insisted Danny. "We just need more gunpowder. We need to find more fireworks."

"I think I might know someone who's got some," said Colin.

"Who?" I asked.

"Better you don't know," said Colin.

We nodded knowingly. Living on the estate there were often things it was best not to ask questions about.

"I've got a book about cannons," put in David. "It's got loads of diagrams in it showing how they work."

"Now you tell us," groaned Gary.

"Bring it round to my house this evening," said Danny. "Mum and Dad are going out to see my Gran so I should have the house to myself."

"We'll all come around," I said. "That way we can make sure we've got everything we need."

We put the cannon back on the set of wheels, pushed it around to Danny's house and carefully hid it at the back of his dad's shed behind the lawn mower.

Later that evening we all traipsed back to Danny's house, making sure his dad's car was out of the way.

"I've got some more ball-bearings," I said, pouring a pile of glittering silver balls into an ash tray on the dining room table.

"And I've got some more fireworks," said Colin, handing over a brown paper carrier bag.

"Wow!" exclaimed Danny, looking inside. "That should be plenty. Who did you get them from?"

Colin just tapped the side of his nose and kept quiet.

"Here's the book," said David, heaving a weighty tome onto the table.

“The History of the English Civil War.” I read out the title. “Trust you Dave, only a swot like you would have a boring history book at home.”

“Do you want to know how to make this cannon work or not?” David asked indignantly.

“Let him show us,” said Gary.

David quickly opened up the book; he’d already marked the page with a bit of paper. There were diagrams of different sorts of cannon, ranging in size from average to enormous, some for use on ships and some on land. Then there were the all important instructions on how to load and fire them.

“That’s what we were doing wrong,” explained David, pointing to a particular diagram. “We needed to put wadding in after the powder and then ram it down.”

“Where are we going to get some wool wadding?” asked Gary.

“I know,” I said. “We can use an old sock. I’m sure we’ve got loads of those.”

“Right,” said Danny. “Let’s meet back here tomorrow, better make it about ten o’clock so our parents are out of the way, then we can have another go.”

It was agreed. Tomorrow we’d blow up the school.

The following morning word had got around that something was on and a more of our friends arrived, all wanting a piece of the action. Eventually about a dozen of us carefully wheeled the cannon over to the war zone. This time we buried the capped end of the pipe in a hole, resting it against a flat stone, at an angle of 45°s and aimed directly at the school. Following the diagram copied from David’s book we loaded up the cannon. Finally we set the fuse.

“If this just explodes we’re all going to get killed,” warned David, the only half-sensible one among us. “We’d better take shelter behind the trees.”

For once there was no argument and no-one called him a cissy, we'd all seen how much gunpowder had gone into the pipe.

"Who's going to light the fuse?" he asked.

"I'll do it," said Gary. "Just the rest of you stand back."

We all retreated behind the large oak tree and waited, and waited.

"Bloody hell," cried Gary in frustration. "The f'ing thing won't light."

Hurriedly we all rushed back to the cannon.

"The earth keeps falling in," Gary explained.

"Here, let me have a go," said Danny, King of Arson Attacks. He whipped out his trusty lighter. Click. The fuse was alight.

Back we rushed to the oak tree and waited ...and waited.

"It must have gone out," I said eventually.

"Someone will have to look," said Colin.

I could feel his eyes on me. "Don't look at me," I said. "I didn't light it, Danny did."

"Yeah," said Gary. "You lit it Dan, you go and have a look at it."

Cautiously Danny stepped out from behind the tree.

BANG!

Dan was lifted off his feet and propelled backwards, coming to rest in amongst the bracken.

The sound was so loud we all just ran, picking up Danny as we went. We knew that such a loud bang would attract attention. Unwanted attention. We legged it. Fast.

Later, as usual, we met up behind the shops.

"Anyone heard anything?" I asked in a whisper.

"I went into Patel's for some lemonade and that Mrs. Cooper was in there," whispered Colin. "She said the police are looking for a gas leak."

"We'd better not go back yet," said Gary.

"Come back to my house," I said. "We'll go back this afternoon when things have quietened down."

That afternoon we got out our bikes and nonchalantly cycled over to the heath.

"Wow! Look at that!" said Danny.

We stared in awe. The pipe, which was made of heavy metal at least an inch thick, had peeled back like an unzipped banana! A crater a foot deep was all that was left of the hole. The tree that had saved us wore a large black scorch mark.

"The school must have been demolished," I said joyfully.

We looked hopefully towards the school buildings, expecting to see a heap of rubble. Nothing! Not a damn scratch. Not even a broken window. We couldn't believe it, all that hard work for nowt.

"Well I don't know what went wrong," said Danny dejectedly

"It certainly made a big enough bang though," said Gary with a grin.

"I wonder if they've have found that gas leak yet." I said, and we all began to laugh.[41]

---

[41] A week later some neighbours whose house was near the school, returned from their holiday, and discovered their chimney stack had fallen from the roof and was now laying in their back garden. They decided it must have been hit by a thunderbolt during a storm – which may, or may not, be the case!

Chapter 37

A Trip to the Big Smoke

It was a struggle getting up for my paper round on Sunday morning. I don't know why people read the news on a Sunday, I thought as I cycled around Kingswood reading the headlines - bombs in Northern Ireland, more strikes, galloping inflation (whatever that was), even Big Ben had stopped chiming. All the news was dire and guaranteed to make you grumpy for the rest of the day. Surely Sundays were meant for fun.

Eventually I was finished and met up again with Danny and Gary outside the Newsagents. We cycled back to Burgh Heath and sat on the bench outside the Surrey Yeoman.

"Back to school on Wednesday," said Danny looking depressed. "Dad's already on to me to work harder and get good GCSE results. He says he can't afford to keep me at home forever, I need to get a decent job."

"My dad's the same," agreed Gary. "And mum reckons I'm eating them out of house and home. I don't know how she can say that, I hardly eat anything."

Danny and I looked at him and burst out laughing.

"Poor Gary, he's starving," I taunted, giving him a slap on the stomach.

"Quick, get him some food before he fades away," Danny joined in.

"Shut-up you two," he said, giving us each a good natured punch. "We ought to do something special to end the holidays."

"Yeah," I said, thinking of those newspaper headlines again. "But where shall we go?"

"We've done Brighton," said Danny. "Shall we go north this time, up to London, spend a day in the Capital?"

"Good idea," I agreed. "But I can't go now, Dad's got a problem with the car and he wants me to help him sort it out."

"And I've got relations coming over," added Danny. "Damn. There'll be ructions if I don't turn up."

Gary and I nodded, Sunday's were like that, we'd be wanting to have fun and some parcel of relatives would turn up and we'd be expected to stay at home and hand around the tea and cakes. Our dads would cunningly retreat to the garden, and then our mums and nans and aunties would start talking about a parcel of people we couldn't remember, as if we would be interested in Mrs. So-and-so down the road, or her auntie's cousin.

"Why don't we go after tea," suggested Gary. "If I say I'm staying at your house Graham, and you say you're staying at mine, and Danny can say he's staying with you, we could stay out all night."

Now that seemed an excellent idea, I don't know why I hadn't thought of it myself. Staying out all night in London would be a brilliant end to the holidays.

We arranged to meet up at Danny's house at six o'clock, then cycle over to my Aunties where we could leave our bikes. She lived near Morden so we could walk from her house to the station and catch the Tube to the City.

For once things went as we had planned. Gary's mum, the only one who might make a fuss, agreed he could stay the night at my house, so at six o'clock we pedalled off with just money in our pocket. We cycled through Banstead to Rose Hill where my Auntie lived. She was used to me just turning up and asking favours, she had two sons of her own and was used to boys.

"Push your bikes around the back out of sight, so they don't get pinched," she said, before giving us all a cold drink and seeing us on our way.

It didn't take long to walk to the Tube. The station was really busy for a Sunday evening and as we lined up at the turnstiles we noticed two boys who kept looking furtively around and then jumped the barriers.

"Come on," one of them said, beckoning us over. "You don't want to pay do you?"

So we jumped over to join them, and then followed as they ran onto the platform. As we watched they jumped into a carriage and were gone, leaving us staring after them.

"I'm hungry," complained Gary, as we waited for the next train.

Dan and I nodded, we all felt hungry, but there was nowhere on the platform to get any food. Then Danny noticed a Pearly Queen, her black skirt and jacket all covered in pearl buttons.

"I expect she'd know where to go," he said, and in his usual friendly way went over to ask her.

"Have you any money?" she asked.

"Not much," we replied.

"OK, go to Tootin' an get a pie an' mash. Best pie shop in London it is. Left out the station, on the corner of the 'igh Street. You can't miss it."

Gary soon navigated a route and we got off at Tooting. A man was collecting tickets so we waited until he had gone, then jumped over the turnstiles and ran out onto the High Street. Just as described the café was on the corner, an old establishment with tiled interior. As we looked in through the window we could see buckets full of slithering eels. Judging by the queue outside the place was popular, attracting all types, young and old, but mainly locals.

Once inside we ordered the special, steak and kidney pie with mashed potato, mushy peas and jellied eels swimming in jelly, which looked like green frog spawn. We ate with the large, heavy cutlery provided and looked out of the window, watching London go by outside. The food was delicious and so abundant that even Gary had difficulty clearing his plate. We were surprised at how inexpensive the meal was, if the café had been nearer to home we would definitely be regulars ourselves.

With full stomachs we headed back to the station to catch another train further into town. It was getting dark when we came up in Soho and walked around, looking in windows, wide-eyed at some of the pictures on display!

"Al' right mate?" The shout came from an alleyway, and we turned to see the two lads from the tube station.

"Thanks for the tip," I said. "We've been all over London for free."

We introduced ourselves and they said their names were Dave and Steve. Dave was a Cockney, and I guess he was a sort of modern day Artful Dodger, with Steve from Camden his accomplice.

"Do you want to help us shift some gear?" asked Dave. "My brother's in a band and we could do with some 'elp."

"Sure," I said. So we followed them down the alleyway to a dodgy looking club with a tatty Morris van parked outside. We helped unload the speakers and amps, carrying them down the stairs into the dark smoky hole below.

The club was small, just one long room with a bar at one end and a stage at the other. The walls were painted black and the ceiling was brown with the tar from a million cigarettes. Loaded down with speakers and lights and what seemed like miles of cables it was difficult to weave our way between the clutter of tables and chairs, but at last everything was set up.

"Stay and listen to the band," suggested Dave. "They're pretty good."

Well, we hadn't anything else to do. We huddled around a small table in the far corner and waited to see what would happen. The club seemed to fill up quickly.

"Do you need a drink," asked Dave, coming over to see if we were OK.

"Will they serve us?" asked Danny, knowing how often we'd been chucked out of pubs for being under-age.

"Sure, just get yourselves an empty glass and follow me," he said, with a knowing wink.

Rather mystified we picked up some dirty glasses from another table and went over to where Dave was standing in a corner, next to a hole in the wall. Soon a drink appeared in the hole, Dave swiftly took it, replaced it with an empty glass and handed the full one to me. Soon we were all standing there with full pint glasses.

"Don't you pay for anything?" Danny asked.

"Nah, never," he said with a grin.

"I'll get some crisps to go with it," said Gary, turning to go towards the bar.

"Don't waste your money," said Dave. "Just tell them it's for the band and you'll get 'em for free."

We could get used to this I thought, free drinks, free food, London was obviously the land of opportunity. As the evening wore on more people arrived and soon the club was heaving. With free drinks thanks to the hole in the wall we were having a great time.

Eventually, at about midnight, the band stopped playing and we lent a hand to put all the gear back into the van.

"Want to go to a party?" asked Dave. "We always go to a party after playing a gig."

A party it was then. Steve and Dave obviously knew their way around, and we followed them through a maze of back alleys until we reached a large house with motorbikes outside and music blaring through the open windows.

Dave's brother and his band were already there, setting up some of their equipment in the garden.

"I'll go and give them a hand," said Dave. "You go and find yourselves some drinks."

Although the house was large, enormous compared to our council houses, it was crowded with all sorts and ages of people. We wandered through the rooms taking in the sheer opulence of the furnishings and trying not to stare at some of the people we passed.

"Was that a man or a woman?" muttered Gary, as we past someone in a blond wig and strident red lipstick.

"No idea," I said, hurrying him past.

"There are two blokes in that corner, holding hands!" exclaimed Danny, his eyes out on stalks. "I hope no-one wants to hold my hand."

"I'll hold your hand, sweetie," said someone in a feather boa, bending down to stroke Danny's cheek.

Hurriedly I grabbed Danny's arm and hustled him out of the room before he started a fight. Or worse, set that feather boa alight!

"Can you see any drinks yet?" I asked Gary.

"There's a punch bowl on that table," he said, pointing to an ornate side table with an enormous glass bowl in the centre surrounded by matching glass cups.

It was difficult to see what exactly was in the punch bowl because the lights were so dim, but we'd all had punch at Christmas parties, so we decided to give it a go. We each took a glass cup and scooped up a generous amount of liquid. It tasted good with lots of fruit floating in it. It was a hot evening, and the amount of people in the house was making us feel even warmer, so that first glass went down really easily.

"This isn't bad," said Gary appreciatively. "I think I could have another cup."

"Good idea," I said, so Danny and I followed suit, gulping the drink down eagerly.

At that moment Steve came in.

"Don't touch the punch," he said. "It's got acid in it. The band has spiked it so that no-one can tell how crap they play."

"Acid?"

"Yeah, acid," he looked at our vacant faces in exasperation. "You know - drugs!"

We stared at each other, remembering the magic mushrooms. This was worrying. Very worrying. There was no way we wanted to start running around naked like Miss Brown, not at this party, there were people here who might get the wrong idea!

"Too late," I told him. "We've all had two glasses."

"Three," corrected Gary. "I've had three."

Steve looked worried. He quickly called Dave over and explained what had happened.

"You idiots," he said. "Never touch the punch at parties, it's always spiked." He turned to Steve. "Get Dee," he said hurriedly. "She'll help."

Dee turned out to be an American hippy who had some experience with this sort of thing, apparently she had been to Woodstock and played with a band. She took us outside.

"You need to be at one with nature," she explained. "That way you'll have a good trip."

We followed her to a park and all sat down beneath a tree.

"What is acid?" I asked.

"L.S.D." she said, as if that explained it.

"What will it do to us?" asked Danny.

"It's a hippy drug and will expand your mind."

That didn't seem too bad, I though. At that moment Gary's eyes began to get bigger, and bigger, and then he fell over giggling.

"He needs body contact," said Dee, climbing on top of him. "Don't panic, just be cool and enjoy it."

I began to feel a bit odd too, so though I'd better lie down as well, perhaps Dee would climb on top of me. That would be nice. I could feel the grass on my arms, it felt smooth, like a green scented carpet. Scent, flowers, I could smell flowers. I could hear the birds. "Tweet, tweet," I murmured happily. "Tweet, tweet." I'm lying on a grass carpet, I thought dreamily, and then I was floating, just drifting gently above the ground. It seemed so natural to be floating, as if I were on my own little magic carpet. Looking up at the branches of the tree they seemed to be waving at me, just me. The tree was my friend. I'd found a friend in the park. That was nice. Where's Danny? Oh, he's floating too; perhaps he's on a magic carpet. He's my friend. It's nice to have friends in the park.

We just lay there all night, not asleep, more like dreaming but with our eyes open. Watching the sky as it changed colour, such beautiful colours, swirling around, making patterns. The night seemed to last forever, and then the sun came up and flooded the world with light – and we staggered to a bench.

"My head hurts," moaned Danny, putting his head in his hands and trying to stop the world spinning round.

"Mine too," said Gary. "I wish those eff'in birds would shut up."

"Why would anyone do this?" I asked. "And where's Dee?"

"Who?"

Danny and Gary looked at me blankly.

"Well, I thought she was here," I said, puzzled. "But perhaps I dreamt her."

"I want to go home," said Danny.

"And I need some water," added Gary. "Lots of water."

"OK," I said, holding my head and trying to think. "Let's find a shop and then catch a bus back to Morden."

So we found a shop and bought some lemonade, thankfully the shopkeeper knew which bus we needed to get back to Morden, and even more thankfully the bus-stop wasn't too far away. On the bus home we sat silently looking out of the window, too ill to utter a word.

This is what it's like to be a Zombie I though, trying not to move a muscle, not even an eyelid.

"You look rough," said Auntie when she opened the door. "Are you sure you can ride your bikes?"

"Just," I replied.

We set off wobbling our way back to Tadworth, cycling at the slowest pace we had ever ridden. It was not been the trip we had expected, but it had been memorable all the same. At least we'd have something to talk about when we got back to school. That essay 'What I did in my school holidays' was going to be interesting!

Chapter 38

Summer's End

We were around at Gary's house tucking in to the beans on toast his mum had made. Mrs Johnson always assumed we were starving and she was generally right.

"Come in here and look at the weather forecast," called Gary's dad.

We all hurried through to the front room. On the TV the weather man was pointing to a map of England and northern France, with a large swirl of arrows at the bottom. "The blocking cyclone[42] which has been causing our hot weather is finally moving," explained Mr Fish. "It is now pushing down towards France and Spain. This will bring in colder air from the north causing widespread storms."

"We could do with a good storm," said Gary's mum, fanning herself with a copy of the Radio Times. "It'll clear the air."

It started that afternoon, as we were riding home from Epsom. We had noticed the blue sky steadily disappearing as we cycled up the hill. By the time we reached the golf course the entire sky looked as if it was covered by a purple bruise. Peddling faster the heavens began to rumble. Suddenly a fork of lightening hit a tree in front of us, running down the trunk and striking the earth. The air filled with the stench of burning as the tree burst into flames.

"Let's make for the Bernie Inn," shouted Gary, as we turned into Tattenham Corner.

---

42 The blocking cyclone which had been causing our hot weather, had got stuck over the English Channel, and its centre was directly over the border between Surrey and Kent. The highest ground, which was the South Downs, was the hottest, so Tadworth, Epsom Downs and Boxhill were the hottest areas of the country at that time.

The front of the restaurant was crowded with diners who had come out onto the porch to see what was going on. As we stood beside them we could see the storm moving across the Downs. The thunder was so loud it shook buildings and broke windows. There was fork lighting that split the sky, bouncing down to earth and setting more trees on fire. Great balls of lighting hurtled across the heavens. But worst of all was the sheet lighting which covered the earth with tiny flames, singeing swathes of grass, scorching everything in its path. The air was filled with the smell of burning and the incessant clang of bells from fire-engines rushing to deal with fires.

We watched the storm pass over Epsom and out over London. It stayed in the Thames Valley and in the flashes of light we could make out the Post Office Tower and St. Paul's Cathedral.

"Let's get home before it comes back," I said.

As we rode we could hear the storm moving to the east, circling around the high ground that we lived on. Gary's house was the nearest, just as we reached his gate the rain started, not normal rain but a torrential downpour. The force of water was so great we felt as if it was trying to push us into the earth.

"You coming in?" he asked.

"No we'd better push on, mum will be worried where we are," I said.

The rain and the wind made it impossible to ride our bikes, so we pushed them up Merland Rise. For a while we sheltered in the lea of the primary school. It seemed strange to be going in that school gate again; it had been such a long time since that first day when we had hated the place so much. Funny, it didn't seem so bad now, looking back.

As the rain eased a little we made a dash for home. The thunder seemed to be following us as we pedalled as fast as we could. The only fault with Raleigh Chopper Bikes was as soon as you tried to increase your pace the gears would slip out and you could easily bang your nuts. It always happened when you were cycling flat out, which was exactly what happened to Danny.

"Ouch," he yelled as the bike suddenly jerked. "F*ck, f*ck, f*ck!" he screamed, lying on his side on the floor, his hands clutched to his groin.

Poor Danny, he'd got it so bad this time he could hardly stand, let alone walk. Eventually he managed to sit side saddle on his bike with his legs wide apart while I walked beside him pushing, all the while trying to hold on to my own bike. We were drenched to the skin by the time we reached my house, and Danny waddled indoors, slowly following me up the stairs. Looking out of my bedroom window we could see the storm was getting closer again and began counting the time between the flashes and bangs.

There was a house at Burgh Heath, just past the traffic lights, that had a metal roof and was always getting struck by lightening and that night was no exception. A huge ball of lightening shot across the sky and landed on the house, there was a terrific 'BANG' and the house burst into flames. The remains of an old elm tree on the hill also got struck, splitting it in half in a shower of sparks.

We were not easily scared, but this storm was different, at times peals of thunder were so loud it seemed as if the end of the world had arrived. We couldn't phone Danny's parents to tell them he was safe as all the phone lines were down, dad got the car out and ran him home, coming back to tell of branches and debris on the roads. The electricity went out, but the house was lit up by continuous flashes of lightening. The storm continued all night, and I don't think anyone got much sleep. Of course our dog, Joe, was terrified and mum had to spend the night crouched next to the broom cupboard trying to comfort him.

Finally morning arrived and something had changed, the air seemed different, cleaner, as if the rain had washed all the dirt away and made everything new.

Danny, Gary and I rode over to see the damaged tree and gazed in awe at the destruction wrought by just one strike of lightening. The tree was split right down the middle, from top to bottom. It was as though it had been smote by a giant fiery axe. The burnt bark was still smouldering and the breeze sent sooty smuts winnowing up into the air.

"What would have happened if we'd been sheltering under that?" asked Danny, looking up in wonder at the dying tree.

"We'd have been burnt to ashes," I replied, peering down into the hole at the charred roots. It was a sobering thought.

We didn't realise then that the storms were not over, we were in for two more days and nights of thunder, lightening and torrential rain. It was as if the Gods were reminding us of their power, the balmy days of warmth and sunshine had lulled us into thinking summer would never end, then the skies had unleashed their mighty thunderbolts to jolt us out of our complacency. The summer of 1976 had certainly finished with a bang, but looking back it was definitely worth it for the memories of that one long, hot, glorious summer.

Authors' Notes

This book is dedicated to my two best friends, Danny and Gary in memory of all the good times we had together.

Tadworth in Surrey is of course a real place, but the area has changed considerably since 1976. De Burgh School has been bulldozed to make way for housing, and the 'Hills and Mountains' have also been built on. The field where everyone played football is in the process of becoming a supermarket and car park. However, Burgh Heath pond is still there, as is Marbles Way pond (although the branch we used to swing from has been lopped by Health and Safety).

We hope you've enjoyed our memories of the Preston Hawe Estate and surrounding areas, if you have any (printable!) memories or photographs of the Estate, please contact us on our Facebook page (https://www.facebook.com/bikesbombsandbunnygirls/?ref=br_rs)

Graham Bone and Vivianne Moore

25238719R00154

Printed in Great Britain
by Amazon